HYBRID MAIZE DIFFUSION IN KENYA

Policies, diffusion patterns and consequences

Case studies from Central and South Nyanza Provinces

Franz-Michael Rundquist

CWK Gleerup

CWK Gleerup is the imprint for the scientific and scholary
publications of **LiberFörlag**, Lund.

ISBN 91-40-05076-9

© 1984   Franz-Michael Rundquist

Infotryck ab, Malmö

(2·11.87

SB
791
M2
RUN

MEDDELANDEN
FRÅN LUNDS UNIVERSITETS GEOGRAFISKA INSTITUTION
AVHANDLINGAR XCIV

WITHDRAWN

ACKNOWLEDGEMENTS

I would like to express my great debt and gratitude to the following persons and institutions:

— The Swedish Humanities and Social Sciences Research Council for having funded part of the expenses during the data collection period in Kenya.

— SAREC — Swedish Agency for Research Cooperation with Developing Countries — also for having funded part of the expenses during the data collection in Kenya.

— Dr. Olof Nordström, my thesis advisor, who has helped and encouraged me throughout the work with the present study.

— Dr. Björn Gyllström, who during the whole project has in discussions and in the reading of manuscripts given many valuable comments that have been adhered to.

— Dr. Richard Odingo, Department of Geography, University of Nairobi, who gave many valuable comments and pieces of advice which greatly helped in the field-work.

— The Director and Staff at the Central Bureau of Statistics, Nairobi, who through their co-operation aided and facilitated the collection of data.

— Mrs. Barbara Lindberg, who helped me in editing and correcting my English.

— My frieds and collegaues at the Department of Social and Economic Geography at Lund and elsewhere.

— Those who knowingly or accidentally kicked me (metaphorically speaking) in the right places at the right time.

— My wife, 'Pixie', who managed to stand me at my worst moments in producing this book.

— Finally, and perhaps most important of all — the innovations of my own life — Sara and Elin, who have contributed more than they realize in the finalizing of the present work.

Again, thank you all.

F-M. R.

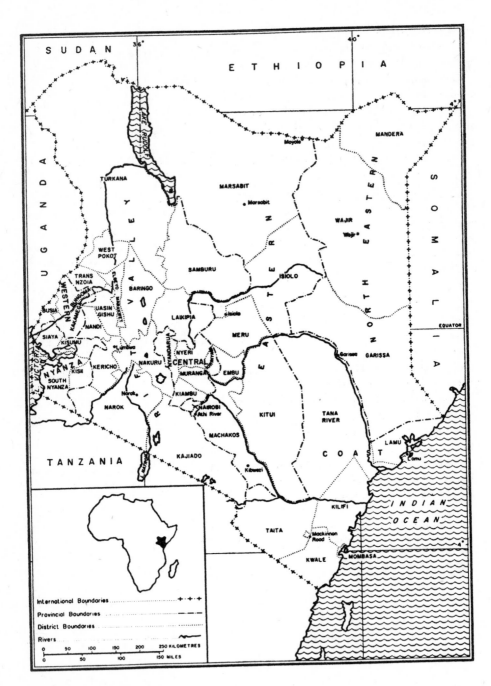

Administrative areas in Kenya
Source: ILO (1972:x).

Contents

I. Introduction

"Development is nothing if it is not
the effective diffusion of innovations." (Mabogunje 1980:114)

1.1 Introduction

The quotation above summarizes much of the underlying
rationalities and philosophies for this thesis. To some the
quotation may, perhaps, seem too categorical and even of-
fensive. This may be the case if one considers the strong
criticism that has been aimed at several large scale innovation diffusion programmes in the last decade (cf. for example Blaikie 1978; Griffin 1972; Lele 1975; Rogers 1983
and Yapa 1977). Much of the criticism has been aimed at the
negative social and economic effects of agricultural projects based on the diffusion of 'Green Revolution Technology' but also at the negative effects and aspects of several family planning projects. In particular the criticism
has focused on the negative effects of the diffusion of
certain innovations in the underdeveloped countries, but
also a growing apprehension towards some of the diffusion
processes in the developed countries e.g. fashion trends
could be noticed in the debate.

Still the quotation contains a general truth concerning
the development process of an almost truistic nature. Despite the multitude of development theories with their vast-
ly different underlying political, economic and humanistic
rationalities (cf. for example Brookfield 1975 and Hettne
1982), what they all have in common is that development is
partly based on the introduction of new types of products
and/or a new type of organization of the productive activities in given societies, viz. development presupposes different types of innovations. Thus, the key words in the
quotation from Mabogunje are <u>innovations</u>, on the one hand,
and <u>effective diffusion</u> on the other. The two concepts entail in themselves the essence of the problem of development. Simplistic as it may sound, this problem consists of
finding appropriate innovations (in the broadest sense,
i.e. not only physically tangible elements but also ideas
concerning, for example, organization and management) and
of diffusing these in a way that satisfies predetermined
political, economic and social goals. Much of the contro-

versy in development matters, then, deals with the definition of the goals to be fullfilled and the innovations that
should be introduced to achieve the goals.

Although the importance of the discussion concerning the
types of innovations and the ends towards which innovation
diffusion processes should strive for, is recognized, these
aspects will not be discussed in detail here. To all ends
and purposes it will be more appropriate to discuss these
aspects in connection with the presentation of the theoretical background for the thesis.

At this stage it will suffice to notice that behind the
choice of subject for the present thesis, lie the recognition of the general truth in the quotation by Mabogunje —
if, however, not as succinctly formulated. At the same time
it must be emphasised already here that, despite the recognition of the importance of innovations in the development
process, a growing apprehension is felt by the author and
many others towards many of the innovations that are being
introduced into the Third World today (see for example
Carlstein 1978 and Lappé & Collins 1982). Although truisti-
cally valid Mabogunjes' quotation also reflects the common
'Modernization' ideals as well as the "Pro-Innovation Biases" (Rogers 1983) so frequently found in both the discussion and the practice of development in the Third World.
The 'Western-rationality' of most innovations being diffused may have detrimental social as well as economic effects on the societies into which they are being introduced. Innovations are rarely neutral — a point which will
be a major theme of the present work.

Before the attention is turned to the details of the
work such as the theoretical background, data collection
and the results, it will however, be necessary to give a
perspective to the whole work. Already here it could be
noticed that the arrival at this publication has been a
relatively drawn out process which has been repeatedly
interrupted for longer or shorter periods and that this has
led to a thesis which is quite different from the one that
was proposed in 1972. Thus, in order to understand the
approach chosen and some of the results it will be necessary to have a general understanding of the course of the
work and the stages through which the analytical work has
passed.

1.2 Background to the work in its present form

As an introduction to the description of the stages
through which this study has passed it could be stated

that, this publication is something quite different from what it could have been. Possibly such statements could be attributed to all, or at least most, academic publications. To a large extent it is only natural that changes in the original plans are made in the light of additional readings concerning the problem at hand and in the light of empirical evidences that appear during the course of the research activities. The problem here, however, is the fairly long time-span that has passed from the time the original project proposals were presented up until today when the final results are made available. Thus, the scope for changes have been quite substantial and the points that are emphasised in the final version are quite different from the points stated in the original plans.

From one point of view the fairly long delay in presenting the results, not least when one is working with empirical material that refers to a specific point in time, could be seen as something negative. In other respects, however, the dealy in finalizing the survey and publishing the results may have had some positive sides too. Implicit in the introductory sentece lies my conviction that the delay in finalizing the work has made it more worthwhile — hopefully this will also be the view of the readers. Had it been finished on time, which should have been around 1978, it would have been a very conventional type of study falling within the mainstream of research traditions of the late sixties/early seventies, to be placed among the others on the shelves for diffusion studies.

At that time it would have contained quite sophisticated analytical techniques borrowed from statistics and applied to a geographical, social or, generally speaking, a development problem. If it would not have contained at least one factor analysis or principal component analysis, it would have contained one, probably several, multiple regression analyses with the residuals properly mapped. The analytical approach of today, at least in a technical sense, is much less ambitious — as will become apparent later. Already here it should be stated that the indicated change of emphasis in the study is not simultaneously a claim to originality. The change of emphasis entails only an adoption of and adaption to the more recent thinking concerning the problems of the diffusion of innovations.

On my return from Kenya in 1976, after having carried out the data-collection in 1975/76, the work progressed at a more than satisfactory rate. In 1977, however, an opportunity to go back to East Africa turned up. The decision

was a bit traumatic — on the one hand the thesis called for
completion and, on the other hand, the possibility of participating in such an interesting and educational undertaking as a population census in an African country ling-
ered on the horizon. The choice was difficult but the urge
to 'go back' got the upper hand and the 1978 Tanzanian
Population Census turned out to be the next assignment.
With our, perhaps usual flair for self-deception, I tried
to convince myself, my family and colleagues that my spare
-time in Tanzania should be devoted to thesis-work. Initially I may have convinced myself, but I doubt if anyone
in my surroundings belived me. As it turned out nothing
concretely was done in terms of work for the present study
for three years — the two years in Tanzania and an additional year after my return to the department in Sweden.
The additional year was devoted to getting into my new
tasks and to finalizing the offsprings to the work carried
out in Tanzania.

All in all this meant that the present work was lying
idle for three years and to take it up again was extremely
difficult. To reread what I had written before 1978 and to
return to the frames of reference that I had had at that
time was difficult and almost painful. More than once I had
the urge to try to find something else, that seemed more
worthwhile, concentrating on. Gradually, however, as I became more familiar with some of the 'more recent' writing
on the subject, my interest in the topic was renewed.

What happened was that I got the opportunity to catch
up on my reading of some publications that had come before,
but also during my stay in Tanzania. The points that came
out of these publications were not completely new to me,
but they helped me to formalize and channel my own dissatisfaction with the rather mechanistic approaches often
found, to the study of the diffusion of innovations — of
which my earlier writing was but one example. A more detailed presentation of the theoretical framework for the
study will be made in Chapter II and thus, it will suffice
to only briefly mention some of the publications here and
to indicate how these have affected the present study.

Basically the reorientation of the emphasis came out of
two related developments to be found in the 'more recent'
literature. First, significant developments had been made
in the spatial theories on the diffusion of innovations.
To a large extent these developments had come out of the
research project led by Professor Brown at Ohio State University. These findings have been summarized in Brown

(1981), but before this the results were largely unavailable in Sweden. Only with the assistance of Professor Hägerstrand in giving me access to his private library could I get a systematic coverage of the theoretical and empirical developments that had taken place within that project. The access to his private library also gave the opportunity to familiarize myself with a lot of writing on the subject which had only been mimeographed and not widely distributed and which, to a large extent was otherwise unobtainable. Some of the writing by Brown — particularly the "Diffusion Dynamics" (1968b) — was very important in the inital project proposals. The ideas presented there have, however, been much expanded upon and developed since 1968 (cf. Brown 1981).

Second, in catching up on the reading, the increasing criticism against some of the earlier theoretical notions, but particularly against the underlying rationalities behind and the effects of the diffusion of innovations, became obvious. This criticism was not a new element in the published works on the subject. What had happened instead was that the criticism had become more widespread, penetrating and based on a firmer empirical basis. Of the particularly influential pieces of work to be mentioned in this connection are first Griffin (1972) — a piece of work that belongs to the early phases of this growing criticism. The importance of the work by Griffin is the pointing out of the differential impact that could come out of an uncritical, or unreflected, introduction of certain innovations. Not least is the work by Griffin important in pointing out that the content of innovations, or innovation packages, may generate different patterns of adoption. The latter is reflected in the terminology used i.e. "Landlord-biased" and "Peasant-biased" innovations.

The terminology used by Griffin (1972) is also used by Yapa (1977) in a paper where he continues to draw some of the consequences of the earlier presented reasoning by Griffin. In particular he discusses the economic benefits from adoption that may accrue for certain groups — "class-rent" — but also the benefits that may accrue from locational factors — "location-profit".

In addition a broader perspective in diffusion research has become obvious. This is, not least, reflected by more explicit considerations of the reasons for non-adoption — see, for example Yapa and Mayfield (1978). Although non-adoption has, of course, been recognized in diffusion studies, the main focus has been on the group of adopters. To a certain degree one often got the feeling, from quite a lot of literature on the subject, that non-adoption was seen as a kind of deviant behaviour that would largely be rectified in due time with a further increase in the adoption rates. In more recent literature, of which Yapa and Mayfield is an example, non-adoption is seen as a natural, or rational, behaviour in certain situations defined by economic and/or social conditions or, in other words, "of the structural arrangements of the economy" (ibid.:146).

Another important paper in changing the emphasis of the analysis, is the one by Blaikie in Progress in Geography (1978). In the refreshing criticism of the spatial theory of diffusion he refers to it as a "spatial cul-de-sac". In particular the criticism is levelled at the lack of recognition of the consequences of the diffusion of innovations, the lack of qualitative assesment of the informational aspects and finally the space concept as such. Although the text is basically critical it does contain critical points to be considered in the establishing of a more useful and relevant set of spatial diffusion theories and these have largely been adopted in the reformulation of emphasis in the present study.

In addition, two major publications dealing with the problems of the diffusion of innovations, have been very important in the process of reformulating the emphasis. These also to a large extent, echo the criticism presented by Blaikie, although no explicit references are made to his 1978 paper. The first of these is Brown (1981) — "Innovation Diffusion, A new perspective". Here the large research project at the Ohio State University, referred to above, is summarized and the results arrived at during the span of the project are presented. The book also points out new directions for continued research within the field of diffusion. In it two chapters of particular interest for the present study can be found — "The Development Perspective I and II" — in which some of the major shortcommings of our traditional theories with respect to the Third World and the problems of the diffusion of innovations there, are discussed.

The second major publication is a very recent one, which has not been so influential in the change of emphasis but rather in giving support to the new directions chosen. This publication is: "Diffusion of Innovations, Third edition" by Rogers (1983). Rogers, a Rural Sociologist, is a major authority on the field of the diffusion of innovations and who has written among other things, several important summarizing books on the 'state of the art' within the field.

The first two, published in 1962 and 1971, are to all ends and purposes, identical. Some of the text had been re-written between the editions and some of the illustrations had been elaborated upon, but the content and messages were largely the same. The latest book, from 1983, represents a fairly radical change in emphasis and content. Over and above general presentations of theoretical and empirical developments within the field of diffusion research, the book contains a chapter dealing with an extensive criticism of 'classical' diffusion research. It also contains a chapter dealing extensively with real and possible consequences of the diffusion of certain innovations. This reevaluation is refreshing and does, to a large extent, accept the criticism levelled at traditional diffusion research in the latter part of the seventies and the early parts of the eighties.

1.3 General presentation of the problem

In the preceding section a reformulation of the emphasis of the present study has been mentioned repeatedly. Having briefly referred to some of the works that have been influential and instrumental in this process, it is time to describe more explicitly the nature of the change of emphasis. It should be noticed, however, that the purpose of this section is not to present the hypotheses to be tested in the analytical chapters. Explicit hypotheses will be inserted in the text at appropriate places in connection with particular pieces of analysis. Instead the purpose of this section will be to describe the course of development in the problem formulations and in doing this, to point at a more comprehensive set of problems forming a basis for the analytical approaches to be found later.

In the original problem formulation, much of the conventional 'knowledge' concerning the diffusion of innovations was taken at face value and the formulated purposes pointed in the direction of a fairly traditional geographical diffusion study. It differed from the traditional type of studies in two respects and these were to be the new elements and the contribution to a greater understanding of the processes. First, the focusing on the individual per se as the adoption unit did not seem completely relevant. To a large extent adoption and non-adoption were interpreted in terms of individual socio-psychological set-ups. Only to a limited extent was the socio-economic 'environment' in which the adopters were to be found, considered as something which could influence adoption or non-adoption decisions. A consequence of the focusing on individual attributes was a lessened interest in the problems of non-adoption — as already mentioned. Non-adoption was largely seen as deviant behaviour and not as the possible outcome of a rational choice based on the socio-economic realities facing a potential adopter.

Second, in much of the traditional studies on the diffusion of innovations the indicators used were of an ubiquitous nature, i.e. once the decision to adopt is taken the innovation materializes. Naturally, this does not refer to all studies (cf. for example Törnqvist 1967), but not infrequently economic, infrastructural and other constraints to adoption have not been considered very explicitly. This critcism was largely influenced by Brown (1968). It has also been summarized and elaborated upon into what is now called the "Market and Infrastructure Perspective" on the diffusion of innovations (Brown 1981).

Basically the criticism rested on the notion that, although every innovation in itself contained one, or several, new ideas on how to e.g. organize and/or produce things, the majority of innovations were physical entities that had to be put together, transported, sold or otherwise made available to the ultimate users. Simplistic as this may seem, it calls for the introduction of other factors than purely individual ones in order to understand a particular diffusion process. Not least does it call for explicit recognition of organizational aspects of production, distribution etc. It also calls for a consideration of policy aspects concerning e.g. government support, prices, subsidies etc. In taking these aspects into consideration the analytical approaches must be broadened to include a complex set of links, and resultant dependencies generated through these, than is the case with a singularly individually oriented approach.

A consequence of the reaction towards the individualization of the adoption decisions, has been that the adoption unit in the present study is defined as the farm, or the farming unit. Naturally, this does not preclude the existence of a decision making hierarchy defined from traditional roles of authority. The purpose of the redefinition of the adoption units is rather that decisions are not taken in isolation by single individuals and that the ultimate decision makers are influenced by a number of factors — e.g. internal and external sources of information, the internal organization of production, the socio-economic position of the family and the farm etc. Thus, adoption is not seen as a process dependent on singularly socio-psychological set-ups of single individuals, but as the outcome of an evaluation process based on a number of influences — external as well as internal. Some of the practical consequences of the redefinition of the adoption units with respect to questionaire design and to the analytical approaches will be discussed later under the appropriate headings.

In addition to the points raised above, it should also be mentioned that the early problem formulation of the study to a large degree was under the influence of the common "Pro-Innovation Biases" (Rogers 1983:92-103). Although not completely insensitive to the possible impacts of different innovations, the implicit value premises of the early approaches rested on notions of a generally positive view of most innovations that could contribute to a 'modernization', increased production, raised incomes etc. Implicit in the approaches were also the ideas that part of the contribution to be derived from the study, was to unravel obstacles to the diffusion of innovations and thus, point out more effective means for continued and increased diffusion. To an extent these views coincide with an unreflected and uncritical intepretation of the quotation by Mabogunje (op. cit.). Such a restricted interpretation of Mabogunje would not be fair to him and, moreover, the reformulation of emphasis consists of a conscious move away from the original "Pro-Innovation Bias".

It should also be mentioned that the theoretical foundations for the early problem formulations were not based on an acceptance of what is generally referred to as "Modernization Theory" (cf. Brookfield 1975; Hettne 1982 and Mabogunje 1980). In particular the early problem formulations opposed the element of 'westernization' found more or less explicitly in the 'Modernization Theories'. This, however, was not made very explicit in the early texts, nor in the choice of analytical approach.

Thus, the reformulation of emphasis consists of a much larger consciousness of the potential dangers, or negative effects, involved in an unreflected introduction of certain types of innovations — as already indicated. On the one hand, in the present problem formulation, the biases that may be built into the technical configuration of an innovation, or a package of innovations, are acknowledged. In the case of agricultural innovations, which are the focus of interest here, the notions of "Landlord" vs "Peasant" biases are recognized (cf. for example Griffin 1972 and Yapa 1977). On the other hand, and this is more basic to the present analysis, the consequences of the introduction of innovations into the kind of societies being studied, are considered much more explicitly in the present analytical approach. The latter, of course is to an extent the outcome of the former, i.e. the built in biases that could be found in the innovations as such. Although not possible to show directly, the consequences could be thought of, or seen, as "windfall profits" (Brown 1981) or "class-rents" (Yapa 1977).

In practice, the more explicit orientation towards the consequences of the adoption of innovations, has had direct effects on the analytical orientation. Thus, a major part of the detailed analyses of the empirical material deals with the questions of if, and then to what extent, adoption reflects an existing social and economic stratification and how this could be further strengthened by the introduction of certain innovations.

In doing this, two interrelated phases of the diffusion and adoption processes are identified and analysed. First, an attempt is made to find signs of a pre-/early-diffusion segmentation on behalf of the various bodies, or change agents, involved in the introduction and promotion of the innovations. Beneath this part of the approach lies, of course, the idea that a deliberate focusing on certain in-dividuals, or groups, in the promotional activities may not only reflect, but also enhance existing socio-economic dif-ferences. Second, an attempt is made to identify signs of a stratification either as the direct outcome of adoption, or as an enhancement of a preexisting one. Naturally, the two concepts are very much related to one another and are difficult to separate. From an anlytical point of view, however, segmentation refers more to deliberate actions in connection with the introduction and the early phases of adoption of the innovations, while stratification is seen more as the possible outcome of the processes.

From a theoretical, as well as practical point of view, the reorientation in the approach towards an analysis of the consequences of the introduction and adoption of inno-vations being studied, also has effects on the overall re-sults of the study. In addition to what can be said with respect to the adoption processes as such and the ways in which this could be facilitated and speeded up, which was the original intention, a major part of the presentation of the results must deal with the questions of the social

and spatial distribution of the benefits derivable through
the adoption. In that respect it is important to consider
non-adoption, and this is also a part of the analysis dealing with segmentation and stratification.

Moreover, the reorientation coupled with discussions of
the distribution of benefits and the 'westernization'
ideals generally inherent in 'Modernization Theories',
calls for a much more concious and explicit discussion of
the content of different types of innovations and the effects these may have in terms of segmentation and stratification. This however, also points to a major problem facing
the whole work in its present form. Basically the problem
consists of the difficulties of being able to draw conclusions of interest for the present analytical approach from
an empirical material that was collected with the intention
of pursuing quite another type of analysis. Although a comprehensive and detailed presentation of the data material
has not yet been made, it has already been said that the
data-collection for the study was made in 1975/76 and,
thus, it was based on and streamlined to fit in with the
purposes in the original problem formulations.

In much of the early problem formulations the purpose
was to look at the interface between the supplying organizations of the innovations and the farmers constituting the
group of potential adopters. In pursuing a more traditional
type of geographical analysis of the diffusion of innovations, which will be seen in Chapter VI and parts of Chapter VII, the available data serves its purpose. In shifting
the emphasis, towards an analysis of the consequences of
the introduction of certain innovations, some of the shortcomings of the available material become obvious.

First and foremost of these comes the problem of causality (see section 4.6). The available data, to a large extent, come from survey material collected by means of a
'one-shot' interview. Thus, longitudinal data giving information on the changes in the values of the 'independent
variables' over a period of time, are not available. In
consequence most of the conclusions drawn, with respect to
real and possible stratifying effects of the innovaions
studied, must be very tentative and can only be based on
the differences found between individuals and groups at the
time of the interviews.

Second, the collected data material deals with a fairly
limited set of innovations i.e. 'Green Revolution Technology', or HYV's (High Yielding Varieties) and related innovations, which here means Hybrid Maize seed, fertilizers

and pest-/insecticides. In the light of the present analytical approach, it would have been benficial to have information on a larger number of innovations, not least innovations of a consumer goods character, and their respective
adoption dates. Had this been available it would have been
possible to juxtapose their adoption with the adoption of
purely agricultural innovations and thus get a clearer picture of the transformation processes that are now only tentatively assumed.

   In Chapter IV a detailed account of the data collection
and the available material will be made. At this point it
suffices to state that in certain respects the available
data material limits the possibilites of drawing far reaching conclusions. In particular this pertains to the processes leading up to the consequences of the introduction of
the innovations studied. Within the framework of the present study it has not been possible to rectify some of the
shortcomings of the available data. Thus, some of the conclusions arrived at must be seen as very tentative. Moreover, they should, to an extent, be seen as hypotheses
pointing in the direction of continued research on the problems being raised.

1.4 Short presentation of the content of the study

   Much of the earlier discussions in this chapter have focused on the changes of emphasis in the problem formulations for the study. In practice, however, this has not
meant that the original intention have been completely dis-
posed of. In actual fact part of the underlying reasons for
the reformulation of emphasis is to be found in the seemingly limited relevance in the explanatory power of the results arrived at in the more conventional analyses. Thus,
in its present form the work reflects the dissatisfaction
with the early results and the familiarization with the
more recent trends in research on the diffusion of innovations. This will become obvious in the following text, but
already here it could be relevant to give an outline of the
content of the work and the way in which the different
chapters are related to one another.

   Chapter I, as is already obvious, gives a brief overview
of the basic problem formulations and of how these have developed during the course of the work. Although the chapter
contains references of relevance for the theoretical basis
of the study, the discussion is held at a very general level. Thus, this chapter should be seen as giving only a general background to the study. In that respect the purpose

of the chapter is to create an understanding for what may be seen as theoretical and analytical inconsistencies in the following text.

Chapter II deals with the theoretical background and foundation for the study. In particular spatial diffusion theories are discussed, but also theories and models developed within other social sciences are discussed when appropriate for the study — of primary interest are the developments within the various branches of sociology and, to an extent, economics.

Based on the more general discussions on the theoretical background basic hypotheses and an Analytical Model will be presented in Chapter III. Presentation of more detailed hypotheses derived from the basic ones will be made at appropriate places in the text in connection with specific pieces of analysis.

Chapter IV discusses methodological questions pertaining to the study. More specifically this means that questions like questionaire design, choice of survey areas, sample design and criteria used in drawing the sample will be discussed. Again more specific methodological aspects will be discussed in connection with particular pieces of analysis.

Questions dealing with validity and reliability of the collected data will also be discussed and how these may affect the analysis and the results arrived at. Finally, and this is of vital importance for the study as such and particularly for the very detailed pieces of analysis, the problem, and possibilities of determining causal realtionships are discussed. A hint of the problems involved in determining causal relationships has already been given above. In this chapter the discussion is continued further and anlytical and methodological consequences are drawn.

In Chapter V — 'Sales of Hybrid Maize — Organization and Development' — the analysis is made at the national level of aggregation. The content of the chapter is quite varied and covers a number of different aspects affecting the introduction and diffusion of Hybrid Maize seed and related innovations. The content ranges from a discussion on the role of maize in Kenyan agriculture including a general discussion of the Kenyan agricultural sector, to an analysis of the development of the sales of Hybrid Maize seed as a reflection of the success, or effectiveness, in promoting the innovation. In between questions are discussed dealing with past and present agricultural policies, underlying policies and rationalities behind the introduction of Hybrid

Maize seed and the building up of a distributional network for the seed. In discussing the building up of this network, short references are also made to the agronomic research forming the necessary prerequisite for introduction and diffusion.

Also in this chapter the spatial organization of the supply network and its development over a period of time, is considered and analysed. Moreover, the distribution of stockists (the lowest link in the distributional hierarchy) is looked upon in terms of the population each stockist should cover in different districts. This is used as a rough measure of the potential for adoption in different areas.

Generally speaking the purpose of this chapter is to outline the overall framework and the basic prerequisites for the introduction and diffusion of the innovations looked at in this study. In more theoretical terms, discussed in Chapter II, the chapter deals with the "Functional Aspects" of the "Cones of Resolution" and with "Propagator Supported Innovations" in the "Market and Infrastructure Perspective" (cf. Brown 1981).

Chapter VI deals with the adoption patterns as they emerge in the micro-analysis areas. Basically this chapter forms the logical continuation of the analysis presented in Chapter V. It is also a continuation of the more conventional analytical approach in geographical diffusion research. The analyses pursued in this chapter are also part of the original problem formulation in which the farmers' response to the created distributional networks was the principal point of interest. Thus, the survey areas are seen as located within the area of coverage for specific distributional nodes and the resulting spatial diffusion patterns are analysed within this framework.

Beside the purely spatial analysis in this chapter, part of the text is devoted to looking at the temporal aspects of adoption singularly and the combinations in which the studied innovations are adopted. The latter is of interest for the future refinement of the analysis into the discussion on the consequences of adoption. The studied innovations are interrelated and complementary and should be seen as 'Bundles', or 'Packages', of innovations. It is however, possible to adopt partial combinations out of the complete 'Bundle' and from an analytical point of view the differences in underlying rationalities for complete or partial adoption are of particular interest. The adoption-categories are defined in Chapter VI, while the analysis is pursued in Chapters VII and VIII.

Chapters VII and VIII are closely related and deal with the detailed analysis of the adoption processes and the consequences of adoption. While in the preceding analytical chapters (V and VI) the emphasis has been on the spatial and temporal aspects of adoption of certain adoption-categories as such, the approach is now broadened to include 'causes' and effects, by considering a number of 'independent variables' pertaining to adopiton and non-adoption.

Chapter VII, more specifically, deals with general aspects of detailed analysis. The discussions focus on the results from a basic correlation analysis, which is made in an attempt to identify critical and particularly important 'independent variables'. The results from this analysis are used as a background to and a steering mechanism for the more detailed approach in Chapter VIII.

Chapter VIII, as mentioned previously, is closely related to Chapter VII and the analysis pursued in this chapter is very much a continuation and refinement of what has been made in Chapter VII. Here the focus is primarily on the adopters of the adoption-categories defined earlier and these are looked at in a temporal as well as spatial perspective. Basically the chapter gives a systematic coverage of the different adoption-categories found within each survey-area. Each adoption-category is analysed following a standardized approach. In practice the analysis follows a course in which the overall population of adopters of a particular adoption-category is 'broken-down' (subdivided) along temporal and spatial criterion variables and the relationships between the values on the 'independent variables' for the created sub-groups are compared and analysed. Generally the analysis focus on the adopters, but wherever possible, or appropriate, comparisons are made with the important group of non-adopters.

Chapter IX, finally, is where the main conclusions should be summarized and presented. Given the analytical approach in which the analysis progresses from a macro-orientation into considering more and more micro-oriented aspects of the adoption processes, it will also be necessary to 'lift' the analysis up into more general considerations of the Kenyan development problems and into more general development theory. Furthermore, in doing this an attempt to evaluate the present results, in terms of their relevance for future developments and development planning in Kenya will have to be made.

II. Theoretical Background; Premisses and Problems

2.1 Introduction

A major breakthrough for a 'modern' type of diffusion studies could be dated back to the early 1940s with the study of Hybrid Corn Diffusion in Iowa, USA, by the Rural Sociologists Ryan and Gross (1943). From then onwards the number of publications on the subject have been growing tremendously and Rogers & Shoemaker (1971) give references to no less than 1653 titles directly dealing with the diffusion of innovations. Despite this interest in the diffusion of innovations, which has spread over a great number of academic disciplines (cf. Rogers & Shoemaker 1971:Ch 2 and Rogers 1983:Ch 2), it has been claimed that diffusion research has been "independently invented" and that "...diffusion researchers...scarcely know of each other's existence" (Katz, Levin and Hamilton 1963:240).

In the second half of the 1960s and the early 1970s, however, an increasing awareness, and knowledge, of developments in the field of diffusion studies within other disciplines than their own became obvious among scholars (see Rogers & Shoemaker 1971:45-48 — particularly Fig. 2.1). Thus, much more about interdisciplinary approaches to the problems at hand was found in the literature. Also the present study tries to transgress the boundaries set by single academic disciplines and thus draws on a number of sources, representing several fields of emphasis, for its theoretical foundation. Naturally, for reasons of academic background and basic training, a 'spatial bias' will be obvious. In addition the theoretical basis is very much coloured by developments within the various fields of Sociology — particularly Rural Sociology, Education, Agricultural Economics etc., which will become obvious in the references cited below.

It is not the purpose, however, to write a complete history of diffusion research, which would lead far beyond any reasonable purpose with the present study. Moreover, papers and books with that particular intent have already been published — see, for example, Brown (1968a), Brown and

Moore (1969), Gould (1969), Hudson (1972), Rogers (1962), Rogers & Shoemaker (1971), Rogers (1983); for short reviews see, for example, Brown (1969), Carlstein (1977), Heine-Geldern (1968), Hägerstrand (1968), Katz (1968) and Törn-qvist (1967). The following presentation will, therefore, restrict itself to a short general review of different trends in diffusion research, with a particular emphasis on studies made with an explicit spatial perspective and studies with a specific bearing on the problems to be dealt with in this study.

2.2 Early theoretical developments
2.2.1 Sociology and economics

Although 1943 was indicated as a very important year with respect to a more modern type of diffusion research, the academic scene had not been completely void of studies dealing with the diffusion of innovations before this date. For example Tarde (1903) was the first to suggest that the adoption of new ideas followed a S-shaped curve, which is now part and parcel of the 'established' knowledge of dif-fusion processes. Many of the early studies on diffusion of innovations, of which Tarde's writing was a part, were the outcome of a scientific 'battle' in the 19th-century between evolutionists and diffusionists among anthropolo-gists at that time (cf. Edmonson 1961 and Heine-Geldern 1968). Interesting in the anthropological studies was the strong emphasis on qualitative aspects of the innovations. This is reflected in the writing of Graebner (1911), who discusses the complexities of cultural traits and how these affect diffusion. Of greater importance for the debate of today may be the work by Linton (1936) who identifies three qualitative aspects of innovations that should be particu-larly considered in diffusion processes:

"Form, which is the directly observable physical apperance and sub-stance of an innovation.
Function, which is the contribution made by the innovation to the way of life of members of the social system.
Meaning, which is the subjective and frequently unconscious percep-tion of the innovation by members of the social system." (cited in Rogers & Shoemaker 1971:336-37)

Despite the early interest in the more qualitative aspects of the innovations being studied, these aspects were not treated very explicitly in the early developments of the more modern diffusion theory. These developments in-

stead focused on the observed empirical regularities found
in diffusion processes, while the innovations as such were,
largely, only seen as indicators of the processes. Although
the qualitative aspects were not completely disregarded,
it is basically in more recent years and as an effect of
the growing interest in diffusion processes in Third World
countries that the aspects have been brought to the fore
again. This reawakening could be dated from the late 1960s
onwards and could be exemplified by two different quotations.

"There is a sparsity of reported studies in which scientists have
tried to measure the rate or extent of practice adoption in relation
to the technical adequacy of the change agent or the technical appro-
priateness of the practice advocated." (Byrnes 1968:1)

and

"But generally speaking, the innovation itself has not been the main
object of interest in diffusion studies, nor the effects of innovations. This has had two noteworthy consequences. Firstly, diffusion
studies have been less useful in planning for development because of
the rather crude implicit assumption that all innovtions contribute
to development and progress and not merely change. ...Secondly, there
is no comprehensive and generic classification scheme of types of
innovations affecting regions. ...Surely, a region is not similarly
altered by innovations such as a new political party, the foxtrot
dance, ..., a new method for checking cattles disease, ..." (Carlstein 1977:3-4)

At this stage it is, however, not necessary to go deeper
into this debate. Further comments pertaining to the qualitative aspects of the innovations to be diffused will be
made later. Instead the attention should be turned to a
short review of the most important findings that came out
of the early research on the diffusion of innovations from
the work by Ryan and Gross (1943) onwards.

Roughly speaking, the results arrived at could be summarized in three different points. First, it was observed
that the distribution (frequency) of adopters over a period
of time tended to follow a bell-shaped curve very much re-
sembling the normal distribution. In its cumulated form the
normal distribution forms the logistic-curve, viz. the S-
shaped curve often found and referred to in diffusion research (see Fig. 2.1). In the 1950s and the 1960s much research interest was directed at the exact nature of the

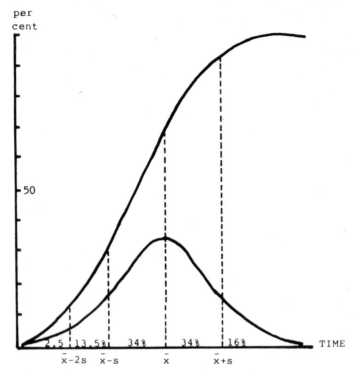

<u>Figure 2.1</u>: Normal and cumulated curves for an adopter distribution.
Adopter categorization. (Adapted from Rogers & Shoemaker
1971 - Figs. 5.1 and 5.2).

curves describing the diffusion processes, the mathematical
functions that could be used in formalizing these curves
and the values of the different parameters in these functions (cf. for example Dodd 1955, Grilchies 1957 and Törnqvist 1967). The underlying logic in the distributions
found and in the S-shape of the cumulative adoption frequencies when plotted over a period of time could be found
in the following quotation by Dobb (1955:394):

"The S-shaped logistic curve of knowers rises slowly at first when
there are few tellers active, then accelerates to its maximum slope
when half the population know and half don't know, and then decele-
rates as the few non-knowers become harder and harder to find. ...The
logistic curve is thus the most probable growth curve for interaction
in pairs in any large and homogenous population of molecules, mice
and men, whereever many independent influences determine the transfer
of the attribute."

Second, many research efforts have been used in identifying, describing and characterizing different adopter-categories. Although it could be readily accepted that there exist differences between early and late adopters of an innovation, the most commonly found definitions of these appear to be slightly arbitrary (see, for example, Rogers 1962:159-192). Generally five different adopter-categories are indicated — Innovators (2.5%); Early Adopters (13.5%); Early Majority (34%); Late Majority (34%) and Laggards (16%). The figures within parentheses refer to their share of the area under the normal distribution curve and, in actual fact, adopter-categories are often operationally defined in terms of positive and/or negative standard score deviations from the mean in a normal distribution (see Fig. 2.1 — cf. also Jones 1963:1; Rogers 1962:161-62 and Rogers & Shoemaker 1971:181-82).

A number of catchwords/catchphrases describing their characteristics have been ascribed to the different adopter-categories. Thus, the Innovators have been described as "venturesome"; Early Adopters as "respected"; Early Majority as "deliberate" and "Be not the first to lay the old aside, nor the first by which the new is tried."; Late Majority as "sceptical" and, finally, the Laggards as "traditional/localite" (Rogers 1962:168-85). Obviously a lot of research efforts have been put into describing the different adopter-categories in terms of Weberian 'Ideal Types'. Added to the more general description of the characteristics of the adoter-categories Rogers (1962, 1971, 1983) presents a number of generalizations pertaining to the different characteristics of the adopter-categories — or, rather, to the differences between them. At this stage, however, it may suffice to indicate that the generalizations deal with "Personal Characteristics", "Communication Behaviour" and "Social Relationships" and how these vary between early and late adopters.

A practical aspect of the categorization of adopters into adopter-categories has been in the field of a deliberate/planned introduction of innovations. The point then is to identify key-individuals with favourable characteristics and that these individuals should be the targets for active promotional activities. The key-individuals should then act as active informants and examples that should stimulate further adoption. The usefulness of adopter-categories as planning instruments is, however, restricted as there is evidence indicating a movement between adopter-categories depending on the type of innovations introduced.

Usually the shifts have been only from one category to the next, but the deliberate diffusion by aiming at key-individuals is made more difficult (cf. Rogers 1962:189). The notion of identifying and actively encouraging adoption by key-individuals (opinion leaders) is, however, prevalent in the literature — see, for example, Naidu (1975).

Lastly, a great deal of research effort has been put into defining the stages of a process leading to adoption. Basically one speaks of five stages today — although there is still a controversy as to the exact number of stages and what characterizes the stages. Agreement has, however, been reached with respect to the fact "that adoption is the result of a sequence of events and not random behaviour" (Rogers 1962:101). The five stages identified are: "Awareness, Interest, Evaluation, Trial and Adoption" (ibid.:81-86).

The model of stages in the adoption process implies a time-lag between awareness and adoption and, thus, that innovations are not instantaneously adopted once they become known to the potential adopters. Various studies have shown that the average time of adoption differs between different types of innovations in otherwise fairly homogenous communities. Furthermore, it has been noted that 'Innovators' spend shorter time from awareness to adoption than do later adopters. This has been attributed to a more favourable attitude towards innovations among 'Innovators', but also to the facts that 'Innovators' usually have better sources of information and are in a better position to evaluate this information (cf. Rogers & Shoemaker 1971: 129-32).

Institutional and/or entreprenurial factors may also be instrumental in affecting the rate of adoption in different areas. Törnqvist (1967:57-59) in his study of TV-ownership in Sweden found differences in adoption rates between different areas. This could be attributed to the sequences in which the network of TV-transmitters was gradually built-up over the country. There are clear indications of a much faster adoption rate in the later included areas compared to the first to be covered. This is ascribed to a greater preparedness to adopt in the later included areas as information on the innovation was already available and the innovation may even had been tried. Similar findings have been reported by Grilchies (1957) in studying the introduction of Hybrid Corn in different communities in Iowa. In this case the time-lag was caused by the entrepreneurs breeding and selling Hybrid Corn Seed. In both instances it is therefore likely that the potential adopters in the

later serviced areas had had the possibility of passing
through several stages in the adoption process before the
innovations were made available.

Finally, and in all fairness, a short additional note
should be made concerning the qualitative aspects of innovations. The existing literature is not completely void of
discussions pertaining to these aspects, but it seems that
their importance has not always been fully recognized. Rogers (1962:Ch.V) and Rogers & Shoemaker (1971:Ch.4) discusses characteristics of innovations that may affect their
rate of diffusion. Again we are facing a division into five
factors, viz. "Relative Advantage, Compatibility, Complexity, Divisibility and Communicability" (Rogers 1962:124-33).
Although implicit in the classification by Rogers, one may
also notice that Grilchies (1957) and Coughenour (1964),
among several others, notice explicitly the economic aspects of the diffusion of innovations. Grilchies (1957:521-22)
notes that "...farmers have behaved in a fashion consistent
with profit maximization". Coughenour (1964:333) emphasises
"cost, size of return in money and labour-saving" as important characteristics of an innovation.

This section has given a very short presentation of some
of the basic theoretical standpoints among the various
branches of sociology and some other academic fields. Given
the purpose of the present study it has not been deemed necessary to go into a lot of details. To a large extent also
the points raised here belong to 'established knowledge'
concerning the diffusion of innovations. This 'established
knowledge' is also part of the basis from which the author
of this study approaches the problem at hand. Thus, some
of the points raised here will be further elaborated upon
later and cross-references will be made back to this section. In particular the points concerning the characteristics of different innovations will be discussed and then
primarily the economic aspects.

2.2.2 Geography

The second major theoretical basis for the study comes
from the field of geography. In terms of a research tradition this field cannot be approached without first mentioning the work of Hägerstrand (1952, 1953, 1965a, 1965b,
1966, 1968 and 1974). Although the original ideas and conclusions presented by Hägerstrand have been to some extent
criticised, they still form a necessary and fruitful point
of departure for any piece of research dealing with spatial
aspects of the diffusion of innovations. Moreover, the im-

portance of his work is not restricted to the field of geography, but has had, and indeed still has, an influence on a more general field of the study of diffusion. Here, the presentation of his main results will be kept very brief due to a couple of pragmatic reasons. First, to most scholars within the field, his findings should be well known and, furthermore, they have been summarized and presented in so many instances already. Second, in light of the assumed familarity with his main findings, still another summary would not serve a useful purpose and would to most readers only be tiring and would take up space that could be used for the discussion of the concrete problems at hand. Thus, another summary is felt to be uncalled for and a good, short and comprehensive one can be found in Brown (1981).

The tendency for diffusion research within different academic disciplines to develop along parallel lines has already been mentioned. To a large extent this is also true for the early developments in geography. In the case of Hägerstrand he was aware of the work done by, for example, Ryan & Gross, but avoided following a similar approach to the problem. He felt the analytical approaches in sociology and economics to be to "concentrated" or restricted in their focus on the "cumulated frequency distribution" (the S-curve) as the analytical instrument, in comparison to the mapped presentation of the diffusion processes (cf. Hägerstrand 1952:9-10). Furthermore, an important motivational factor for Hägerstrand was his reaction towards the often very static analyses found in several of the available studies — not least in ethnological studies. By definition the diffusion of innovations is a spatio-/temporal-process, which could not be captured by a static analytical approach.

The criticism against static approaches to the problem has been very constistent throughout Hägerstrand's writing on the diffusion of innovations, which is obvious from the following two quotations.

"The historical facts, however, only exceptionally admit a statistical treatment. ...Usually it is feasible only to settle where a certain cultural trait was to be found — but not to what degree. The changes in spatial distribution with time have to be expressed by means of displacements of culture boundaries." (Hägerstrand 1952:3)

and

"In most cases available information has not allowed consideration of the distribution of a particular item at more than one isolated point in time. From this single spatial picture one has had to make guesses about that probable historical process which could be supposed to have led up to the known situation." (Hägerstrand 1966:27)

Thus, one of the underlying motivations in Hägerstrand's work was to come to grips with the dynamic aspects of an innovation diffusion process. In doing this Hägerstrand set about studying a number of diffusion processes and worked out three different models which could simulate the processes. From the first simulation model, in which a purely random process is assumed, the models were gradually refined to include a larger number of restricting assumptions on the steering factors in the processes. The results from subsequent runs of the simulation models were compared with empirically established diffusion patterns in order to determine the extent to which the simulation models reflected actual adoption patterns (Hägerstrand 1953).

Refraining from going into details of the simulation models and their testing, it could be stated that Hägerstrand first concluded that the diffusion of innovations could not be explained by purely random processes. The following model tests were based on the assumptions that the willingness/possibilities and the information of the new items were unequally distributed and that these factors singularly, or in combination, would capture the underlying driving forces in a diffusion process. Hägerstrand's conclusion from the subsequent tests was that the economic factors implied did not explain the adoption patterns, but rather that the critical variable was the availability of information (ibid.:152). The focus on the accessibility to information as an explanatory variable is, furthermore, evident already from his study in 1952.

"If economic conditions alone were active, there is no reason why every cell without time lag should not closely follow the general increase in ratio up to saturation limits at different heights. Such a uniform raising of the 'ration surface' however, requires an evenly distributed information about the new item from the very beginning. In fact the information seems to extend only to restricted distances around the places where the novelty already exists. The information seems to flow mainly in the network of social contacts." (Hägerstrand 1952:13)

In sum, and this has had a very strong impact on diffu-

sion studies in geography and other academic fields, Hägerstrand concluded that the main explanatory factor in diffusion processes was the informational factor — i.e. the
availability of information and how this was transmitted
in different social networks. Thus, although economic factors were not completely neglected by Hägerstrand and other
scholars, a major share of the emphases in much diffusion
research has come to focus on factors of an almost socio-
psychological nature — i.e. the availability/access and re-
sistance to information among various groups of potential
adopters. Naturally, the fact that information forms a necessary prerequisite in an innovation diffusion process is
not refuted here. The question — to which we will return
later — is, however, the extent to which information forms
a sufficient prerequisite for diffusion. It is felt that
a strong focus on the informational factors in much of the
fairly early diffusion research, may have obscured from
view other, equally important, factors (cf. in this context
for example Blaut 1977).

Another equally, if not more, important aspect of the
results arrived at by Hägerstrand, is his conceptualization
of the stages in which adoption patterns are often found
to progress. Hägerstrand notices three stages in the diffusion process. First come the "primary stage" in which the
initial diffusion centres are established around the early
adopters. From these occurs a "centrifugal increase" causing a radial expansion of adoption around the initial diffusion centres, but also the establishment of secondary
diffusion centres. This is called the "diffusion stage".
Thirdly the process enters the "condensing stage" when the
innovation is commonly known and, finally, it enters the
"saturation stage" — "when furhter increase is impossible
in the given conditions" (Hägerstrand 1952:16-17).

The important factor in the conceptualization from several empirically determined spatial diffusion patterns, is
the so called 'neighbourhood effect', which is used to account for the contagious nature of very many diffusion patterns. To many, the working of the 'neighbourhood effect'
has been taken to signify the friction of distance influence of the spread of information. The exact nature of distance-decay functions and thus the 'neighbourhood effect'
as to the impact on diffusion processes, has however, been
a subject of a lot of debate and controversy in geographical diffusion research. Of interest for the present study,
is that much of the discussion on the 'neighbourhood effect' point in a direction away from a too strong depen-

dence on the informational factors as explanations and towards the importance of economic and socio-economic factors.

To mention only some of the works where the concept of
the 'neighbourhood effect' is put under scrutiny, one could
start with Nordström (1957). In studying the diffusion of
the plough in parts of southern Sweden from the late eigh-
tenth century onwards, he notices adoption patterns that
conform to Hägerstrand's conceptualization of the process.
On a further probing into the data he also notices some important additional aspects. First, although the plough is
introduced into the area in the 1790s no wider diffusion
is noticed until the mid-ninetenth century. Second, the
early adopters are found among the farming nobility and
among the larger land-owners. Third, a more general adoption does not occur until production of ploughs is taken
up by local black-smiths and when the local iron-works are
starting to sell ploughs. Thus, he notices that first when
the initial barrier has been broken and the supply is organized through local and familiar channels, does adoption
gain momentum. Once this has happened, however, an obvious
'neighbourhood effect' is at work. Furthermore, he notices
a social-class barrier in the case of other innovations
e.g. glass-ware. These were used among the upper classes
but did not diffuse to the lower classes, although they
were familiar with them through work in the local glass-
works. He writes on these phenomena:

"An innovaticn does not only have a spatial distance, which must be
surpassed, but also certain social barriers. The fact that an object
— be it of an every day character — had been used by the higher social-classes could at least in the conservative peasant society prevent its spread to wider layers of society." (Nordström 1957:30 —
authors translation)

A second study to be mentioned here is the one by Törnqvist (1967) in which he studies the spread of Television
in Sweden. The study was carried out at different levels
of aggregation, viz. national, regional and local level.
In the study at local level it was hypothesised that distance should play a role in the forming of the actual adoption patterns, but the hypothesis could not be verified.
Törnqvist writes:

"The probability of contact between differnt households did not, however, depend on the physical distances between them. The information

was spread in a complicated network of social relationships which we are unable to survey.

Previously inquiries have shown that contacts in such networks decline with increasing physical distance. It should be noted, however, that in these inquiries we have worked with distance relationships that are quite different from those existing in our detailed study area. We therefore assume in conclusion that the factor of distance is more or less inoperative in such a small region as the one worked with in this inquiry." (Törnqvist 1967:222)

Similarly Maclennan (1973) does not find signs of a 'neighbourhood effect' based on differences in the availability of information at local, or micro, levels. Instead he emphasises that the indications of the working of a 'neighbourhood effect' should be based on economic criteria rather than informational. He claims that: "The neighbourhood effect is not typically produced by local diffusion processes." but, at the same time, asserts that it "may still be operative at higher levels of the...settlement hierarchy." (Maclennan 1973:30-31).

The mainstreams in the discussions on the 'neighbourhood effect' should be fairly clear from the discussion presented above. Two additional quotations may, however, shed further light on the nature of the debate and, moreover, point forward towards a more recent debate on the 'neighbourhood effect'.

"These observations suggest that where interpersonal communication underlies diffusion the neighbourhood effect operates within a population group that is homogenous with respect to certain characteristics, but between such groups to a lesser degree. ...Both very small populations and very small areal units, for example, are likely to have a greater tendency towards a random mixing among the population, or network and social relationships which are not distance dependent. ...When phenomena other than interpersonal interaction underlie the diffusion, the spatial pattern(s) of diffusion will follow the special pattern(s) of the critical phenomena. Frequently the resulting pattern will be of a contagion sort, but the conclusion that distance-biased interaction has taken place may be spurious" (Brown & Cox 1971:533)

and

"First of all the functional reasons which make a particular innovation attractive of feasible at all are not constant from one decision-maker to another and often vary over space in a non-random man-

ner. ...Similarly spatial variations in production opportunities of
farms occur, which affect the rate of innovation adoption. This point
seems almost too obvious to make, but these variations have been stu-
diously neglected by geographers obsessed with the neighbourhood effect (in spite of the explicit warnings by Grilchies, 1957; 1960a;
1960b). The geographer's approach has been beset by a common weakness
of a rather narrow one-discipline approach — if one looks for contagious effects, and more specifically the neighbourhood effect in innovation diffusion, one will find it, and this is as true as it is
with kinship patterns, variations in social organization related to
the quality of entrepreneurship (see for two quite different approaches Hagen, 1961, and Barth, 1959), or other communication variables (as exemplified by the studies reviewed by Dubey, 1969). In the
case of agricultural innovations variations in physical and social
access to marketing outlets in towns, transport costs of marketed
produce (both distance-dependent), land tenure and the quality of
government extension and the timely provision of complementary inputs
all serve to encourage agricultural innovations nearer larger markets
in economies such as India's (Clark and Haswell, 1966; Haswell, 1969;
Harrison and Vietorisz, 1971). The whole infrastructure versus inter-
actance controversy can be followed in Grilchies, ibid.; Rogers and
Havens, 1962, and is mentioned in Brown and Moore, 1971. The important point is that all these factors encourage innovations to occur
in clusters. Simplistic scanning of a map of such innovations (or
testing by statistical means for a point pattern more clustered than
random) might suggest a predominance of the neighbourhood effect
working in an isotropic area — when, in fact, spatial variations in
production opportunities without serious knowledge dearth are the major controlling variable." (Blaikie 1975:138-39).

The discussion on the so called 'neighbourhood effect'
has deliberately been made fairly long. The reason for this
is that this particular debate has a direct bearing on the
present study. As will become evident later, a large part
of this study deals with diffusion processes in very small
areal units and, thus, constitutes indeed a micro-level
analysis. The problem implied in determining the working
of a 'neighbourhood effect' at low levels of aggregation
will thus be of critical importance here.

Before the attention is turned to the more direct theoretical aspects pertaining to the present study, one more
aspect of the established theoretical framework within geography should be briefly discussed. This is the concept of
hierarchical diffusion, which lifts the level of aggregation in diffusion studies and deals with diffusion in international, national and regional systems/networks. Geo-

graphers often clearly distinguishes between hierarchical and contagious diffusion (cf. i.a. Brown & Moore 1969; Gould 1969 and Morrill 1975). Similarities exist between the two, but enough differences exist to justify a separate treatment.

Hierarchical diffusion is often found in urban systems (international and national) and this implies that diffusion is proceeding from larger to smaller centres (Brown 1981:21). Hierarchical diffusion could also take place between social-classes i.e. in a social hierarchy (Gould 1969:5). Basically the concept of hierarchical diffusion rests on the notion that there exist within a population informational-/contact-networks, built up by other criteria than spatial proximity. In these, information and impulses could be channelled upwards and downwards from, for example, national to local levels and vice versa (cf. Hägerstrand 1953:240-43; 1965a:263-64 and 1965b:371). The concept is, obviously, very much related to the scale at which a diffusion process is being studied. Around the nodes in a hierarchy e.g. an urban hinterland "diffusion is expected to proceed in a wave-like fashion outward from the urban centre, first hitting nearby rather than farther-away locations, and a similar pattern is expected in diffusion among a rural population." (Brown 1981:21)

A large number of studies giving evidence to the occurrences of hierarchical diffusion patterns could be mentioned: Hägerstrand (1966) on the diffusion of Rotary-clubs in Europe; Huang-Gold (1974) on the spread of Rotary-clubs in the urban hierarchy of the USA; Pyle (1968) investigating the spread of cholera in the USA; Gould (1960) on transport development in Ghana; Riddell (1970) on the diffusion of "Modernization" in Sierra Leone; Pedersen (1971) on the diffusion in the urban hierarchy in Chile and also, the diffusion of innovations between countries in South America; Girling (1968) on the spread of banking in early USA and Zelinsky (1967) on the spread of classical names in the USA.

Findings from the research, referred to above, are strikingly similar despite the fact that they have been carried out in different areas and at different levels of aggregation. The implications are that innovations tend to move very much in urban hierarchies emanating, or entering, at higher levels and then gradually filter down through urban centres of smaller sizes. There are also some evidences indicating that innovations entering, or emerging, at middle- or low-levels in the urban hierarchy 'jump' upwards to the principal centres from where a subsequent diffusion take place (cf. i.a. Semple & Brown 1974:16). There are also implications to the fact that innovations are filtered down along major arteries of transportation e.g. coastal shipping and river transport (Girling op.cit. and Pyle op. cit.). Furthermore, Riddell (op.cit.:92) shows the impact of the railway in moulding the "modernization surface".

Parallel to the hierarchical diffusion, however, a contagious diffusion process take place around the nodes in the hierarchies being studied — something which has been observed in all the studies mentioned. Thus, spatial diffusion studies often have to account for simultaneous and interrelated diffusion processes that, to an extent, are conceptually different and where different explanations will have to be sought depending on the part of the processes where the main focus is set. Obviously, and naturally, this is very much related to the scale, or the level of aggregation, at which particular studies are carried out.

2.3 Theoretical premisses for the present study

First, it should be emphasised that no definite logical break in the theoretical development concerning the diffusion of innovations in geography exists that justifies the separation made here. From a practical point of view, however, some of the more recent developments have a stronger bearing on the present study than do the earlier works, and this may justify their separate treatment. In particular the discussions will deal with the problem of scale, or more appropriate — Cones of Resolution, and the "Market and Infrastructure Perspective" (cf. i.a. Brown (1981:Ch.3-4). The discussion will also take into account a number of empirical studies on diffusion made in a Third World context. Concerning the latter, two aspects will be particularly emphasised. First, the role of government support in diffusion processes — particularly the role of agricultural extentsion services and agricultural research. Second, the consequences of the introduction of innovations will be considered.

Gould (1960:25-26) in discussing Cones of Resolution refers to these as simply "geographical scales" manifesting themselves as e.g. national-, regional- and local-levels. To Brown and several of his co-authors this is too narrow a distinction, that within itself contain a number of contradictions (cf. i.a. Brown 1981:37-40; Brown and Cox 1971; Brown and Lentnek 1973; Hanham 1974 and Semple & Brown 1974). These authors stress more the mechanisms generating

diffusions. In doing this they note different types of decisions i.e. "those pertaining to the establishment of diffusion agencies and those pertaining to the strategies by
which the diffusion agency reaches the individual adopter."
(Brown 1981:38). This, in turn, leads to the fact that
'functional aspects' — over and above singularly spatial
aspects — must be introduced and explicitly considered in
order to properly understand diffusion processes.

Brown (1981) elaborates on the distinction between the
functional and spatial aspects of a diffusion process into
a more complex conceptualization of the Cones of Resolution
in diffusion studies. In this he distinguishes between the
"Functional perspective" and the "Spatial perspective" and
writes:

"...the functional perspective which encompasses the mechanisms and
the decisions that drive the diffusion process to its various out-
comes. The second is the spatial perspective which encompasses one
manifestation of the functional." (Brown 1981:40)

Brown's model of the Cones of Resolution (ibid.:41) is
a synthesis of much of the research at Ohio State University in the seventies and then particularly Semple & Brown
(1974) and Semple & Brown & Brown (1975). From these an important conceptual basis for the analysis of the functional
aspects of a diffusion process has emanated. A primary distinction has been made between "propagator" and "non-propagator" supported diffusion processes. A propagator supported innovations involves a decision-making body with a
commercial and/or political interest in promoting the diffusion of specific innovations. Non-propagator supported
diffusion then implies a decision made by the adopter independently or after having been give the impulse to adopt
from a previous adopter. The previous adopter has no special interest in the latter's adoption. Moreover, agencies
with commercial and political interest in the adoption are
not involved in the process.

On a closer examination, few innovations are found to
belong to the non-propagator supported innovations. Still,
many early diffusion studies in geography and e.g. sociology have tended to overlook this fact and, thus, have treated innovations as ubiquitous commodities in space and time.
Obviously the profit-motive, generally associated with a
propagator-supported innovation in a free market-economy,
could substantially influence diffusion patterns both in
their temporal as well as their spatial manifestations (cf.

i.a. Grilchies 1957).

In addition the propagator-supported diffusion could be divided into "polynuclear" and "mononuclear" diffusion. Basically the difference between the two pertains to the number of propagators involved in the decision process in locating diffusion agencies. The polynuclear case refers to the case when "the responsibility for locating these agencies is decentralized and the decision carried out by more than one propagator" and the mononuclear case for which "a single propagator is responsible for the decision to locate a set of diffusion agencies" (Hanham 1973:8). Rationalities and underlying motives for agency establishment and location could, naturally, vary between different propagators and this could lead to differences in the possibilities to adopt between otherwise homogenous areas. Thus, in order to grasp the complexities of a diffusion process, the set-up of propagators and the rationalities pertaining to these must be explicitly considered. Hanham writes on the decision processes faced by the propagators and the effects on location patterns of diffusion agencies resulting from these:

> "Although, theoretical, it is possible for propagators to develop objective utility functions and assign utilities to all locations, it is more likely that biases arise through variations in perception. The propagator's awareness space will be determined to a large extent by the amount of information available to him, together with his past experience. Not only will the number of potential locations be less, but so will knowledge of the attributes of those locations. The marketing surface therefore becomes a perceived surface, and the utility function a subjective one." (Hanham 1973:9)

and

> "...., the utility function and decision rule of the propagator will both be influenced by the existence of a set of agencies that have previously located. Such agencies will not only afford the propagator with more information, and hence enable him to re-evaluate his utility function, but will also limit the number of agencies to be located and to some extent force the propagator to channel the innovation into previously established directions." (ibid.:10)

The latter quotation could make it possible to speculate on the regularities often found in diffusion processes, not least with respect to hierarchical diffusion patterns. This, however, would go beyond the purpose of this section.

As a final distinction, diffusion processes could be divided into "monophasic" and "polyphasic" diffusion. "The former is distinguished by the fact that potential adopters are influenced in their decision to adopt only by factors occurring prior to adoption. Polyphasic diffusion is characterized by influential factors occurring both prior and after adoption." (ibid.:13). Of the two the monophasic is the simplest and contains a single link between agencies and adopter. Once the link has been established and used by the adopter, be it for transmitting information or supplying a needed commodity, this is sufficient for adoption (cf. Brown & Lentnek 1973). The polyphasic case, however, involves more steps and could therefore make adoption more difficult.

The important factor in the polyphasic diffusion is that secondary links will also have to be considered. Brown & Lentnek (1973:5) use "the change from traditional agriculture to commercial agriculture" as an example of a polyphasic diffusion process. If the same example is used here, the secondary links would constitute marketing channels for the output resulting from an initial adoption. If the same propagator controls both the primary and secondary flows, it is reasonable to assume that provisions are made for these in the form of e.g. processing units, collecting points/routes etc. (cf. Gyllström 1977:Ch.7 and App. VII). If this is not the case the picture becomes more complicated. A likely outcome, however, is an adaption of policies between the bodies involved (Hanham 1973:15 and pp. 18-19). Still, the latter situation may lead to sub-optimal solutions that could have a negative effect on adoption.

Much of the discussion on the different aspects of the diffusion process is, in several of the works referred to, parallelled by a discussion on the "scales" (macro-, meso- and micro-scale) at which the aspects manifest themselves. Details of that discusion is, however, not necessary for the present purpose. Instead it may suffice to note that Brown (1981:42-45), after having discussed the "Functional perspective" of a diffusion process, distinguishes between the "spatial scale" and the "spatial form" at which these are manifested — "Regardless of whether the diffusion of an innovation is propagator or non-propagator supported, ..." (ibid.:42). The spatial scale of diffusion is thought of as "National, Regional and Local" and the spatial form of diffusion in terms of "Random-, Neighbourhood- and Hierarchical-patterns". Moreover, it should be pointed out that Brown advocates that "we ought to speak of cones of resolution for the functional perspective as distinct from those for the spatial perspective." (ibid.:44).

The discussion on the functional aspects of the diffusion of innovations leads naturally into the "Market and Infrastructure Perspective" on the diffusion process (ibid.:Ch.3 and 4). The nature of the factors involved in this perspective are obvious from the name of it. Thus, what is considered are the "supply" and "demand" factors of the diffusion process. Furthermore, the perspective could be seen as a reaction against the often implicitly assumed ubiquitous nature of the innovations studied and the strong focus on the individual adoption decisions found in several of the early diffusion studies (ibid.:50).

It is possible to follow the development of the Market and Infrastructure Perspective in Brown's writing from the late sixties onwards. In his study of the diffusion of TV-sets in a part of southern Sweden Brown (1968b) considers the location of distributors of these and introduces what he calls "Market Factors" in his explanations of their influence on the resulting diffusion patterns. He writes:

"An understanding of innovation adoption must, under these circumstances, consider the shopping trip behaviour of the potential adopter. Furthermore, it must also consider the distribution policy of the propagator of the innovation, since it is necessary to know whether a market utilized by the potential adopter is one chosen as a distribution point by the propagator." (ibid.:37)

and

"Since most shopping trips are made to nearby centres (for necessity-type goods), the residents of centres not containing distributors of the innovation will have less opportunity to purchase the innovation and less contact with distributors of the innovation, who are themselves persuasive agents." (ibid.:38)

In a later study by Brown (1975:203 and pp. 208-12) the infrastructural aspects are introduced more explicitly. Here a distinction is made between "Diffusion Agency Establishment" (creating supply nodes) and "Innovation Establishment" (promoting the spread of the innovation). These are then related to the infrastructural set-up round a given market and the discussion centres on how this could affect and shape the actual diffusion pattern. As mentioned already, much of the early writing by Brown and others is synthesized in Brown (1981) in which he writes on the

"Market and Infrastructure Perspective":

> "...., the diffusion agency enters into the diffusion process in two
> ways. On the one hand it provides a point of distribution for a given
> geographic area. Thus, the location of the agencies and the temporal
> sequencing of their establishment determine where and when the inno-
> vation will be available and provide the general outline of the spa-
> tial pattern of diffusion. This is conceptualized as the _first_ stage
> of the diffusion process, _diffusion agency establishment_.
> The second way the diffusion agency enters into the diffusion pro-
> cess is by conceiving and implementing a strategy to promote adoption
> among the population in its market or service area. The _agency ope-_
> _rating procedures_, the _second_ stage of the diffusion process, contri-
> bute further detail to the spatial pattern of diffusion by creating
> differing levels of access to the innovtion depending upon a poten-
> tial adopter's economic, locational, demographic and social characte-
> ristics. The establishment of diffusion agencies and the operating
> procedures of each agency are, more generally, aspects of marketing
> the innovation. This marketing involves both the creation of infra-
> structure and its utilization. Thus, the characteristics of the rele-
> vant public and private infrastructure, such as service, delivery,
> information, transportation, electricity or water systems, also have
> an important influence upon the rate and spatial patterning of diffu-
> sion.
> Together, then, these _market and infrastructure factors_ comprise
> the _supply_ side of diffusion and shape its course. These factors also
> affect the _demand_ side of diffusion by establishing constraints with-
> in which _adoption_, the _third_ stage of the sequence, occurs." (ibid.:
> 50-51 — underlinings by author to indicate italics)

Obviously the present study leans strongly on the theoretical developments in the spatial diffusion theory by
Brown and others at Ohio State University. The focus on the
'Functional aspects' of diffusion and on the 'Market and
Infrastructure Perspective' will be particularly obvious
in Chapters V and VI in the following text. The analysis
in Chapters VII and VIII, however, is less concerned with
the actual adoption patterns and how these could have been
affected by market and infrastructural aspects. Here, instead, the focus is largely on the consequences of adoption. Thus, it will also be necessary to make a short presentation of the theoretical premisses for that part of the
study.

Basically this part of the analysis draws on the discussion of the consequences of the introduction of the so called 'Green Revolution'. The first reference to that discus-

sion should be Griffin (1972). This discussion is also followed up and summarized in, for example, UNRISD (1974) and Pearse (1980).

Griffin (1972) introduces the concepts of "Landlord biased" and "Peasant biased" innovations with which he indicates the potential stratifying mechanisms that are built into much of the 'Green Revolution Technology' as such. Pearse, for example, write on the new "new technology":

> "The widespread introduction of a genetic-chemical technology is inseparably linked to major structural changes in the society and it is therefore unwise to talk about 'technological neutrality' in this connection. In another sense, however, a technology is neutral in that the significance of its use depends on the purposes and situation of the user. In theory at least, governments are able to make the new technology serve their chosen development policy. In fact, the social forces upon which government rest set parameters for technological policy." (Pearse 1980:7)

Griffin's terminology is based on the notion of the lack of neutrality in the 'new technology' in terms of differential access to essential factors of production — land, labour and capital — in agriculture between the "Landlords" and "Peasants". He notes, quite naturally, differences in access to land through e.g. tenurial arrangements. Also in terms of labour, differences exist in the sense that the 'new technology' may presupose a certain amount of mechanization, which is too expensive or otherwise unavailable/inaccessible for the group of peasants. Finally, he notes differences in interest rates for the two groups depending on whether they can get capital/credits from formalized credit institutions or if they have to rely on local 'moneylenders'. Singularly and in combination all these factors point to the fact that access to and the incentive to adopt the 'new technology' is easier and more favourable for 'Landlords' rather than for 'Peasants'.

Although no detailed discussion is presented here, it should be noted that at the core of Griffin's discussion lie the notion of "fragmented factor markets" generating different "costs" to 'Landlords' in comparison to 'Peasants'. It should also be noted that Griffin distinguishes between different types of innovations in terms of "Labour-augmenting innovations" (peasant-biased); "Neutral innovations" and "Material-augmenting innovations" (landlord-biased). The 'new technology' is 'Material-augmenting' and, thus, more likely to be adopted by the 'Landlords' who then are more likely to benefit from these innovations.

Yapa (1977) draws directly on Griffin's conclusions and conceptualizations. Yapa, however, continues the analysis and introduces a couple of additional elements to the ori-ginal analysis. First, he introduces the concept of "class-rent" (ibid.:353-56). In doing this he makes an eco-nomic analysis of the cost of production of a similar quan-tity of output for landlords compared to peasants based on the assumption of unequal factor prices in the fragmented factor markets. In this analysis he concludes that there exists an "excess profit...due to the privileged access to resources enjoyed by the class of landlords as reflected in the inequality of the prices of material inputs." (ibid.:354).

In addition to the discussion on how benefits are gene-rated and distributed in connection with the introduction of the 'Green Revolution Technology', Yapa discusses spa-tial implications of this — i.e. locational patterns of adopters/producers. The discussion here is phrased in terms of the Thünian rings and Ricardian islands and deals with the revenues created in different locations for the two groups — landlords and peasants. It will not, however, be necessary to go into details of this discussion. Instead it may suffice to quote Yapa's own conclusion from his discussions:

> "In summary, there are at least four basic forces which determine the course of diffusion of 'material-biased' innovations. First, there is the monopoly of land ownership with its manifold implications for the political economy, but particularly for the area of factor pricing. Second, there are the spatial gradients of location profit. Third, there are the variations in land quality which influence adoption through differential profits (or Ricardian rent). Fourth, although the economic facts of discrimatory factor pricing and location pro-fits define the equilibrium state toward which the pattern of diffu-sion is tending at any one time, the actual realization of that state will depend on space-time related rates of information flow." (Yapa 1977:358)

Obviously Yapa attempts to combine elements of a more conventional approach towards the understanding of the dif-fusion of innovations (the informational aspect) with aspects of political economy and social-structure. Such trends are also obvious among other authors e.g. Blaikie (1975, 1978), Brown (1981) and Rogers (1983). In combina-tion, the writings of the mentioned authors point towards

future research where the consequences of the introduction
of innovations will have to be considered much more explicitly. Moreover, these consequences will have to be analysed when considering the political-, economic- and social-
settings of the areas into which the innovations are introduced.

At this stage it will not be necessary to discuss these
authors at length. References will be made to them in later
chapters when the results from the empirical analyses are
being discussed. Thus, some brief comments will suffice.
First, Brown (1981) discusses the relationship between the
diffusion of innovations and the problems of development
in the the Third World in terms of what he calls "The Development Perspective" (ibid.:Ch.7 and 8). In the first of
these chapters Brown discusses the applicability of the
'Market and Infrastructure Perspective' in Third World settings. The premisses of this chapter are that, although a
lot of research on the diffusion of innovations has been
carried out in Third World settings, these have largely
worked in what Brown calls "The Adoption Perspective"
(ibid.:197-98 see also pp. 5-7). A singular focusing on
adoption aspects only does not (according to Brown) completely catch the complexities of diffusion processes and
their manifestations. In very many instances it is also im-
perative to consider the market and infrastructural aspects
of the diffusion process in order to understand the processes and forces involved.

This is shown by Brown in his Chapter 7 by two fairly
detailed presentations of studies in Third World countries
where an explicit 'Market and Infrastructure Perspective"
has been used — Garst (1972, 1974a, 1974b) and Brown and
Lentnek (1973). In addition a theoretical model of the diffusion of Cash-Crop Innovations is presented in this chapter. The points raised by Brown here will be discussed at
greater length in Secition 2.4, however, when attention is
focused more directly on the problem formulations for the
present study.

In the second chapter on the "Development Perspective"
Brown discusses "The Interrelationship Between Development
Processes and Diffusion". Initially the discussion focuses
on the consequences of innovation diffusion and draws upon,
among others, the works of Yapa and Griffin. From this
Brown continues to present a theoretical model on the diffusion of innovations in a rural hinterland. In this model
he incorporates the structural aspects defined earlier and
discusses the consequences of these on the diffusion pro-

cess. Finally, he discusses "The Regional Impact Of Innovation Diffusion" and "Development Impacts Upon Innovation Diffusion". Although interesting, it will not be necessary to discuss these at length here.

A short reference should also be made to Rogers (1983) who devotes a chapter to the discussion of the "Consequences of Innovations" (ibid.:Ch.11). Again it will not be necessary to penetrate the details of what Rogers writes. One may notice, however, that Rogers, like the other authors mentioned, bases his line of reasoning on the increased realization of the importance of the structural aspects for the outcome of a diffusion process. Thus, Rogers discusses "Windfall Profits" (ibid.:381), while Brown used the concept "Adoption Rent" and Yapa "Class Rent".

Rogers' chapter on the Consequences of Innovations is fairly long and contains theoretical discussions as well as empirical examples. Parts of Rogers' discussions focus on the role of change agents in the diffusion processes and how their actions may actually contribute to a strengthening of existing socio-economic stratification by focusing on certain strata of the population. This has, to an extent, already been discussed above and there will be reasons to return to this in several places in the following text.

There may be reasons, however, to pause briefly at one point in Rogers' discussions – i.e. for "A Model for Studying Consequences" (ibid.:375-76). In principle the model is very simple and emphasises only that the consequences of innovations will have to be introduced as a new set of independent variables, over and above the direct measurements of innovativeness used in more traditional studies. In defining the new independent variables Rogers separates between the "Functional, Direct or Manifest Consequences" and the "Dysfunctional, Indirect or Latent Consequences" (ibid.:376). The former are further subdivided into: "1. Increased production or effectiveness; 2. Higher income; 3. More leisure and 4. Others", while the latter are subdivided into: "1. Greater expense; 2. Need for more capital; 3. Less equitable distribution of income, land or other resources and 4. Others" (ibid.:376).

Following his discussion of the model Rogers continues to discuss the question "Why Haven't Consequences Been Studied More?" and the reasons given by him are of a general interest, as well as a particular interest in the present study. Rogers mentions three points:

"1. Change agencies, often sponsors of diffusion research, overem-
   phasise adoption per se, tacitly assuming that the consequences of innovations decisions will be positive.
2. Perhaps the usual survey research methods are inappropriate for
   the investigation of innovation consequences.
3. Consequences are difficult to measure." (ibid.:377-78)

Under each of these headings Rogers discusses the implications briefly. The first point is in the direction of a
point discussed earlier by Rogers — "The Pro-Innovation
Bias of Diffusion Research" (ibid.:92-100). With this he
implies that much diffusion research has been influenced
by implicit and explicit value premisses that innovations
should be adopted and rapidly diffused in social systems.
Moreover, according to Rogers, the positive views of innovations have restricted research designs and, thus, limited
knowledge of diffusion. In this respect, of course, change
agents with a political and/or economic motive in promoting
adoption could further bias research designs, if and when
by sponsoring research they have a vested interest in the
outcome of the research.

The second point dealing more explicitly with survey and
research designs also has a bearing on the present study.
This point leads into a much wider discussion on research
designs within the social sciences as a whole and, not
least, with respect to diffusion research (cf. Rogers
1983:114-116; see also Section 4.6). The basic issues raised here are: First, that commonly the problem formulations
in diffusion research focus on the adoption process as
such. This, in turn, often generates a research design focusing on the factors leading up to adoption, while post-
adoption factors are not considered. Second, and this is
very much related to the first point, information is often
collected in 'one-shot' surveys. Such surveys, on the one
hand, actually give a very restricted basis for the answer-
ing of questions concerning why a process takes place and
on the other hand, an almost neglible basis for the study
of more long term consequences of e.g. innovation adoption.

Concerning the third point given by Rogers it will not
be commented upon here, but more or less be left as self-
explanatory. It may suffice to say that a lot of Rogers'
lines of reasoning centre around the concept of "cultural
relativism" and its implications in terms of cultural-
values, political-values and individual-values. Obviously
the interpretations of what is desirable and not-desirable
may vary extensively between different value-bearers and

this, of course, will be even more strongly felt if an outside researcher tries to evaluate the consequences of innovations in a society other than his own.

2.4 Problem formulation
2.4.1 Introduction
From the more general description of the theoretical
background to the present study, it is necessary to concre-
tize the more direct implications for it and also to formu-
late the basic hypotheses. In doing this it will be necessary to use a much more 'empirical' approach to the problem, than what has been made above. The actual problem formulation has been strongly influenced by concrete and empirical research, carried out in different Third World countries. Initially it will, therefore, be necessary to briefly present these pieces of research before the attention
is turned to the actual problem formulations.

2.4.2 Diffusion studies in a Third World setting
As a first approach to the problem, a model showing dependencies and linkages affecting potential adopters was
construed (see Ch.III). The model was based on a fairly extensive reading of available studies dealing with the diffusion of innovations in Third World countries. As a pre-
lude to the problem formulation it is thus necessary to
give a very short synopsis of some of these. It should be
noticed, however, that the presentation makes no claims on
being complete or even very systematic.
The first thing to notice is that relatively early studies draw heavily on the theoretical frameworks and conceptualizations developed in the First World, or the West.
Notable examples in this genre are Misra (1968) and Ramachandran (1969), both studying diffusion of innovations in
the agricultural sector of India. Ramachandran in summarizing his findings writes:

"The important finding here is that the spread of innovations in
India can be analysed on the basis of conceptual tools developed in
the West; ..." (Ramachandran 1969:166)

The conceptual tools referred to are, basically, research findings in the traditions set by Hägerstrand and
Ryan and Gross. To a great extent these early diffusion
studies only confirmed established knowledge, rather than
adding knowledge that would pertain to the particular settings that could be found in different Third World coun-

tries. In one sense the finding of Ramachandran pointed in a direction that shifts the focus from the individual adopter towards the incorporation of marketing factors. He noticed that his adoption patterns were partly dependent on "the availability of the innovation at various points in time" (ibid.). Similarly Huke & Duncan (1969), in a study of the diffusion of improved rice varieties in the Phillipines, noted a hierarchical diffusion between municipalities and a neighbourhood effect diffusion around them, which is in line with established knowledge. At the same time they found that the transportation network was important and influential in channelling the diffusion patterns. Moreover, in incorporating additional variables, they could show that the transport cost of fertilizers had a negative impact on adoption, while the presence of irrigated land worked in the opposite direction. Thus, while still working within an essentially westernized conceptual framework, early studies increasingly started to point in a direction where it would be necessary to include variables pertaining to market factors and structural relationships.

A study which could have been referred to much earlier due to its importance for the early problem formulations of the present study, is Blaikie (1973), dealing with aspects of the diffusion of agricultural innovations in the Ziz Valley in southern Morocco. To an extent this study has a very technical bias, in the sense that large parts of the text deal with mathematical and statistical problems in the use of multiple regression analyses and then, not least, with the problem of including dummy variables in regression equations. For our present purpose, however, it will not be necessary to deal with the more technical aspects but rather concentrate on the assumptions and the findings.

In the theoretical basis for the study, Blaikie criticises conventional geographical diffusion theory for being "no more than information diffusion models" (ibid.:84; compare also Blaut 1977). To a large extent, he claims, that the importance of the information variables have been derived from "pseudo-contagious diffusion patterns" that are actually dependent on the different production opportunities on the farms themselves and the spatial variation of these different production opportunities (Blaikie 1973:84). Equally important are the differences in production opportunities dependent on infrastructural variables where increasing distances from cities, or markets, causes e.g. "increasing transport costs, increasing risk of unstable prices, poorer physical and social access to the market, problems of timely supply of inputs etc." (ibid.:84). Thus, a higher incidence of adoption around cities and markets, is not necessary a reflection of an informational supremacy over more distant locations, but could equally well be a reflection of the spatial organization causing a lower incidence of adoption in more remote locations due to rational economic considerations.

In addition Blaikie notes that innovations are rarely left to develop 'naturally' and, thus, he introduces and emphasises the importance of the change agent locations into his model and as a critical factor in understanding a diffusion process. Having defined the theoretical framework Blaikie goes on to discuss aspects like the data collection, testing procedures etc. These matters should not be discussed at length here. Attention should instead be focused on the results arrived at. Furhtermore, it will not be necessary to go into details of the results and thus, these could be discussed in a general form.

As a starting point Blaikie concludes that "information is the absolute pre-requisite of innovation" and that "A farmer cannot innovate without first hearing of the innovation" (ibid.:97). From these statements he goes on to discuss the relative importance of the informational variables in comparison with economic variables — primarily farm sizes. Basically in this comparison he notices that the economic variables take precedence over the pure informational variables in explaining adoption patterns and particularly early adoption.

He also notices, which is interesting in the perspective of conventional spatial diffusion theory, that the informational networks differ between larger and smaller landowners and, thus, also in the informational sphere, unequal opportunities for adoption are created. In a sense the differences found in the informational networks resemble the basis for the so called 'two-step hypothesis' of information flow i.e. a limited number of individuals are centrally placed in an informational network, while the majority receive their information through secondary sources and which is then often filtered through the centrally placed opinion leaders. In combination the finding that the economic status is related to position in informational networks indicates a situation where different factors interact in a way that furhter strengthens initial unequal opportunities for adoption of innovations.

In the case of Zis Valley, Blaikie also finds that the economic variables have "a spatial pattern of their own" (ibid.:102) and that this furthers the 'pseudo-contagious adoption processes'. As an overall conclusion he finds that the economic factors dominate as explanatory variables for the adoption patterns found. The informational aspects could, of course, not be dismissed as explanatory factors, but they had to be put into perspective with the economic variables. As a general conclusion it is possible to quote directly from Blaikie's text:

> "...this analysis of informational networks, diffusion and innovative behaviour shows the danger of deducing spatial processes from spatial form without adequate knowledge of the former. It also shows the differing importance of spatial factors in the process of diffusion of information and innovation." (ibid.:87)

The presentation of Blaikie's paper is slightly more detailed than the other works dealing with diffusion of innovations in the Third World. This is due to the strong influence this particular paper had on the original problem formulations. Before attention is turned more explicitly to these, some additional studies will be reviewed briefly.

The so called 'Modernization' studies form part of the basis for the original problem formulations, although the general implications concerning the development process in these are not in accordance with the purpose of the present study. Being basically diffusion studies, however, they give some insight into the processes involved. Worth mentioning here are the studies by Soja (1969), Riddel (1970) and also to a certain extent the one by Lundqvist (1975). Additional sets of studies dealing with the diffusion of innovations in the Third World that have had an impact on the problem formulations, although they are not possible to trace directly are e.g. Fuller (1974) who looks at the spread of family planning in a Chilean Community; Fawcett, Somboonsuk and Khaisang (1967) demographers and medical scientists who studied the effects of a family planning clinic in Bangkok and in doing this noted a 'neighbourhood effect' in the diffusion patterns; also Mayfield & Yapa (1974) who investigated information fields in a rural area of Mysore, India have had a general impact on the present study.

Of greater direct importance for the present study are, however, the studies by Garst (1972, 1974a, 1974b); Gerhard (1974, 1975) and Jonsson (1975). Garst worked very explicitly within the theoretical framework developed at Ohio State University. To a great extent his study was a test

on the applicability of the 'Market and Infrastructure Perspective' in a Third World setting and for this purpose he
chose a part of Kisii District in Kenya.

Garst worked with six different types of innovations
that in varying degrees could be said to be market and in-
frastructurally dependent. All the innovations were actively promoted by various propagating agents — government,
co-operative and/or private. In addition the diffusion of
some of the innovations e.g. coffee, tea and pyrethrum was
affected by different sets of rules defined by the propagating agencies. Garst managed to show very clearly how the
various factors interacted in way that they formed distinctly different adoption patterns for the six innovations (for a short summary of Garst's findings see Brown
1981:198-215). Market and infrastructural factors played
an overwhelmingly important role in the shaping of the diffusion patterns. At the same time, the sets of rules could
reduce or enhance their importance and, thus, directly influence the actual diffusion patterns.

Gerhart, an economist, also worked in Kenya and primarily in Western Kenya. Gerhart looked at the diffusion of Hybrid Maize and innovations related to the adoption of Hybrid Maize — fertilizers, pesticides and management aspects
related to these. In terms of diffusion theories he was
very much influenced by the sociological tradition in the
field.

Primarily Gerhart's approach is one in which he tries
to establish the economic relationships involved in the
diffusion of Hybrid Maize. He also introduces the concept
of availability of the innovations, but treats this factor
at a very high level of aggregation and is not able to
establish a relationship between this factor and adoption.
This was partly due to the research design and his difficulties in getting useful data on the availability aspect.

Gerhart's findings are of general interest for the present study, as one of the areas chosen for a detailed analysis in this study is situated in the areas where Gerhart
was working. Of more specific interest for the present study, however, is Gerhart's risk hypothesis. This hypothesis
is based on the notion that peasant farmers generally are
risk minimizers (cf. i.a. Dickenson et al. 1983) and that
farmers' risk perception affects their adoption behaviour.
Gerhart defines the real risk by dividing his study area
into ecological zones based on rainfall and rainfall probability. He also defines a proxy for the farmers' perceived
risk factor, by looking at their crop-mix and the presence

of drought-resistant crops. In testing this hypothesis he found that the farmers' perception of risk was negatively related to adoption. From this he concluded that, unless the farmers are fairly confident in the profitability of adoption, they hesitate before they spend money on purchasing seed and additional inputs making up the innovation package related to Hybrid Maize.

One additional study in the genre of more general diffusion studies in a Third World setting, could be briefly reviewed and that is the one by Jonsson (1975) dealing with the impact of the so called CADU-project in Ethiopia. The CADU-project being a good example of integrated rural development projects implies that the study is an example of the effects of actively propagator supported innovation diffusion. Like other studies dealing with a similar framework — e.g. Garst — the findings indicate a clear relationship between the location of supply nodes and change agents on the actual diffusion patterns. In addition to the spatial aspects Jonsson also looks at a fairly large number of socio-economic factors. Of the large number of conclusions drawn from these data two could be mentioned briefly. First, Jonsson notices a tendency towards a higher adoption rate of credits among farmers with relatively larger families. He also notices a higher adoption rate among relatively older farmers which runs counter to findings from diffusion studies in more developed countries where innovativeness is often assumed to be related to youth. In a way the age factor could be related to family size and, thus, form part of the explanation for the first observation. A higher age could mean a larger family, implying a higher dependency burden which makes these farmers more innovative. Secondly, the relatinship between adoption rate and age may be a reflection of a cultural trait commonly found in an African society, where the status of the individual and the weight of his opinion is very much determined by his age. Higher age implies more accumulated wisdom and, thus, the examples for adoption have to be set by the elders (Jonsson 1975:113-21). The latter could be an interesting point to consider in the formulation of propagator supported diffusion programmes in an African setting. It should be mentioned, however, that Jonsson has a long and detailed discussion concerning the difficulties in getting accurate information on the age variable (see Section 4.3).

The presentation of diffusion studies made within a Third World framework could be made much longer, but this would not contribute to the understanding of the problem at hand. To a great extent the findings arrived at in the more general studies are very similar. Of the findings from the studies reviewed the most important points could be that the importance, and relevance, of the market and infrastructural aspects on the diffusion process have been clearly shown and, furthermore, that cultural and local factors must be considered in order to understand the details of the diffusion patterns found. Moreover, in considering the latter factors, it also becomes evident that models of diffusion developed in a western setting are not directly applicable in a Third World setting (cf. i.a. Blaut 1977).

The list of studies presented is, naturally, in no way exhaustive. Quite a large number of studies on the Third World deal with aspects of the function of change agents in the diffusion process. Another set of studies, that have also had an influence on the initial problem formulations, are diffusion studies with an explicit Time-Geographical perspective. These will, however, not be presented here. Instead the implications from these, with a special bearing on the present study, will be dealt with below in connection with the problem and model presentations.

2.4.3 Basic problem formulations

In fact, the discussion so far should have given quite a good picture of the problems of particular interest in the present study. It should, therefore, be possible to make a fairly brief presentation of these.

At the time of the formulation of the original plans for the project, the author's notions of the change processes needed in the Third World were very much in line with the implications found in the introductory quotation from Mabogunje (1980:114). To an extent they still are, but they have been modified by a greatly increased awareness of the potential risks involved in an uncritical diffusion of innovations into Third World societies. Much of what should be presented here, however, deals with the original problem formulations and then also with the basis for the analysis that will be presented in Chapters V and VI. Beneath these original plans was the notion that an important part of the overall development process lay in the necessity to increase agricultural productivity. On the one hand, in order to create a better nutritional basis for the population at large, but also, on the other, in order to create surpluses that could feed a growing urban/industrial population and at the same time contribute to the capital formation needed in the restructuring of the general economy (cf. i.a. Dickenson et al. 1983 and Lewis 1978).

With this background the studying of the diffusion of agricultural innovations came fairly naturally. In addition the choice of indicators — an innovation package based on the adoption of Hybrid Maize — also came naturally. Other indicators could have been chosen, of course, but Hybrid Maize and the related innovation had all the qualitative aspects in them that were of interest for the present study. At the time, Hybrid Maize was very actively promoted as an agricultural innovation in Kenya (the country in which the ideas in the problem formulation were to be tested). The package based on Hybrid Maize is possible to adopt fully, or in parts, and depending on the actual adoption patterns the innovations put different demands on both the adopter and the supporting/supplying organizations. Finally, adoption of the package based on Hybrid Maize seemed to be a farily simple and rapid method of creating an intesification process, as well as paving the way for further adoption of innovations that could contribute to a more self-generating transformation process.

In general the problems to be looked at consist of identifying the critical mechanisms in the diffusion process and in doing that focus particularly on factors that could be obstacles to adoption. Implicit in this general problem formulation is also the idea that the means by which the obstacles to adoption could be removed, or reduced in importance, should be identified. In more specific terms the problem formulations were based on an acceptance of the importance of the 'Market and Infrastructure' factors in the promotion of innovations and, for that matter, in making adoption possible at all. Adopting a 'Market and Infrastructure Perspective' also implies the recognition of two parallel, and to an extent simultaneous processes. On the one hand, the innovations have to be made available through the building up of a distributional network. On the other hand, the potential adopters will have to 'respond' to the distributional network by starting to use the nodes in the network as supply points in their adoption. Rationality and efficiency criteria most certainly differ for the agents in the two parallel and interrelated processes and this forms the basis for more detailed problem formulations.

In these, the two sides of the overall process are looked at separately. First the focus is on the building up of the distributional network — i.e. the creation of the preconditions for adoption. It is recongnised that the underlying rationalities on behalf of the propagating agents, are critical in the forming of the opportunity set for adoption and, thus, also largely determine the resulting adoption patterns. The propagator rationality is, however, in turn determined by legislation and/or other actions taken by responsible central authorities and by technical constraints inherent in the innovations to be promoted. All these factors interact and the problem is then to try to indentify their relations and see how these interact to form the actual opportunity set for adoption.

The second aspect in the more detailed problem formulations, is the response shown by potential adopters to the distributional network and the extent to which the important factors in the creation of the network also influence the response. The applicability of the 'Market and Infrastructure Perspective' on diffusion patterns in a Third World setting have been fairly well shown by e.g. Garst (op.cit.) and Jonsson (op.cit.) and it could, of course, be questioned whether yet another study would add any important new insights to the problems at hand.

The two studies referred to, and this is common in many geographical diffusion studies, operate at a farily high level of aggregation. In this perspective it could also be noted that most of the spatial diffusion theory, or the empirical regularities in spatial diffusion patterns, is based on the observations made at a fairly high level of aggregation. In particular this concerns the frequently used wave analogies, which form an important basis for the spatial diffusion theories. The approach chosen here, however, is to work at a much lower level of aggregation than one usually finds in geographical diffusion studies. An indication of the micro-character of the present study could be given by mentioning that the sizes of the study areas are approximately 21 and 14 square kilometers, which could be compared with the size of the 'floating grid' used by Hägerstrand — it being 25 square kilometers.

Two particular problems are of primary interest. First, the purpose is to investigate the ways in which the potential adopters respond to the establishment of one or several supply nodes in their areas. The primary interest, of course, being to identify the critical mechanisms involved in the process — i.e. the elements involved in the linking of the farmers to the wider distributional networks.

The second purpose/problem consists of trying to establish the extent to which the regularities observed in spatial diffusion patterns, are a cumulative response to simi-

lar processes also taking place at lower levels of aggregation. It is possible that the empirical regularities are
only observable at higher levels of aggregation and that
the micro-processes forming them are actually fairly random
processes in which e.g. the friction of distance plays an
insignificant role. The latter would point at threshold
values at which certain explanatory parameters manifest
themselves and thus that the theories may be scale dependent. Also, if the aggregated results are made up of random
micro-diffusion patterns, this would further emphasise the
importance of market and infrastructural factors in shaping
the more general adoption patterns. Naturally, the lower
the level of aggregation the more difficult to separate general processes from random influences — still it would be
possible to draw some more general conclusions from this
part of the analysis.

Finally, the problem of the consequences of the introduction of innovations was part of the original problem
formulations, but not as a point of major interest. In the
present form of the study, however, these questions form
a major part of it.

III. Analytical Model

3.1 Introduction — Study objects

The original problem formulations were strongly centred around two important concepts in the diffusion of innovations, i.e. the 'Market and Infrastructure Perspective' and 'Innovations Bundles'. The latter describing the fact that innovations seldom appear as singular entities (see Ch. VI). In order to capture the interrelationships between the two concepts, an analytical model was constructed and a set of innovations fulfilling the requirements of the model were selected. The innovations selected as study objects were Hybrid Maize seed, fertilizers and insect-/pesticides — the three being related, from a usage perspective, as they have been presented as an integrated package in the promotional activities for Hybrid Maize in Kenya. While still important in the conceptualization of the problem in the present work, the analytical model is not given the role it originally had. Still the analyses of Chapters V and VI are based on the implications from the model and these form an important background to the later analyses in Chapters VII and VIII. Given this, the empirically oriented analyses below can be seen as comprising two interrelated layers — a point which is also emphasised in the general layout of the study.

In practice the actual adoption of the innovations used as indicators here, is affected by a number of agronomic considerations. Actually it is not possible to talk of Hybrid Maize seed in a general form as different varieties are developed for different ecological conditions. Similarly with fertilizers and, to some extent, pest-/insecticides it is not really possible to discuss these in general terms as the actual brand used is dependent on variations in local conditions. These distinctions will be discussed in Chapter V. At this stage it is sufficient to notice that the three innovations chosen as indicators, are all good examples of the types of innovations being diffused in the rural areas of many Third World countries and that they all posses qualities that are of interest for the present study.

First, it is possible to notice that they are all based on a set of ideas pertaining to their function and use. Thus, on the one hand, they have been developed in order to increase yields but, on the other hand, they also presuppose changes in farm management in order to obtain the yield benefits. Second, they are not singularly ideas, but also tangible physical objects that have to be made available to potential users. Third, as physical objects they also have to be transported from the supply nodes to where they should be used. Finally, they all carry costs i.e. they have to be purchased by potential users and, thus, their use would be dependent on the availabiltiy of capital and/or credit facilities. Furthermore, costs could also be incurred in transporting the commodities, thus, raising the total need for capital or credit.

3.2 Analytical model
3.2.1 General description of the model

In approaching the analysis pertaining to the original problem formulations, an analytical model was construed (see Fig. 3.1). The purpose of the model is to identify and to describe the links, dependencies and constraints that will affect the potential adopters of the innovations being looked at. As is already obvious from the graphical presentation of the model, and this will be further elaborated below, the model rests on ideas related to the frequently mentioned 'Market and Infrastructure Perspective' but also on Time-Geographical ideas.

As a starting point for the conceptualization of the model the notion of the dual economies in Third World countries could be used. In the dichotomy defined by this notion, agriculture would be found within the traditional sector (cf. Gyllström 1977a and IDR 1973). Empirical research has shown that economic relationships are often much more complex than the simple dichotomy in modern and traditional sectors suggests (IDR 1973), but this need not be discussed here. It may suffice to notice that Carlsen (1980:92) indicates that "between 20 per cent and 30 per cent of the rural labour force in developing countries has its main occupation in non-farm activities...", thus pointing at a larger economic diversity than the simple dichotomy suggests.

In narrowing the scope to individual farms the conceptualization could be used, however. In this perspective, the traditional sector could be thought of as containing tradi-

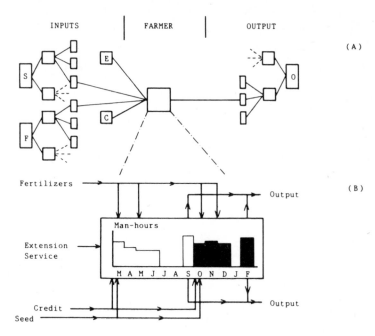

INPUTS | FARMER | OUTPUT

Fertilizers

Extension
Service

Credit

Seed

Figure 3.1: (A) shows how the farmer is linked to organizations with a
hierarchical structure on the input as well as the output
side.
(B) shows the seasonality of agriculture (white: long rains
and black: short rains; Adapted from Upton 1973). The use of
different inputs being confined to certain well defined
periods out of the agricultural production cycle is also
shown.

tional agriculture in which the individual farms would
largely be closed economic units. Again this is not completely true as, for example in an African context, contracts
and dependencies were created within the extended family
and the clan, in undertaking more labour demanding activities like land clearing and house building (cf. Kenyatta
1938:Ch.III). Also some long distance trading took place,
but was probably not very significant with respect to volume and impact (cf. Kenyatta 1938 and Soja 1968).

By thinking of the farm as a closed economic unit it is
possible to see the production activities as more or less
circular. Labour is largely recruited within the farm unit,
food is produced and consumed within the same unit, seed
for planting is taken from the previous harves and manure,
if used, is produced by the livestock on the farm. In this
perspective the farm has a large amount of autonomy as well

as control over the production functions. The introduction
of innovations of the kind being discussed here would radically alter the production relationships and the degree of
autonomy.

As indicated in Section 3.1 the farmers will have to
link themselves to supply networks of the innovations.
Thus, a number of dependencies will be created i.e. the
farmers will be dependent on rationalities and decisions
pertaining to the establishment and function of the supply
networks. Given the structure of these, viz. the networks
will often be defined at a national and/or regional basis,
the farmer will largely be dependent on decisions outside
his direct control. This, however, is as necessary in any
change process in the rural sectors of the Third World, as
it has been in the transformation processes in the more developed countries. Here one could notice some of the writing by agricultural economists. First, Mosher (1969:2) in
discussing Modern Agriculture describes "Each Farm Business
as an 'Assembly-Line'". Second, Mellor (1966:289) writes:

"..., one of the key features of a modern agriculture is that its
current level of production and, to an even greater extent, incre-
ments in production are based on a set of purchased inputs of a form
not found in traditional agriculture."

Usually the individual farmers will only be in touch
with units at the lowest levels in the hierarchical distribution networks. To a very large extent the actual adoptions will be affected by the trust the potential adopters
put in the proper functioning of the supply networks. Given
the often intricate couplings that exist between the parts
of an 'innovations-bundle' malfunctioning in one of the
networks may very well lead to discontinuation or non-adoption.

Figure 3.1 shows how a farm unit will be tied up in such
networks if and when adoption takes place. The figure has
been divided into two figures where Figure 3.1A shows a
'macro-structure' in which individual farms are tied up on
both the input and output side into hierarchically struc-
tured networks. The present study deals singularly with the
networks on the input side. It is, naturally, recognized
that the factors pertaining to these networks are equally
applicable to the networks on the output side. Figure 3.1B
shows aspects of the internal production organization on
the farm and thus indicates some of the possible problems
that could be found in fitting the innovations into an ex-

isting production-system. For the sake of clarity the number of different links has been limited to those of principal interest here. It is easily conceivable that the mapping of an empirical situation could show a much more complex web of links and dependencies.

Figure 3.1A shows two types of input networks — here fertilizers and Hybrid Maize seed — and in addition extension- and credit-services. The latter could, of course, have a hierarchical structure as well, but showing this would only add details to the figure without adding any explanatory value. Figure 3.1B, in addition, shows that there are also temporal aspects linked to the use of the innovations. Given the characteristics of the innovations being studied here, it is obvious that they come into the agricultural production organization at different points in time. Thus demands will be put upon the different supply organizations in a similar temporal sequence.

Starting with Figure 3.1B, it is obvious that the information provided through the extension service, being a necessary prerequisite for adoption, has to come in first — mostly before the production cycle starts. Secondly, in very many cases credits will be an equally necessary prerequisite for adoption and, thus, credit has to be available at the time, or before, the inputs needed have to be acquired. Finally, adoption/use could take place and following the natural crop production cycle as well as the recommended managerial practicies suggested for the use of the innovations, this too will follow a definite temporal sequence. In the figure a second cropping season, suggesting a bi-modal rain regime, is shown, this also indicates a repetition of the sequences. Each individual coupling in the overall pattern will, however, be facing particular problems and constraints, which will put the farmer in quite a complex planning situation when deciding whether to adopt or not. In order to show the intricacy of this planning situation the different elements could be discussed separately.

3.2.2 Information and sources of information

As pointed out in the theoretical discussions, information is a necessary prerequisite for adoption. It should, however, be noted that information could come from several different sources and it will always be difficult to establish the relative importance of different sources of an actual adoption pattern. The two-step hypothesis on communication, mentioned earlier, indicates some of the problems.

In this perspective the focusing on the extension service as the source of information in the model, and in much of the analysis to follow, is not completely realistic. Two reasons could be put forward, however, for the particular emphasis used in this study.

First, in the agricultural transformation process which is being initiated in most of the Third World countries, the extension service is playing a very important role. To a great extent the extension service is used for the dissemination of what Mabogunje calls control information (Mabogunje 1980:Ch.11). This implies that the extension service is used for transmitting desired messages from central bodies to the farming population. A major portion of such messages constitute information on innovations which the central bodies support in their development programmes. Furthermore, in many instances the extension service has been given a number of important functions in the overall transformation process, not least in determining the credit worthiness of potential credit seekers.

The second reason for the emphasis put on the extension service in the model, and the analysis, is of a more pragmatic nature. Given the data collection situation, described in Chapter IV, it was difficult to collect information on the intricacies of interpersonal information networks. Questions with the intent of capturing aspects of the more informal information networks were asked, but the results from these are not possible to use in a systematic analysis of the relative importance of different informational sources on the actual adoption. The results from these questions can only be used for very rough and tentative conclusions with respect to interpersonal and informal information networks.

There exists a large literature on the role of extension services in the development process. A major emphasis in the available literature on the subject, is on the relationships between extension agents and the potential adopters. Thus, the focus is on the direct role played by extension agents in the diffusion process. This part of the literature is well described by Rogers (1983:Ch.9), who also has a large number of references. There will be reasons to return to the lines of reasoning followed by Rogers in the analytical chapters.

Part of the available literature, however, also deals with some other aspects of the role of extension workers. A part of the focus here has been on agronomic research and the possibilites of applying findings from Agricultural Re-

search Stations on a large scale and then particularly in
the conditions faced by small-holders (see Campell 1975;
Heyer 1976 and Mbithi 1972). The general conclusion drawn
by these authors, is that there exists a large gap between
Agricultural Research Stations and the realities faced by
small-holders. The main emphasis in the research lies on
the most advanced and modern methods of agriculture which
are far beyond the managerial and financial capabilities
of the average farmers. Mbithi, for example, refers to the
Research Stations as "Ivory Towers" as far as the small-
holders are concerned (Mbithi 1972:11).

One aspect of the relationship between Agricultural Research Stations, extension agents and the farmers, is the
way in which research findings are presented to the users.
Often research findings are presented to the extension
agents as packages and this is also the way in which they
are further presented to the potential adopters. The divi-
sibilities (cf. i.a. Rogers 1962:Ch.V) often found in non-
mechanical agricultural innovations are not utilized in
promoting an adoption in stages. Packages are often presented in a 'take it or leave it' fashion, possibly discourag-
ing a number of potential adopters. The responsibility of
splitting a package is often passed over to the change
agents in the field, something which they are usually ill
equipped to do (cf. i.a. Mbithi 1972).

A particular problem with the extension service which
has been noted by several researchers, is the educational
level of the agents. The range of topics on which the extension agents have to inform farmers is very wide, which
would call for a broad and deep-reaching education in agricultural practices and the related skills needed in a modern agriculture. In practice, the educational level often
lie far below the desired standard. Several studies have
reported that the agents' level of knowledge sometimes lies
no higher, or even lower, than a better informed 'average
farmer'. In many instances the formal education of many
agents consists of only the most basic courses at agricultural colleges. A greater emphasis on more policy directed
research and a greater emphasis on practical knowledge rather than paper qualifications is also called for (cf. i.a.
Byrnes 1969; Heyer et al. 1971:Ch.5 and ILO 1972:Technical
paper No.13).

Roling, Chege and Ascroft (1973) and Lele (1975) have
discussed the efficiency in the frequently used individua-
lized techniques in reaching the potential adopters of innovations. These authors all suggest a greater use of

group-extension techniques as a mean of achieving a greater
efficiency in the extension efforts. Roling et al. also emphasise that the increased social pressure found in a
group-extension situation could be a stronger incitement
to adoption than an individual approach (Roling et al.
op.cit.:42). Lele is also in favour of group-extension
techniques. She, however, stresses that "a group approach
can work only when there is a relative equality in the
socioeconomic status of the target population" (Lele
op.cit.:80).

Related to a discussion on individual and/or group-extension, are the biases in the functioning of extension
agents which have been found in several instances. On the
one hand, it has frequently been found that extension
agents have a tendency to concentrate on already progressive farmers (cf. i.a. Rogers 1983). Additional biases
could be introduced when considering the means and modes
of transportation available and used by extension agents.
The agents often face transport problems and are required
to go on foot and/or by bicycle when covering their areas
of responsibility. With the overall transport problems
found in several Third World countries, the limitations in
these respects may introduce spatial biases as well, in
which the agents 'cover' the population (cf. Brown 1981).
The latter question will be discussed in greater detail in
the following analysis and, thus, no detailed discussion
is presented here.

In summarizing this section, it should be obvious that
the extension service does play an important role in an innovation diffusion process which must be included in the
model as well as in the analysis. Furthermore, the role
played by the extension service is influenced by a large
number of 'intervening' factors that could affect the efficiency of the agents in performing their tasks, as indicta-
ted. This, in turn, makes it even more interesting to include the extension services in the analysis in order to
try to determine their real impact on diffusion processes,
or at least some aspects of this. This will definitely be
of interest as their importance as sources of information
is not likely to be reduced for quite a long time. ILO
(1972:154) writes on the role of the extension service.

"In a country with a fair amount of illiteracy and inadequate mass
communication (sic), extension workers are likely to remain a major
source of information on new farming techniques and practicies for
many years to come."

3.2.3 Cash use and the need for credit

The types of innovations studied here presupposes an increased dependency on inputs purchased and also an increased dependency on cash or credit for the acquiring these inputs. Incidentally, this might in itself be looked upon as an innovation in a community previously organized on a subsistence basis where the majority of transactions have been based on bartering. The latter, not being an important aspect for the present study as available information, indicates that "the average Kenyan rural household received as much as 43 per cent of its income from non-farming activities" in 1974/75 (Carlsen 1980:99). Thus, indicating an already existing integration into a monetarized economy.

The integration of the farming population into a monetarized economy was for the most part introduced already during the colonial era in Kenya. The colonial government introduced a number of taxes − hut- and poll-tax. Partly to rise funds for the running of the colonial administration, but primarily as a means of getting African labour to the European owned farms (cf. Carlsen 1980; Cone & Lipscomb 1972; Manners 1962; Miller 1973 and Odingo 1971). Despite this already existing integration into a market economy, a further integration involving greater cash-use and a dependency on credits is qualitatively different.

Basically, there are five sources of capital for the purchase of the new inputs making up the innovation packages. First, capital could be raised directly by the sale of farm products. Second, private money-lenders could supply the capital needed. Third, government credit institutions could step in. Fourth, co-operative credit institutions could supply either cash or, more commonly, the inputs needed in kind. Fifth, commercial banking institutions could be utilized.

In actual fact, however, the sources of capital are much more limited for the average farmers than the list may suggest. In the case of more formalized credit institutions, a number of restrictions exist for the acquisition of credits. These restrictions consist of the need for membership (in the case of co-operatives), minimum acreage and title-deeds − over and above a general credit-worthiness. Naturally, this leads to biases in the availabilty of credits, possibly limiting the availability to groups that are already in a favoured position. Carlsen indicates that less than 10 per cent of the peastants have been able to obtain credits from Commercial Banks and suppliers of agricultural inputs, primarily fertilizers (Carlsen 1980:83). The situa-

tion for the overall sector of more formalized credit institutions is probably not very much better.

Using capital acquired from the sale of surplus products, or capital received from non-farm labour, is of
course one way of acquiring the new inputs needed. The
group of farmers which would have to do this would largely
be those without the possibility of acquiring credit. Thus,
the purchase of the inputs would compete with other consumption needs in a situation where liquid assets are probably a major problem. In such a situation the purchase of
agricultural inputs may not be the first priority.

Lastly, turning to private money-lenders would lead to
a situation where the investment costs would be very high.
High interest rates may act as a deterrent in this case.
It should already be mentioned here, that the use of private loans for the financing of the purchase of the innovations, plays a very marginal role in the areas looked at,
as found from the empirical material. It can therefore be
assumed that short-term private loans are used more for urgent consumption needs, rather than for investments in
agriculture.

Although the investments required for the purchase of
the commodities making up the innovation package are not
very high, they still may be beyond the means of the average farmer. Formal credit institutions are probably of
great importance in influencing the overall adoption rates
and adoption patterns. Furthermore, credit from such institutions is probably the most advantageous to the farmers
and to the economy as a whole. Still a number of problems
face the farmers in their gaining access to the services
offered by the credit institutions. These are partly the
same problems that face the suppliers of the inputs, i.e.
accessibility and timeliness of supply. Partly the often
rigid and cumbersome practices in receiving credits may act
as a deterrent to many farmers. A revision of these practicies in favour of small-holders and their need for short-
time credit could be very important in promoting changes,
including the adoption of innovations. Mellor discusses
these problems at length:

"Short-term credit must be timely, it must have a convenient repayment program suited to the money flows from the cropping cycle, and
the procedures for obtaining it must be reasonably simple. In contrast with these needs, co-operative credit tends often to involve so
much bureaucratic red tape than none of the conditions are met — many
trips to the office may be required of the farmer, thereby making it

less convenient, adding to the real cost, and quite possibly reducing the timeliness with which credit is provided. Rigidities of procedure may force repayment patterns which do no suit the particular production cycle facing the farmer." (Mellor 1966:321)

Mellor only discusses co-operative credit organizations, his line of argument, however, is applicable to the majority of formal credit institutions.

3.2.4 Input supply organizations

Similar to the problems facing credit institutions the input supply organizations are facing the problems of accessibility for the farmers and the timeliness of supply. In the overall framework of the hierarchical organization of the supply networks there is the logistic problem of having the correct supplies available at the right time in the places directly serving the farmers. Generally, the farmers' situations are such that they are dependent on getting their supplies from one or two suppliers and they cannot spend time and effort in searching for alternative sources of supplies. This, of course, puts a great responsibility on the proper functioning of the supply organizations as failure to meet the farmers' demands may have a negtive effect on the overall diffusion process. Two quotations may illustrate the problems:

"...it is quite clear that a modern type of agriculture not only presupposes the existence of markets where products can be sold, as well as markets where inputs can be purchased, but it is necessary that both types of markets should be spatially dispersed in such a way that they will be within satisfactory distance and travel time of farmers, for the simple reason that farmers' relative mobility is always limited by their space-bound occupation." (Johnsson 1970:181)

and

"The problem of credit and of the inputs delivered at the requisite time is evidently essential: the studies that I have received very rightly insists on this point, which is absolutely essential. It requires better co-ordination between those in charge of credit, supplies and the technical advice. A number of credits become impossible to recover, not because of the farmer, but because of the delivery of manures, insecticides or other inputs. An important difficulty rests in the prior estimating of the necessary quantity of these inputs, of which many have to be ordered from overseas, and therefore long months in advance." (Dumont 1969:50)

With the introduction of additional elements into the model the picture gradually becomes more and more complex. To a large extent the steering mechanisms are the crop production cycles facing the farmers. This is shown in Figure 3.1B and a short discussion on the implications to be drawn from this is necessary as well.

3.2.5 Crop production cycles and time-use in agriculture

Given the setting of the present study, Kenya, the following discussion will mainly deal with particular aspects of tropical agriculture.

The most striking feature, perhaps, of tropical agriculture is the strong seasonality prevailing. Seasonality, of course, is a feature of all agriculture, but it could be claimed that the sharp dividing lines between the wet and the dry seasons have a much more profound impact on the agricultural cycles than the more gradual change from winter to spring in more temperate climatic regions (cf. i.a. Webster & Wilson 1966:Ch.1). Among several factors, two stand out as critically important in determining crop patterns and yields. These are soil-moisture and soil-temperature. It is possible to determine an optimal combination of these with respect to yields and, thus, it is also possible to determine an optimal time of planting.

Soil-temperature is rarely a problem before the rains when, of course, soil-moisture is the critical factor. The onset of the rains, however, supplies the necessary soil-moisture but simultaneously lowers the soil-temperature. In this perspective the optimum time of planting in tropical areas is usually at the onset of the rains, or shortly before. Thus utilizing both the high soil-temperature and the moisture supplied by the rains to ensure proper germination of the seeds (cf. Scrimpf 1966:53-59). The farmers then find themselves in a farily delicate situation in which they have to try to evaluate if and when the rains are going to start. Failures to find the right time could have profound effects on the yields received or, for that matter, could in some situations lead to crop failures.

Added to this problem is also the problem of soils and soil-structures (cf. Webster & Wilson 1966:Ch.2). During the dry seasons the soils often dry out and a hard surface is created which is sometimes impossible to break until the first rains have fallen and softened the soil somewhat. Combining this with the requirements set by the optimum conditions for planting and germination, generates a situation of peak labour demands at the time of the start of the rains. Dumont writes:

"Early sowing, especially in tropical climates with a single short
rainy season, remains the prime factor in any improvement. This is
absolutely indispensable, and without it none of the other advances
will be profitable. A sufficient density of sowing or of planting is
the next essential for a good yield, as is the early and careful
cleaning of the land." (Dumont 1969:10)

The combined picture from the quotation and from the
discussion above is that the already existing peak labour
demands found at specific points in the crop production
cycle are further aggravated by the introduction of innovations into the system. In the recommended managerial practicies for Hybrid Maize seed, are found exactly the same
points as those raised by Dumont for the improvement of agriculture i.e. early sowing, increased plant population,
careful and regular weeding. This, in turn, increases the
demands that have to be put on the proper functioning of
the different organizations that have to supply inputs,
credit and also information. All these will be needed at
a time in the production cycle when the farmers will be extremely busy with seed-bed preparation and planting. Thus,
the possibilities of searching around for needed inputs and
the time available for multiple visits to credit offices
will be further restricted.

In discussing time-use and labour constraints in the agricultural production systems, a short note of some time-
geographical aspects should be made. It should be noticed,
however, that no explicit time-geographical analysis is
made in the present study. Still some time-geographical
aspects are of interest for the understanding of underlying
rationalities behind adoption behaviour. First, a lot of
time-geographical writing deals with different types of
constraints of a temporal and spatial nature. The different
constraints interact in such a way that they form restrictions on the potential activity-set faced by individuals.
In particular two of the constraints discussed are of interest here and these have been described by Thrift as:

"Capability constraints limit the activities of the individual
through both his own biological make up...and also the capacity of
the tools he can command.
Coupling constraints arise because it is necessary that individuals,
tools and materials are bound toghether at given places at given
times..." (Thrift 1977:7)

The two types of constraints actually pertain to both the potential adopters as well as the supply organizations. Capability constraints for the supply organizations could be thought of as production capacity of inputs needed, transport capacity to supply all nodes in the system, storage capacity at the nodes etc. In the case of potential adopters they would constitute e.g. labour constraints, technological levels in the productive activites, financial aspects etc. The coupling constraints would refer to aspects of the time-use in agricultural production cycles under a set of restrictions set by agro-ecological factors. The effects on both the supply organizations and the potential adopters will be defined by the definite sequences in which the different inputs will be needed. Added to this will be the restrictions set by the capability constraints, thus forming a hierarchy of restrictions which may limit the possibilities for adoption.

Linked to the discussion on the different constraints is also aspects of the innovations themselves and the "displacement effects" they exert on the present organization of the society (cf. Carlstein 1970a, 1970b, 1973, 1974, 1977 and Hägerstrand 1974). First, the demands put by the innovations may have effects on the type of constraints discussed. With respect to the present study the demands put by the innovations would imply following all the recommended managerial practices, which in most cases would mean an increased labour demand compared to previous practices. Naturally, this would further aggravate the already existing capability and coupling constraints faced by the potential adopters. This together with the fact that innovations are new elements of a given culture lead to "displacement effects", i.e. the innovations replace old cultural elements and/or the time-use organization is adapted to fit in with the demands put by the innovations. Again it should be pointed out that no explicit time-geographical analysis will be made in the present study. The purpose of the short discussion of some time-geographical concepts is to support the conceptualization of the problems and also to give some insight into the processes initiated by the adoption of innovations as well as pointing out some additional restrictions for adoption.

3.3 Application/use of analytical model

The model attempts to describe a relatively broad framework within which innovations should be introduced. To cover in detail all the points raised in the discussion of the model will, however, be almost impossible in a single study. Rather the model should be seen as the broad conceptual framework, within which some aspects could be looked at in greater detail. Moreover, the implications drawn from the relationships shown in the model could, and should, be used as explanations for the empirically established adoption patterns to be presented in the analysis.

The earlier discussion has already in several places indicated the chapters in which the more explicit analyses based on the model will be made. As is obvious from these indications, the initial phases of the analysis deals with the functional aspects of the relationships in the model. The model, however, also has a certain relevance in the later stages of the analysis, where the primary focus is on aspects of the consequences of adoption. The focus of interest would then be the structural aspects of the links shown in the model, rather than the functional ones.

IV. Data Collection

4.1 Introduction

The basic problem formulations and the analytical approach chosen in the study clearly indicate that a large number of data sources will have to be used. On the one hand, official information in the form of reports and published statistics is used for the more aggregated and general pieces of analysis. On the other hand, it has been necessary to carry out an interview survey in order to obtain data pertaining to the micro-aspects i.e. the part of the analysis dealing with the response of the farmers to the supply networks and the consequences of adoption.

The first part of the data collection creates no major problems, apart from the general problems of cutting through bureaucratic red tape. The latter, although frequently annoying, is seldom a completely insurmountable problem. The discussion in this chapter will, however, not deal with such problems.

Basically, then, this chapter will deal with aspects of the interview survey, which is a very important set of data but also the one which could be the most debatable. To a great extent the discussion here will focus on definitional and technical aspects of the data collection by means of surveys. In particular the discussions will centre on questions like the definition of the adoption units, selection of study areas, sampling procedures, questionaire design and field work organization. Questions pertaining to the quality and usefulness of the collected data will also be raised in terms of the validity and reliability of the data and in terms of the possibilities of determining casual relationships from the data.

Particular aspects pertaining to the use of the data in speicific pieces of analysis will be made in the analytical chapters. Similarly, methodological, definitional and interpretational questions related to particular pieces of the analysis will be raised in connection with the presentation of that part of the analysis. This chapter, thus, will only deal with the more general aspects of the data collection that are of relevance for the study as a whole.

4.2 Choice of adoption unit

The first point to be discussed is the choice, or definition, of adoption unit. Defining the adoption unit, obviously, will affect the following steps in the data collection procedure and then particularly the sampling
frames. In addition, of course, the choice of adoption unit
will influence the types of analyses made and the interpretation of the results from these.

The adoption unit used in this study is the farm rather
than individuals, which has been the most commonly used
adoption unit in diffusion studies. The principal arguments
for the choice have already been presented in Section 1.3
and they should not be repeated in detail here. The essence
of the line of argument presented earlier, is that the focusing on individual attributes as explanations of adoption
behaviour run the risk of overlooking important environmental, organizational and structural relationships which influence the adopter. In addition the focusing on individuals as adopters runs the risk of overlooking important
characteristics of the innovations being diffused — characteristics affecting the setting of the individual adopters
and, thus, affecting adoption decisions in a way that go
beyond factors pertaining to the inidividual only.

In all fairness it should be pointed out, however, that
the adoption units used in many geographical diffusion studies have not been defined as individuals (see i.a. Brown
1981; Hägerstrand 1953 and Törnqvist 1967). Still explanations and conclusions have often been worded in terms of
individual behaviour, probably a legacy from the sociological tradition in the field.

It may, perhaps, also be necessary to underline the fact
that the choice of adoption unit is not a denial of the importance of individual decisions in the adoption process.
The thrust of the argument is, that individual decisions
are made in a context, as shown in the analytical model,
which is wider than the frames of reference defined for individuals on socio-psychological criteria. The adoption
process is perceived here as one where ideas, pieces of information on the innovations and individual competences are
weighed together with organizational and economic aspects
on the farm in question. Beneath these concepts, factors
like labour avaialbility, product-mix etc. are thought to
hide themselves.

The second reason for the choice of the farm unit as the

adoption unit, is of a more pragmatic nature and boils down to the problems of data collection in the kind of areas investigated here. At the core of the more pragmatic considerations lie the limitations set by the available funds for carrying out field surveys. The only feasible option in the data collection procedure was one of making 'one-shot' interviews. In these it was necessary to try to capture the important pieces of information at one and the same time and the possibility of returning for complementary information was very limited.

In a 'one-shot' interview situation it is not possible to cover every single piece of potentially interesting information. Decisions have to be made concerning the questions that should be included in the questionaire or not. A guiding factor in this process was the assumed reliability of the information that could be collected and the decision was in favour of questions dealing with easily observable facts, or facts that could fairly easily be checked. Implicit in this selection process was the recognized fact that questions dealing with certain individual attributes e.g. age, education and also incomes have a strong tendency towards not being very reliable (cf. Jonsson 1975:47-50).

In addition discussions with staff at the Central Bureau of Statistics in Nairobi, particularly those responsible for the IRS 1974-75 (RoK 1977) led to advice to concentrate on data pertaining to farm characteristics rather than individual ones, unless the latter could be easily corroborated. Still, some pieces of information relating to individuals were collected e.g. attendance at Farmers Training Centres (FTC). In the analysis, however, these are rather seen as an addition to the set of farm characteristics.

4.3 Questionaire design

The questionaire consists of three separate forms of which two were filled for every respondent. First, general information on farm characteristics was collected in the basic questionaire, which was used for all respondents. Depending on the adoption or non-adoption of the innovations being studied, additional information was collected for each respondent in the A- or B-questionaires. This was determined by the answer to question 11 in the basic questionaire and the A-questionaire was used for adopters and, consequently, the B-questionaire for non-adopters. To a great extent the A- and B-forms contain the same questions, but the A-form contains a set of additional questions dealing with the acquisition and use of the innovations.

The wording of the different questions is found in Appendix 31 and it should not be necessary to go into details here. A broad outline of the different categories of questions should be made, however. Basically the questions deal with aspects of:

a. Demographic aspects and labour availability;
b. Socio-economic farm characteristics;
c. Farm- and crop-management;
d. Access to and availability of information;
e. Adoption and general purchase/marketing behaviour.

Deliberately the questions have not been put in strict order in the questionaires with respect to the main headings under which they are presented above. Some of the potentially 'sensitive' questions, for example those refering to incomes and economic transactions, have been separated from each other by more 'innocent' questions. This has been made with the intention of 'relaxing' the respondents and making them less suspicious of the purpose of the questions and the interview as a whole. A number of control questions have also been built into the questionaire with the purpose of checking the reliability of the answers to some of the 'sensitive' questions. In the latter case the questions have been separated from each other too, and the questions have been given different wordings, while they actually refer to aspects of one and the same thing e.g the amount of money spent on a specific commodity and the volume purchased.

A close examination of the questionaires will, however, reveal the absence of, at least, two types of questions that are usually included in diffusion studies i.e. questions pertaining to age and education of the respondents. In retrospect it could be lamented that they were not included despite the problems of reliability they would have caused. In light of the earlier discussion on the choice of adopotion units linked to the advice given by the staff at the Central Bureau of Statistics in Nairobi, they were excluded from the questionaire. Particularly in the analysis on the consequences of diffusion, the answers to such questions could have been used in order to more fully understand some of the factors leading to a stratification of the general population into adopter and non-adopters, often with very different characteristics.

There were basically two reasons for the exclusion of questions about age and education. First, as already indicated, the choice of adoption unit and the resulting focus on farm rather than on individual characteristics. The second reason relates to the assumed reliability of the answers given to such questions. These problems have been touched upon in the preceeding section and, furthermore, they will be discussed at greater length in Section 4.6. A short note of some of the problems involved could, however, be already given here.

Jonsson in his work on the Diffusion of Agricultural Innovations in Chilalo Awraja, Ethiopia (1975) has a discussion on the reliability of age data (ibid.:48-49 and Figures 3.4; 3.5). He notices that age data are not very accurately stated and that there exists a strong clustering tendency in age reporting towards certain ages, particularly ages ending with 0 or 5 e.g. 30, 35, 40 etc. To a degree this problem could be solved by using age groups, but the uncertainties with the reliability of the age data could not be completely reduced by this. The tendency to over- or under-report age would be dependent on the way in which the respondent perceives the purpose of the interview and the impression he wants to convey to the enumerator. These tendencies may differ for different age groups, thus, making even an age group classification a blunt instrument in trying to cope with the problem.

4.4 Selection of study areas and sampling technique
4.4.1 Selection of study areas
The first selection of study areas was made at a high level of aggregation. At first a selection of districts was made, within these a further selection of a number of sub-locations (the smallest administrative unit in Kenya) is made. Due to fund limitations the population studied had to be limited in various ways and the sub-location was deemed an appropriate areal and population unit for the data collection. Populationwise, a sub-location ranges from approximately 1,500 to 9,000 inhabitants, which gives between 500 and about 1,000 farms — depending, among other things, on family size (RoK 1970).

Furthermore, the sub-location has other advantages as the base unit for a study dealing with micro-aspects of behaviour and location. The sub-locations are the smallest units on which disaggregated statistics are presented e.g. basic population statistics. Of importance for the present study is also the fact that the existing land registration is based on sub-locations. This includes detailed maps in the scale 1:2,500 showing borders and location of registered holdings. Thus, for every sub-location where land adjudication and registration has been completed two relevant sets of data are available. The Land Registry give information on the names of owners, size of holdings, further sub-dividing of the holding since the original registration and whether the farm has loans in arrears. Combined with the maps the information form an excellent sample-frame in registered areas. In addition the maps helped in the fieldwork to locate the sampled farms. From a researchers point of view, however, the slight disadvantage of the two data sets is that they are not available at one and the same place and that different rules concerning access to them were applied. The Land Registries have district offices, while the maps are kept at the Survey and Mapping Division in Nairobi. This must, however, be regarded as a minor inconvenience and it did not pose a major problem for the present study.

Returning to the more general aspects of the selection of the study areas, it could be noted that at the more aggregated level the critera for selection were not very strictly formalized and were more qualitative than quantitative. To a great extent the first phase in the selection process was based on the outcome from discussions with various persons. The criterion applied at this stage was to find areas where the diffusion process was still under way, i.e. it should not have reached a very clear saturation stage. In addition diffusion should not be at too early a stage, i.e. the possibilities for adoption should have been present for a couple of years.

The second criterion used was based on a qualitative notion of the general level of 'development' in different areas. Included in this criterion was a notion of the commercialisation of the agricultural sector based on the possibilities and actual cash-crop production. Thus, it was assumed that adoption would be faster in an area where farmers had cash incomes from, for example, the sale of cash-crops. The choice was affected by the possibility of comparing areas that 'scored' differently on the 'development' criterion. In applying the criterion, different studies such as for example Soja (1968), were used in trying to find 'modernized' as opposed to less 'modernized' areas. Also the opinions of the people directly involved in the actual promotion of the innovations being looked at, were used in deciding on areas with a fast as opposed to a slow adoption rate.

A possible complication which was considered but not ad-

justed to was differences in soil fertility and other ecological variables. Naturally, these factors affect the
adoption rates, but considering the usually relatively
small size of sub-locations this was not thought to be a
major problem. The majority of the Kenyan sub-locations
have an area of less than 50 square kilometers in areas
with a potential for permanent agriculture (RoK 1970). Some
problems could emerge, however, in areas with a very undulating terrain with distinct catena formations. In such
areas leaching and sedimentation lead to differences in
soil-structure and -fertility at different altitudes and
also at very short distances. It was assumed, that such
differences should be fairly evenly distributed over the
population studied and not seriously affect the possibilities of drawing conclusions.

The final criterion for the initial selection was a refinement of the criterion that the selected areas should
be areas where the adoption process was under way. This
concerns the possibilites for adoption and then primarily
the temporal aspects of these possibilites. The first introduction of Hybrid Maize seed suited for small-holders
was made in the season 1966/67. Prior to this, so called
synthetic varieties had been released for certain areas.
The latter has occasionally caused some definitional con-
fusion with respect to the true dates for the introduction
of Hybrid Maize in some published studies. Although, synthetic and hybrid varieties have many things in common,
particularly concerning the demands put on supply networks,
they are also qualitatively different in these demands.
Synthetic varieties are less complex from a genetic point
of view and do not call for replenishment every year, which
is the case for the proper use of hybrid varieties. From
a general point of view, however, the distinction is probably not very important for the small-holder adopters.
Adoption of hybrid varieties may incur higher and more re-
current costs. At the same time a shift from synthetic to
hybrid varieties is probably perceived by the adopters as
changing from one improved variety to another.

Returning, however, to the introduction of Hybrid Maize
seed proper, the areas for the first introduction were
broadly defined as Central, Eastern and Western Provinces.
In addition to these, Kisii District was included (KSC —
Kenya Seed Company 1967). Within the provinces a further
concentration to certain districts was made. Despite this
the number of stockists in the initial phases was fairly
small and they were, thus, thinly spread over the areas

(see Ch.V). In the selection process for study areas the districts of initial concentration were avoided. Based on the frequently used wave-analogy, the underlying idea behind this was to also try to identify long range influences on adoption into areas adjacent to the original core-areas before the distribution networks were expanded into these. Implicit in the line of thinking was, of course, the notion of studying a more 'natural' diffusion process, viz. a process that was not directly influenced by the promotional activities following the first introduction.

In considering the criteria set up, the process led to the selection of Nyeri and South Nyanza Districts. In terms of the last presented criterion, Nyeri borders on Muranga and Kirinyaga Districts and South Nyanza borders on Kisii District, the bordering districts all being areas of initial introduction of the innovations. The selected districts also fulfilled the main points raised in the other criteria.

4.4.2 Sampling technique

From the initial selection process of districts, the process of chosing sub-locations and individual respondents was based on random selection techniques. As already indicated, co-operation was established with the Central Bureau of Statistics at an early stage of the planning process for the study. The co-operation was primarily on technical and practical aspects in carrying out surveys in rural Kenya. This co-operation greatly facilitated much of the preparatory work for the survey. Still the financial and practical responsibility for the data collection rested with the author. Within the Bureau the co-operation was mainly with the staff carrying out the IRS 1974/75 (RoK 1977) and this had a certain bearing on the sampling procedure.

The IRS-data were collected at sub-locational basis in the more important agricultural areas in Kenya. The overall sampling procedure in the IRS is very similar to the one followed here. Within each province a number of districts were selected. Within the selected districts a classification of the sub-locations into agro-ecological zones was made based primarily on the main cash-crops grown in the area. Once the classification was made, a two-step random selection of first sub-locations and subsequently twelve small-holders in each chosen sub-location was made. For the whole of the IRS 139 sub-locations and 1,668 households were selected (RoK 1977:8-9).

The sampling made for the present study was to an extent

based on the one made by the IRS. First, it was agreed that the sub-locations used in the IRS should not be included in the sample-frame for the present study. This was naturally dependent on the assumed danger of interview fatigue that could result from having numerous surveys conducted in the same sub-location. The IRS sub-locations were, however, used in another respect in determining the sample-frame for this study. Due to the similarities between the data collection in the IRS and some of the data to be collected here, it was deemed as beneficial if the newly selected sub-locations bordered onto the ones already interviewed. This, it was felt, would broaden the base for comparison and analysis. With the unfortunate delays in finalizing the present study (see Ch.I) this argument is not as valid now as it was at the time of the sampling.

The next step in the sampling procedure was to decide on the number of sub-locations to be sampled and the sample size within these. The first part of this procedure was not difficult, as it was very much guided by the financial restrictions facing the data collection. It was decided to select one sub-location in Nyeri District and two sub-locations in South Nyanza District. From certain points of view, particularly with respect to coverage and the testing of the problem formulations in different settings, a larger number of sub-locations would have been preferred. In retrospect, however, which will be obvious in Ch.VI, one of the selected sub-locations is not used in the analysis due to the limited number of adopters found.

The second step was to decide on sample sizes within the sub-locations. The decision here was to draw a 20 per cent sample in each sub-location. As a practical norm the sample sizes in each sub-location were set at 200, which in the case of the selected sub-locations containing less than a thousand holdings would give a sample slightly above 20 per cent. This was made in order to leave a margin for absentee land-owners and for the cases where a selected unit was farmed under the management of another unit. The latter turned out to be fairly frequent and the actual number of farms interviewed in each sub-location is less than 200.

As it turned out the three selected sub-locations had all been adjudicated which greatly facilitated the drawing of the final sample. Adjudication had not been included as a prerequisite in the general sample-frame, but as this was the case for the selected sub-locations it also meant that a lot of the time-consuming registration and mapping in order to create a sample-frame was not necessary (see Section 4.4.1).

The actual sample was then drawn randomly in three steps. Within each district chosen the sub-locations used in the IRS were listed and numbered. By using a table of random numbers one of the IRS sub-locations was chosen in Nyeri District and two in South Nyanza District. In the next step all sub-locations bordering on the first selected ones were identified and numbered. From there the process was repeated as in stage one.

Having identified the actual sub-locations to be used in the data collection and also having found out that they were all adjudicated, the sample-frame for the sample of respondents was created. The necessary information for the sample-frames were collected from the appropriate Land Registries and from the Survey and Mapping Division. Having compiled the information from these sources it was possible to make a list of farm units. These were then numbered and a random sample was drawn from the overall list.

Having concluded the sampling procedure a list was made of the sampled farms. In addition the sampled farms were marked on the detailed land-ownership maps. These two devices were later used in the field and did much to facilitate the identification of the units to be interviewed. Particularly the detailed maps turned out to be very useful in this respect.

4.5 Validity and reliability of data —
   Field-work organization

The questions on the validity and reliability of the collected data are of course vital for the possibilities of drawing relevant conclusions from the analyses. At the same time these questions are not separable from the conditions under which the data have been collected. The discussions under this heading will, therefore, also contain a description of the field-work organization where this is appropriate for a judgement of the quality and usefulness of the collected data.

Discussions on validity and reliability can be found in several places in the available literature and to give a very detailed presentation here would not serve a very useful purpose. The problems in these respects are usually very similar for scholars collecting data in similar settings — here a rural African setting. It will thus be possible to draw on other writers who have faced similar problems. One such source is Rudengren (1981:103-110) and the following discussion will, in its more general form, be based on his writing.

The first point to be discussed is the question of validity i.e. if the collected data are relevant to the questions/problems presented. Generally speaking this is a very difficult question to answer. Moreover, it is possible that the question should not be put before the results of the analyses have been presented viz. validity should be judged in the light of the results.

Rudengren (ibid.) discusses the question of validity as partly a question of the possibilites of generalizing from the results. The lack of this possibility may jeopardize the validity (according to Cambell & Stanely 1966/1973:5 − cited in Rudengren ibid.:109). Given the fairly extreme micro-character of parts of the analysis made here, the question of the possibilities of generalizing the results is relevant. The research questions at hand may call for generalizations if and when one wants to use the results in a more normative way − particularly within a planning framework. Still, the answers sought are, most probably, only possible to find at the micro-scale of analysis and the possibilities of generalizing results obtained at this level are usually limited − at least with respect to generalization in a statistical sense.

Results arrived at in micro-level studies may have general implications and could form the basis for general conclusions. Furthermore, the concept of generalization in a statistical, or probabilistic sense, e.g. intervals of confidence, could always be questioned. From a policy point of view more detailed results that point in a general direction could be equally useful in forming the basis for policy discussions. In sum, and in regarding the similarities between this and Rudengren's study it is possible to take a similar stand on the question of validity and generalizations as was made by him:

> "Because of the uniqueness of each case study, the processes observed may contain many confounding factors that prevent generalization, even if some of the results and conclusions from case studies can be generalized." (Rudengren ibid.:110)

Turning to the questions of the reliability of the collected data these may be more tangible, although still difficult. Rudengren (ibid.:105-109) presents the problems under a number of sub-headings and it is possible to use his headings as a kind of check-list here.

First 'language' − the questionaires were all in English

and this may have created interpretational problems in the interview situation. The enumerators, however, were all se-lected from the general area in which the interviews were to be coducted and had a thourough knowledge of the local language. Moreover, before the actual start of the field work an intensive training period of one week for the enu-merators was held. For the period of training they were li-ving at a local FTC (Farmers Training Centre). The week was used for the giving of theoretical and practical lessons relating to the content of the questionaires to be used, interviewing techniques, measurement techniques etc. A large part of the lessons were devoted to the thourough ex-planation of the questionaires and the purposes behind the questions. Still, and in spite of the preparations, it is possible that the translation of the questions from English into a local language and then back into English may have caused some distortions in the original purposes of the questions affecting their usefulness for the present analy-tical purposes. It is, however, impossible to assess the extent and directions of these possible distortions on the available material.

Second in the check-list comes 'understanding of the question(s)'. Basically this is a sub-problem to the one concerning language. Regardless of the language in which a question is worded it does carry a meaning and if this is not conveyed to the respondent in the intended manner it could be a source of error. These difficulties could be further emphasised in the multiple translation processes described above. Again the way out of the problem, or at least a way of trying to minimize it, is through training. A major part of the training sessions were used to describe the meaning and purpose of the questions asked. Moreover, in these sessions the enumerators were asked to make trans-lations of the questions into the local language which was to be used in the interviews. The latter exercise was su-pervised by experienced senior statistical officers with a thourough knowledge of surveys in rural areas, on the one hand, and a thourough knowledge of the local language, on the other. Despite the measures taken to avoid it, the un-derstanding of the questions may be a source of error and the only way out of the problem is through training and standardization of wording and interviewing techniques.

Third, Rudengren raises the question of 'courtesy' in giving the answers. This problem is one with two dimen-sions. First, it has an 'interviewer aspect' viz. the be-haviour of the enumerator in the interview situation may be such that the respondent wants to please him/her and, thus, give the answers that the respondent thinks the enumerator wants to get. Second, there is a cultural dimension to the problem in the respect that "people are particularly keen to please a stranger with their answers" (ibid.:106).

An aspect of the 'courtesy' problem is the giving of 'incorrect information'. If and when this is made unconsciously it is rarely possible to take any corrective measures. It could, however, be made consciously for a number of reasons. First, the respondent may not know the piece of information asked for but out of the fear of losing face, or wishing not to disappoint the enumerator, an answer is given. Second, a special category of this problem is the way the respondent identifies the enumerator and the 'vested interest in the outcome' this identification may lead to.

Before the interviews started in any of the sub-locations, the project and the enumerators were presented at a 'Baraza' (a general gathering arranged by the local administration in a sub-location). At this meeting special emphasis was placed on ascertaining that the project was not a government one. However much such things are emphasised, the most common impression by the local population, of people coming from the outside and conducting data collection, are that they are tied in one way or the other to the authority structure viz. government. The possibile biases due to the 'governmental identification' may lead in the direction of understating some pieces of information due to a possible fear of taxation or the fear or the introduction of restrictive measures in certain areas, e.g. limitations in the number of livestock. In other respects a bias may be introduced from this 'identification' in the sense that the answers to some questions dealing with obstacles to development, e.g. the availability of credit, infrastructural problems etc., may have been too pessimistic. Behind such answers lie, of course, "the hope that the government might come and help people remove them" (ibid.: 107).

Continuing down the check-list a number of points raised by Rudengren can be discussed without going into too many details. 'Reluctance to answer' — actually only one refusal was encountered in the whole of the data collection (in Igana) and the general impression by the enumerators was that the respondents were willing, not to say eager, to answer the questions. In all sub-locations some farmers not included in the original sample, came and asked to be interviewed. In order to keep a good relationship with the respondents in the areas, these farmers were interviewed but their answers have not been used in the analyses.

'Giving the same answers as they heard others giving' — generally speaking this should not have been a reliability problem in the present study. All interviews were carried out in private with the head of the household. Still, one may assume that the survey as such may have been a topic for discussion in the area and that views on the questions asked have been exchanged in the area during the course of the survey and this may, naturally, have affected some of the answers.

'Confidentiality' may be a problem in surveys of this kind. Again the impression from the interviews is that this has not caused any problems. A quick glance through the questionaires does also reveal that very few questions could be seen as 'sensitive' ones.

Three points remain on the check-list and these are of particular interest for the present study. First of these come the question of 'retrospective assesment' — in fact only a few questions in the questionaire deal with matters that demand of the respondents that he/she should remember things that have happened earlier. From an analytical point of view these questions are very important and deserve special treatment. In the actual interview situation the enumerators were instructed to check the information that a particular farm had adopted some of the innovations asked about. The checking was done by having the respondents show empty bags and packages for the innovations as well as by signs of use that could be spotted in the fields. Actually, adoption in the survey was defined as use at the time of the interview so that the statement could be checked. One-time adopters who had ceased to use the innovations have been treated as non-adopters in the analyses. The occurrences of such cases was, however, very limited.

Having established the reliability of the adoption, the problem of the reliability of the stated time of adoption is, however, not solved. In fact the reliability of the latter is not possible to ascertain and the answers have to be taken at face value. The only possible check is whether adoption has been possible or not at the time claimed (cf. Ch.V). Also when the time of adoption is plotted in a cumulative graph the results point in a direction that is well known from other diffusion processes and this may be taken as a tentative indication of the reliability of the information given (cf. Ch.VI). Generally speaking it may be possible to assume a general reliability, but that the exact year (particularly when the time given lies in the fairly distant past) may not be absolutely correct.

The actual time of adoption was established in discussions between the enumerators and the respondents, where the former had information on the time of occurence of events that should also be known to the respondents. The technique is, thus, similar to the one used in population censuses where events are related to points in time that can be clearly defined. Still, it is not possible to ascertain an absolute reliability, but the reliability of the information should be such that it is useful for the analytical purposes of this study.

'Estimating quantitative data' is still another aspect of the collected data to be discussed. Deliberate attempts were made in the construction of the questionaire to avoid 'sensitive' questions and questions that could be difficult to interpret. Still, such questions had to be asked and the problem is to try to ascertain the reliability of the answers. It has often been established that the reliability of such information is fairly low i.e. information on acreage, expenditures, incomes etc. (cf. Pipping 1976:32 — cited in Rudengren ibid.:108). The method of trying to ascertin the reliability here has been through the two measures of training and the use of 'cross-question'.

In the training the enumerators had to practice the measuring of acreages through ocular inspection and by means of pacing the boundaries of fields. The 'cross-questions' dealt with information that could be put against quantitative pieces of information given at other places in the questionaires, e.g. volume purchased against the amount paid, children in schools against the payment of schoolfees etc. Continuously during the interviews the questionaires were checked for inconsistencies and when ambiguities arose that could not be solved immediately, the enumerators were sent back to the farm in question in order to seek out acceptable information.

A particular problem of reliability is found in the question dealing with the relative share of total income/turnover constituted by the expenditure on certain specified headings. The information provided here is used for quite an important part of the analysis in the form of the variable Annual Income/Turnover (INC/ATO). The information on that particular question is used as a weight factor for the 'blow up' of the sums stated on expenditures. Naturally, such a question could not have absolute reliability and

the interpretation of the information has to be cautios.
The instructions to the enumerators regarding this question
were to spend a lot of time on it and to discuss thourough-
ly the indication of the annual turnover that should be the
result of the stated relative figure. The impression of the
enumerators was that the information provided here, reflected fairly well the true values and nothing in their reports points in a direction that should justify a total re-
jection of the results of this question. Thus, again we are
faced with a situation where the information may be assumed
to have a general reliability, while the exact figures have
to be treated with great caution.

Lastly, the question of 'measurement stability', a point
that has partly been discussed above. This point also refers to the transformation of the information in its original form in the questionaires into the numerical form used
in the analyses. Concerning the purely numerical information this does not create a major problem, while the situation is more difficult with respect to the more qualitative pieces of information. Again it is not possible to
state categorically that changes of content and intent have
not taken place. All coding from the original questionaires
was, however, made by the author, which could be assumed
to have created a consistency of interpretation and then
also a measurement stability.

As a conclusion to the discussion on validity and reliability it may be approriate to once again quote Rudengren
(ibid.:109):

> "In conclusions, the overall reliability of the data is high enough
> for the type of analysis applied and the type of conclusions drawn.
> However, a general problem in this connection is that, while the
> data-gathering process is much more difficult in developing than in
> developed countries, the norms for evaluating the quality of the data
> are the same as if the data were collected in an ideal situation."

4.6 The problem of causality

In Chapter I a description was given of the 'stages'
this study has gone through up until its present form. An
important part of the reconsiderations and the changes of
approach described there, was the realisation of the 'im-
possibilities' of doing the kind of analysis initially intended. The analytical problem could be stated in one word
— 'CAUSALITY' — which refers to the applicability of the
survey data to the relationships postulated in the problem
formualtions and the hypotheses.

Due to a widespread inertia in the study of the diffusion of innovations, information is commonly collected in 'one-shot' interviews. Research traditions play an important part in the formulation and the carrying out of research within a particular field of interest. Research traditions — the proper word to use today is probably paradigms — define what is 'normal science' and it is within this that most research is carried out (cf. Kuhn 1962; Aquist 1981). To break out of 'normal science' and to cause a paradigm shift may be the wish of every aspiring researcher. To really do this, however, is only possible for a few. In consequence this study, as most others, follows the path laid out by the 'founding fathers' — if not Tarde (1903), at least Ryan & Gross (1943), Katz in the fifties and many others. The early scholars studying the diffusion of innovations, collected their data largely in 'one-shot' interviews from which they drew their conclusions that now have acquired the status of common knowledge in the field. The followers in the field have kept pace with the established tradition in data collection as they have in so many other respects (cf. Rogers 1983:Ch.2-3).

The problem with the 'one-shot' interview, or similar types of data collection, is that information on both the dependent and independent variables is collected at one and the same time. Survey designs often miss the fact that information referring to the two sets of variables should be quite different. Basically the problem lies in the disregard of the temporal aspects of the problems at hand and the data used in testing hypotheses pertaining to it. The assertion that the temporal aspects are disregarded in diffusion studies may sound a bit strange — to all ends and purposes, however, that is the essence of the problem.

Invariably the temporal aspects of diffusion processes must be recognized. Information on the time of adoption, which is the most common dependent variable in diffusion studies, is often collected as recall data in the same interviews where information on the independent variables is being collected. Recall data are generally very difficult to handle and their reliability is a constant source of worry for the researcher. The use of recall data are then limited to fairly simple, or at least fairly unambiguous, categories of data where reliability could be assumed to be fairly high. In the construction of questionaires the focus has often been set on the data as such and less on the problems at hand. This has led to data collection processes where information on the variables to be used in the analysis, are collected at the time of the interviewing rather than at the time of adoption, which is what they are supposed to refer to.

The core of the 'causality problem' should now begin to appear. What is often made in data collection, may be seen as 'natural' given the concern for the quality of the data. Hypotheses, however, are often phrased in terms of 'cause of adoption', 'adoption behaviour' etc. and this is where an established causality concept is pinpointed. With the exception of some very recent developments within quantum physics, models of causality are phrased in terms of cause leading to chains of effects. An important aspect of the models is that the cause precedes the effect. Preceding has a temporal quality, it is possible to let the difference in time come infinitely close to zero, but it will never be zero — however small there is always a difference in time between cause and effects.

The matter is made even more complicated if one goes further and looks a bit more closely at the kind of variables that are used as independent variables in many diffusion studies. Very often these refer to aspects of status, income, education etc. Particularly where the economic variables are concerned the problem is made more acute as these are often variables that are supposed to be affected in a positive direction by the adoption. The latter may be due, again, to too strong a reliance on established research traditions and "pro-innovation biases" (Rogers 1983:92-103). "Pro-innovation bias" refers to the generally very positive connotations associated with the very word innovation and that innovations should be rapidly diffused and adopted for the benefit of all. Very little research has dealt with the diffusion of 'bad' innovations and the possible negative consequences of adoption (for some examples see Rogers ibid.:Ch.11).

Returning to the causality problem as such, it is possible that a lot of diffusion research has got caught in a paradox that is difficult to come out of. Bearing in mind the two notions that the adoption of innovations is often seen as directly related to an enhancement of the social and economic situation of the adopters and that information on economic and social status is often used as independent variables in diffusion studies. Furthermore, the test-procedure is often one where information — 'ex-post-facto — on economic and social status is used to test underlying causes of adoption behaviour which is defined by recall data referring to a time before, sometimes long before, the data collection. Regardless of the actual type of test used, this leads to the paradox that: THE ASSUMED EFFECTS OF AN EVENT (the adoption) ARE CAUSES OF THE EVENT.

Some may feel inclined to discuss the paradox and its implications in the light of a positivistic research tradition and an overemphasis on quantitative methods that have tended to obscure important factors. The discussion will, however, not be pursued here. Here it will suffice to say that no simple way out of the paradox exists if one wants to discuss causes of adoption of innovations and is stuck with a set of data of the kind described above.

Returning to the 'stages' the present study has gone through, the 'causality problem' became the major concern when the work was taken up in earnest again. Initially attempts were made to wriggle out of the trap, and a number of seminars were held in order to discuss the problem. Judging from unpublished seminar papers it was brought up already in September, 1981 (worknotes 26/6/81). In the light of this it is interesting and also comforting that Rogers (ibid.:114-116) discusses the problem as well.

Although the realisation of the 'causality problem' was not a complete surprise, it caused a lot of uneasiness and a lot of time and energy were used in trying to find a solution. Most probably there is none, at least if one wants to discuss causes of adoption in the perspective outlined above. The only feasible analytical approach to solve the problem is a 'probabilistic' one viz., a reasoning on possible causes of adoption from the information available on the situation of the adopters at the time of the survey.

It should be pointed out, however, that only parts of the total analysis are affected by the implications drawn from the 'causality problem'. In particular the analyses in Chapters VII and VIII will be faced with the problem. Furthermore, the problem of the reliability of recall data, a sub-problem of the overall 'causality problem', will affect the analysis of the spatial adoption patterns presented in Chapter VI. In the latter context they cause a lesser problem than when used in more complex analyses.

V. Sales of Hybrid Maize - Organization and Development

5.1 Introduction

Although the main emphasis in the study lies on the more micro-oriented aspects of the diffusion of Hybrid Maize seed and related innovations, it is necessary to describe and define the setting in which the small-holders found in the micro-analysis, have to act if and when they chose to adopt. Also, given the theoretical perspectives (see Chapter II), it will be necessary to analyse the rationalities and policies behind the creation of the supply networks. These, in addition, will be influenced by factors such as the role of innovations in the overall agricultural economy, characteristics of the innovations and other factors. Moreover, factors influencing the creation of a supply network interplay with those affecting adoption decisions of the small-holders. In reality the whole process is characterized by the interrelationships between the different levels. From an analytical point of view, it is more convenient to work from a macro-perspective downwards towards more and more micro-oriented aspects. This, hopefully, will also give a clearer picture of the overall diffusion patterns and the factors influencing these.

The data available for the macro-aspects mainly consist of reports and papers from Kenya Seed Company (KSC) — the only producing and selling body of Hybrid Maize seed in Kenya. In addition to the material available from KSC information is found in various research reports and officially puplished statistics. Here it should be noted, however, that also the non KSC sources of data sometimes draw heavily on KSC for their data. Despite the fairly limited number of data sources no grounds exist to assume that the data should have a low reliability. From the KSC-reports and from discussions with managerial staff at KSC, a very active interest in the development and promotion of Hybrid Maize seed in Kenya is obvious. The interest, moreover, is not only restricted to the development of sales, but also to the mechanisms involved in the adoption of seed by the farmers. Also from the company's point of view the introduction of Hybrid Maize has been very successful and there should be no need for it to either over- or understate the true development of their actitivites.

The available data varies in terms of coverage, levels of detail and aggregation. Concerning the decision process and its underlying rationalities, it is only possible to look at this at certain points in time and at a high level of aggregation. Some of the data give a lot of details, although still only at certain points in time. The latter particularly refers to stockist location, where it is possible to describe fairly accurately the structure and development of the supply networks. The data on stockists does not allow an analysis of the functioning of the distribution channels and of the stockists. This can only be inferred from the development of sales of Hybrid Maize seed, which will be discussed later in this chapter.

Some of the data is also organized in a way that suits the purpose of KSC, while at the same time making them difficult to compare with other sets of data. This is particularly evident for the data on sales and the acreage planted with Hybrid Maize. The information here is based on depots used by KSC to supply different areas with seed. It is difficult to make a breakdown of the figures to a level which fits in with e.g. the administative organization of Kenya. KSC tries to indicate the areas that are thought of as being served by each depot, but in this breakdown several overlaps occur and it is difficult to assign the certain amount of seed sold to districts. The development of sales can only be described at a regional level, defined by the statistics presented by KSC (see Map 5.4) and at the level defined by the depots.

Also the level of aggregation at which the sales data are presented makes it difficult to look into the relationships between the number of stockists, who are presented at district level, and the development of sales. Such an analysis should not be attempted due to the lack of clear boundaries of the areas of coverage for the depots. The types of analyses possible from the available data are descriptive analyses at farily high levels of aggregation. The possibilities of comparing different sets of data are limited, which makes it necessary to make separate pieces of analysis for each set of data. An analysis of the relationships between the development of sales and the total build-up of the distributional network would have been preferred. An attempt to analyse these relationships will be made, but that part of the analysis cannot be very penetrating due to the problems incurred by the data available.

5.2 Maize in Kenyan agriculture

As a background to the discussions on policies behind the promotion of Hybrid Maize and the building up of a distribution network, a short discussion on the introduction and importance of maize in the Kenyan agricultural economy is necessary.

Maize is not an indigenous crop in Africa. Archeological evidence indicates that Central America and the Andean Region in South America are the areas in which maize originated and was first used as a food crop (cf. Schrimpf 1966:19). It was brought to Africa by early explorers and later on by early settlers. In East Africa maize was first introduced by Portugese traders in the sixteenth and seventeenth centuries (Acland 1971:124). Initially maize growing was limited to the coastal areas up to the end of the nineteenth and the beginning of the twentieth century when white settlers introduced new varieties which were better suited to the inland climate (ibid.). From then onwards maize has spread very rapidly among the African population and has grown to be the most important staple crop in Kenya (cf. i.a. Gerhart 1975:1-3).

Table 5.1: Percentage of area planted with ten major food crops grown in the small farm sector 1960, 1970 and 1975.

Crop	1960 % of total	1970 % of total	1975 % of total
Maize	44.0	51.4	46.6
Pulses	25.7	25.8	32.0
Sorghum	7.3	6.8	5.7
Millet	5.8	2.9	-
Cassava	4.4	4.2	1.9
Finger Millet	4.2	1.8	2.1
Bananas	2.7	3.7	3.6
English Potatoes	2.0	1.5	7.2
Sweet Potatoes	2.5	1.3	0.9
Yams	1.1	0.3	-

Sources: Gerhart (1975:3) for 1960 and 1970. The figures for 1975 are calculated from the IRS 1974/75 (RoK 1977). Figures for 1975 are based on only 8, food crops such Millet and Yams were not included in the IRS.

The importance of maize in Kenyan agriculture is evident from Table 5.1. Almost half of the acreage used for food crops in the small farm sector is used for planting maize. A major share of the maize produced in this sector is directly consumed by the producers, which is an additional indication of the importance of maize as a staple crop.

Table 5.2: Home consumption of maize in the small farm sector. Percentage by province.

Province	Local Maize	Hybrid Maize
Central	50.3	93.5
Coast	75.5	44.0
Eastern	82.4	84.4
Nyanza	33.7	67.4
Rift Valley	66.9	49.2
Western	96.2	50.6
Total	52.4	62.1

Source: IRS 1974/75 (RoK 1977) - Tables 9.2 and 9.3

There are great variations in the consumption figures, but a general conclusion that can be drawn from Table 5.2, is that a great portion of the maize produced in the small farm sector is also consumed there. Moreover, there is no great difference between Local and Hybrid Maize with respect to consumption patterns. This may indicate that Hybrid Maize is not so much looked upon as a cash-crop, but rather is an ordinary food crop similar to Local Maize. Actually what is evident from Table 5.2. is that the consumption of Hybrid Maize does exceed that of Local Maize. This is also reflected in the fact that a smaller share of the produce from Hybrid Maize is sold in comparison with the produce from Local Maize, i.e. 27.8 per cent and 32.8 per cent respectively (RoK 1977:80). Of the other important staple crops in the small farm sector, only beans show a higher home consumption rate than Local and Hybrid Maize, i.e. 72.2 per cent (ibid.:84).

Of the marketed output only a minor share is sold through the official channels, i.e. National Cereals and Produce Board (NCPB) which is the only authorized purchasing body in the country. It is difficult to obtain exact figures concerning the sales through official channels. The quantities sold through these vary very much from year to

Table 5.3:   Value of gross marketed production at constant prices
             (1976) for Maize (figures in K£ '000).

1975	1976	1977	1978	1979	1980[1]
18,682	21,628	16,237	9,048	9,257	8,344

Source: Statistical Abstract 1980 (RoK 1980) and Statistical
        Abstract 1981 (RoK 1981a).

Note 1: Provisional

year depending on the existence of surpluses and local
price variations. It is estimated that between 5 and 15 per
cent of the maize crop is marketed through official channels (Gerhart 1975:1-2; see also Swedish University of
Agricultural Sciences 1981:61). Over the last few years the
value of the gross marketed production has, furthermore,
declined wich can be seen from Table 5.3.

The problems that could be inferred from Table 5.3 with
resepect to the national supply situation of food, have
been noted by the Government and in 1981 a Sessional Paper
on National Food Policy was published. Initially this paper
tries to identify the underlying factors of the decreasing
trend:

"The shortfall in maize supplies in 1980 resulted from a series of
events beginning with the heavy crops of 1976 and 1977. Delay in ex-
port of surpluses left the NCPB with full stores and unable to purchase all that farmers supplied. The private trade was unable to ab-
sorb fully the surpluses remaining on farms due to restrictions on
the private movement of maize. In response, farmers, reduced the area
planted. The consequent decline in production was reinforced by a
shortage of fertilizers. Discontinuation of the GMR seasonal credit
system in early 1979 together with a lowering of the NCPB purchase
price further discouraged farmers from planting maize. This coupled
with adverse growing conditions in the 1979/80 crop year, led to an
exceptionally low harvest, estimated at 18 million bags." (RoK
1981b:6)

The paper continues to discuss problems in the whole
food sector of Kenya, and then goes on to discuss policy
measures that could lead to a greater self-sufficiency in
this sector. There will be reasons to return to this in
later chapters. Here the discussions should centre on the
more direct implications from the falling trend in maize
marketing.

Maize sold through the NCPB is made up of maize produced

both within the large and small farm sectors. In the small
farm sector most of the maize produced is used for subsistence needs and only surpluses in excess of these are marketed. On the other hand it could be assumed that most of
the produce in the large farm sector is marketed and that
the output in this sector is more affected by the price
structure and the termination of certain credit systems.
Between 1978 and 1979 the price paid to a farmer for 100
kilos of maize was reduced by 13 per cent, while the prices
between 1977 and 1978 were kept at a constant level. This
is reflected in a reduction of the acreage under maize in
the large farm sector from an overall high figure of approximately 85 thousand hectares in 1977 down to about 57
thousand hectares in 1979 (cf. RoK 1981a:105). In 1980 it
is assumed that the acreage will rise again, but these figures are still provisional (ibid.).

The reduction in acreage under maize explains some of
the reduction in gross marketed output, but the size of the
reduction is such that major changes in marketing behaviour
must also have taken place in the small farm sector. On the
one hand the reduction in sales to NCPB could be a reflection of a worsening subsistence situation in small farm
areas.

On the other hand this may be due to a reaction against
the price structure. The IRS 1974/75 (RoK 1977) indicates
that about 30 per cent of the maize crop was sold and of
this only 5-15 per cent was sould through NCPB. The obvious
response to a dissatisfaction with the official prices offered, would be to sell a greater share on local markets
where the prices often are higher than the official ones.
Usually there are great seasonal price variations on the
local markets where the prices are highest immediately before the harvest periods (cf. i.a. Gerhart 1975:14-15).

The available statistics do not make it possible to
distinguish the quantities of maize marketed through NCPB
with respect to source i.e. large and small farms. A substantial reduction in overall sales is obvious, however,
and it is assumed here that this is largely a reflection
of the changes in prices affecting both sectors. In the
case of the small farm sector it could also be assumed that
a worsening subsistence situation affects the prices paid
at local markets thus making it even less attractive to
market the maize through the NCPB.

Despite the fact that maize is such an important crop
in Kenyan agricultural economy, it is difficult to obtain
detailed information about procurement and consumption of

maize. Still, the discussion on the role of maize in Kenya could be much protracted. This has, however, been done in many other publications and it may be a bit superfluous to dig deeper into the data here. To round of the string of figures, a limited final set of figures could be given. The value of gross marketed production of maize (Table 5.3) is the second highest of all marketed cereals. Maize is second only to wheat and then only in 1978 and 1979. Before these years maize, valuewize, was the most important marketed crop. In 1978 and 1979 the value of maize marketed makes up between 30 and 40 per cent of the total value of marketed cereals. Prior to 1978 this figure was even higher, being around and even above the 50 per cent level (see RoK 1980, 1981a). Finally, it should be stated that maize is the basic foodstuff for about 90 per cent of the population (Gerhart 1975:14). The last figure, perhaps, summarizes the whole discussion on the role of maize and, of course, clearly indicates why so much effort has been made to develop and promote the production of maize in Kenya.

Lastly, the discussion here has, as far as possible, been brought up to date by using recent information, while the diffusion studies to be discussed later refer back to 1975/76 and earlier. The available statistics indicate that the mid-seventies may have been very favourable years for maize production in Kenya. Still maize is of primary importance as a food crop in Kenya and bringing the analysis up to date could be important in order to give some perspective to the analyses made in the following chapters.

5.3 Breeding programme

Deliberate maize breeding in Kenya first started in 1955 (Ogada 1969:5). The starting point for this breeding programme was a local maize variety called Kenya Flat White, which was the variety commonly grown by Kenyan farmers. The Kenya Flat White was a developed one, through self-pollination from the varieties brought in by early settlers from South Africa (Acland 1971:126). This variety is best suited to highland climates and for altitudes between 900 and 2,300 metres (ibid.).

The initial objectives of the breeding programme was to increase yields of the maize varieties already present in Kenya and this work focused a great deal on the highland areas with a research station situated in Kitale. The programme developed rapidly, however, and after a few years only the programme was extended to include also early maturing maize suited for the drier lowland areas. This work was started in 1957 at the Katumani research station in Eastern Province (Ogada 1969:8).

In the Kitale research station work progressed and in 1959 germ plasm was brought in from different Central American sources. The introduction of these new genetic lines into the programme led to rapid results and in 1961 a variety called Kitale Synthetic II was commercially released (ibid.:5). From the first synthetic variety the programme developed further and in 1964 the first classical hybrid was released. This first hybrid had a yield potential advantage of at least 30 per cent over the Kitale Synthetic II. In the initial breeding programme the intention was to develop both synthetic and hybrid varieties as it was believed that small-scale farmers would not be prepared to buy seeds every year (see Section 5.4). Due to the yield advantage of hybrid seed, however, it became more or less impossible to sell synthetic varieties after 1964 (Harrison — quoted in Gerhart 1975:4).

Since the release of the first hybrids the programme has been further developed into breeding not only classical hybrids but also so called composite varieties. The purpose of the latter programme is to retain a greater amount of genetic variability in the seeds than in the more classical hybrids. In the words of Ogada the problem of the classical hybrid is: "...once the hybrids are produced there is not then much hope to increase their yields because the final product has no more genetic variability left in it to produce for any scope for selection." (Ogada 1969:7).

Developments were also made in the Early Maturity Programme and from its commencement in 1957 it was possible to release a variety called Katumani Composite A in 1966. In the programme it was deemed unfeasible to develop hybrid varieties for the lowland areas in which Katumani seed should be used. The composite varieties developed are synthetic/synthetic crosses (cf. Ogada 1969:5; see also section 5.4).

With the successes of the breeding programme and with the purpose of obtaining high quality seeds for all major ecological areas in Kenya a third breeding programme was started in 1965. This was the programme for the development of Medium Maturity Hybrids, which came to be located in Embu. The work focused on developing a cross between the late maturity Kitale types and the early maturity Katumani types. Again, this work was successful and already in 1967 it was possible to release Hybrid 511 which had a 24 per cent yield advantage over the locally grown varieties and the same maturity length (Ogada 1969:8).

The three programmes covered most of the maize producing areas in Kenya and the only remaining one was the coast. This was the most difficult for which to breed an improved variety and it was not until 1973 that a composite variety, Coast Composite X-105 was released.

Having produced the first hybrid and composite varieties, the breeding programme has continued into producing double-cross and/or three-way cross hybrids from the varieties earlier developed (ibid.:8). The programme has also been geared into breeding high lyceine maize, which from a nutritional point of view could be very important. The latter type of work has been going on since 1966 in Kitale and has also been incorporated into the programmes of Katumani and Embu (RoK 1972:77-81). Initial progress was evident in this programme up until 1970, no later information has been found, however, to indicate that specific high lyceine varieties have been released on the Kenyan Seed Market.

The present situation is that no such major breakthroughs as were made in the 1960s can be expected. The present targets are set at increasing yields by about 4 per cent per annum through genetic improvement. Also an emphasis will be placed on short-maturing varieties suited to double-cropping systems as well as developing varieties suited for intercropping (cf. RoK 1981b).

5.4 Seed and management characteristics

The results from the breeding programmes in the form of Hybrid, Synthetic and Composite varieties are produced in different ways and, furthermore, different managerial demands are put upon their use. Before the attention is turned to the actual creation of a distribution network for these, it is necessary to describe some of these characteristics, as they will have an impact on the possibilities for adoption.

A hybrid is produced by crossing different varieties in two-steps, thus reaching a new variety which contains the genetic qualities of the so-called inbreed lines. Parts of the process is shown in Figure 5.1.

In the process of crossing, deliberate selections are made of the inbreed lines with respect to the particular qualities one would like to have in the final hybrid. In making this selection it is possible to create seed varieties adapted to specific environments. A primary focus in the breeding programme was to adapt seed varieties to the

Figure 5.1: Production of 4-way and 3-way hybrids.

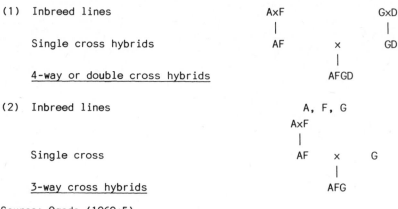

Source: Ogada (1969:5)

wide differences in altitudes and subsequently, differences in rainfall and temperature.

With classical hybrids, however, yields drop in succeeding generations and in order to retain the yield advantage of hybrids over local varieties fresh seed should be purchased for every planting season. Thus, it is not possible to select seed from the preceding harvest, which is the common practice in the use of local varieties. From an adoption point of view this, of course, has implications for the farmers as well as the suppliers.

Synthetic varieties that are formed from a large number of inbreed lines and have a greater genetic variability, are not faced with the same restrictions concerning the need to purchase seed every year (ibid.:5). A development from the classical hybrid are the composite varieties, varietal crosses, with the intention of retaining a larger genetic variability than what is found in the classical hybrids. Composite varieties may be crosses of classical hybrids, crosses between hybrid and synthetic varieties or hybrid crosses with single inbreed lines. These are also less sensitive to yield reductions in subsequent generations, but preferably, new seed should be purchased every year in the case of composite varieties (ibid.:6). Again it is obvious, that above all other factors affecting adoption the genetic characteristics of the improved seeds will have consequences for the farmers and suppliers and thus influence adoption.

A second aspect of the improved seed varieties is that they demand certain management, or crop husbandry, practices that differ from the traditional if the full yield potential should be realized. As already indicated the presentation of Hybrid Maize as an innovation has been made in a package form, also involving fertilizers and pest-/insecticides. The presentation of the package revolves around a set of nine recommended management practices. A leaflet describing these is included in every package of Hybrid Maize seed. The recommended ideal practices are:

"Land preparation: this should be made well in advance of planting and ensure a ready seed-bed clean of weeds at the onset of the rains;

Time of planting: planting should be made at the beginning of the rains, or shortly before;

Choice of hybrid: the right hybrid variety with respect to altitude and rainfall should be chosen;

Population and spacing: a high, but not excessively high, number of plants should be grown, this is achieved if planting is made in rows with a 100 cm between rows and 25 cm between plants;

Planting: two seeds should be planted in every hole and a later thinning should be made when the plants are 15 to 20 cm high;

Fertilizers: these should be used at two times, first at planting and then later as top-dressing when the maize is knee-high;

Weeding: in addition to having a clean seed-bed early weeding is recommended and weeding should be a continuous process keeping the fields clear of weeds until the maize flowers;

Stalkborer protection: in order to prevent stalkborers (an insect attacking the maize) insecticides should be used on the growing maize;

Storage treatment against weevils: it is recommended that insecticides are applied to the harvested cobs before they are stored to reduce storage losses."
(quoted and adapted from KSC instruction leaflet)

As discussed in Chapter III when the analytical model was introduced, the recommended practices may have a profound influence on the existing farm management organization, labour utilization etc. Also in reality it is very likely that the recommended practices are presented as imperatives to the farmers in order to realize the increased yield potentials. In practice, however, agronomic research on Hybrid Maize has shown that some of the points are optional and are dependent on what has been done regarding some of the other points.

A number of studies including Local and Hybrid Maize varieties grown under different quality management conditions, plant populations and fertilizer application have been carried out by Allen (1969, 1970, 1972, 1974). The basic finding from these studies is that the most important factor influencing yield levels is husbandry practices. Linked to husbandry practices is plant population, which Hesselmark (1976) has shown as being a critical factor in affecting yields. Also linked to husbandry practices is early planting in order to take full advantage of high soil-temperatures in the first phase of germination (cf. Scrimpf 1966 and Acland 1971:125-26).

The use of additional inputs, Hybrid Maize seed and fertilizers, but no improvement of husbandry, gave only minor increases in yields as compared to the criterion factor combination: Local Maize seed, bad husbandry and no fertilizers. Not suprisingly the best yields were obtained with a factor combination comprising good husbandry, Hybrid Maize seed and fertilizers (Allen 1969:1). A combination of Hybrid Maize seed and fertilizers but with bad husbandry actually gave lower yields than good husbandry with Local Maize and no fertilizers (ibid.). Allen's findings point in a direction away from an overemphasis of the material aspects of the innovation package. Instead the emphasis should be put on the managerial aspects. He writes:

> "The main conclusion to be drawn from a consideration of these five diamonds is that maize yields, output and profits per acre can be increased tremendeously by adopting the 'package deal' of good husbandry, hybrid seed and fertilizers. The optimum return from each part of the combination can only be obtained if the others are also at the correct level." (ibid.:3)

and

> "...what it does require is more hard work in the field. They should spend their limited cash firstly on improved husbandry, second on improved seed, and any balance on fertilizers. ...The aim is to ensure that money spent on fertilizers is profitably spent. Therefore, it is not wise to advise farmers to use fertilizers on poorly grown maize, as this is usually unprofitable and a waste of scarce money. In addition, there is a big risk that when farmers see that fertilizers have not increased their yields under these poor, bad husbandry conditions, they will blame the fertilizers instead of blaming the conditions, and may become prejudiced against fertilizers in future years." (ibid.)

The importance of good husbandry has been further emphasised in additional studies in Kenya (cf. i.a. Allen 1970 and Hazelden 1976). Substantial yield benefits could, thus, be reaped from the teaching of good husbandry, which should be a major task for the extension service. The presentation of the package, however, has been as a connected unit and alternative approaches have not been suggested (cf. instruction leaflet). Also the instructions issued to the extension agents have stressed the package as a unit. With their often fairly low level of education (see Section 3.2.2) they may not be able to suggest deviations from the recommended practices.

Some short notes on the recommended practices could be of interest. Starting with the material components of the recommended practices it could first be noted that insecticides could be a very important component of the package. Pre- and post-harvest losses of maize in Kenya are estimated at 10 to 20 per cent — a figure which in some areas under certain conditions could be substantially higher (cf. i.a. Hesselmark 1976:22). Second, fertilizers the prices of which rose by 340 per cent between March 1972 and March 1976 (information from staff at the Ministry of Agriculture). The increased price of fertilizers has led to a decline in usage and the value of fertilizers used went down despite price increases between 1974 and 1975 (RoK 1976: 81-2). The adaptive measures taken by the farmers against the increasing prices, where to cease using fertilizers; to use less — sometimes at such a low level that the use could be questioned; finally a selectivity in use i.e. only some crops were given fertilizers. At the same time an increase in manure use has been noted and then sometimes in combination with fertilizers. With the common managerial practices in livestock rearing, manure in sufficient quantities is difficult to collect and, furthermore, it is not available to all farmers.

Finally, a short note on the recommendation to plant in rows and linked to this, to plant single crop stands i.e. to refrain from intercropping of the Hybrid Maize. The basis for these recommendations is to ensure better weeding. More recent agronomic research, however, shows a greater understanding of some of the advantages of intercropping — not least from an ecological point of view. The present stand on intercropping with Hybrid Maize is that interplanting with nitrogeneous fixating crops (certain legumes) could be beneficial and could reduce fertilizer requirements (conversations with managerial staff at KSC).

5.5 Creation and organization of the distributional network
The breeding programme has been closely knit to the com-

mercial production of maize seed through a link with the Kenya Seed Company (KSC) — "...a locally owned commercial enterprise in which the government, through Agricultural Development Corporation, is a major share-holder." (Gerhart 1975:9). KSC has its headquarters in Kitale and since starting in 1956, it has been closely connected to the activities at the National Agricultural Research Station in Kitale, first through its activities in improving and selling grass seeds and later in the improved maize seed programmes (ibid.).

Initially, KSC was very much geared to servicing the large-scale farmers in the highland areas. The distributional network available was based on terminals at the main centres along the railway in the highlands. Before 1963/64 the company had not been involved in the selling of maize seed. In 1963, however, the company made an agreement with the Kenyan Government to start producing Hybrid Maize seed. As mentioned above, the first Hybrid Maize seed was released in 1964, but then only in a small quantity. It is estimated that the quantity released was only sufficient for about 3,000 acres — about 1,320 hectares (Verburgt 1969:1). This quantity was sold mainly to large-scale farmers through the already established distributional network.

Gradually the capability of the company was increased first through the implementation of a seed growing programme and later through the development of the distributional network. Farmers in the area surrounding Kitale were contracted to grow seed. All these farmers are within a distance of 30 miles (50 kilometers) from Kitale, which makes it possible to carry out regular inspections of the seed and of the husbandry practices exerted by the outgrowers (ibid.). With the development of an increased number of improved maize seed varieties the outgrower programme has had to be expanded into other parts of Kenya as well.

In 1966 decisions were taken with the objective of radically increasing the availability of improved seed and to make it available to the small-scale farmers (KSC 1967:1 and Verburgt 1969:2). In order to reach the small-scale farmers the distributional network had to be expanded quite dramatically. The existing network could well cater for the needs of the large-scale farmers who could arrange the transport themselves from the depots to the farms even over fairly long distances. In the case of small-scale farmers this would not be possible and it was decided that seed, fertilizers and chemicals should be made avaialable within "walking distance" for the farmes — "walking distance" being defined as 5 to 8 miles (8 to 13 kilometers) (KSC 1967:1).

To achieve a wider coverage of the distributional network and to be able to fulfil the intentions of getting supplies within 'walking distance' one had to design a more complex network with a considerably large number of nodes than in the existing one. To achieve this a "Method of Operation" was designed which included the existing structure but also extended this by including new levels in a hierarchical fashion. The layers in the new network were:

"a) Existing K.F.A. (Kenya Farmes Association) Branches and Depots;
b) Co-operative Unions and Societies where available and viable;
c) Reputable African Traders." (ibid.)

The levels that are supposed to cater primarily for the 'walking distance' aspects are b and c. Whereever possible one tried to utilize the existing co-operatives, but in areas which lacked these or where they were deemed not to be functioning properly, one tried to rely on local traders and their already established 'dukas'. The latter category is commonly referred to as 'stockists' which will be used henceforth.

At the first stage of the operation attempts were made to identify areas where an effective demand for Hybrid seed existed. This was made by contacting Provincial and District Agricultural Officers who were asked to list markets and areas where they thought such a demand existed. One also asked Co-operative Officers and Trade Officers at district level to recommend societies and traders who could be used as stockists (ibid.:2).

After the initial soundings it was decided to start in a limited number of areas. Broadly speaking these areas were Nyanza Province except Siaya District, Western Province, Machakos, Embu and Meru Districts in Eastern Province and Central Province except Nyandarua District. It should be remembered, however, that the coverage was not complete but was restricted to a number of nodes in the areas involved (cf. Map 5.1). The chosen areas could be supplied through existing K.F.A. branches with the exception of the districts in Nyanza and Western Provinces. For these areas one had to let Godowns in Webuye and Kisii (ibid.:4).

Involved in the first stage were also a number of technical arragements dealing with financing, accountancy and the documentation of sales. These matters are, however, not

Table 5.4: Number of stockists per district in 1966/67, 1971/72 and 1975/76.

Province/District	66/67	71/72	75/76
WESTERN			
Bungoma	1	88	331
Busia	7	31	45
Kakamega	13	109	344
Total:	21	228	720
NYANZA			
Siaya	-	52	56
Kisumu	-	22	33
South Nyanza	3	58	51
Kisii	16	140	222
Total:	19	272	362
RIFT VALLEY			
Turkana	-	-	-
West Pokot	-	13	28
Tranz-Nzoia	-	12	60
Elegoy-Marakwet	-	19	37
Baringo	-	28	65
Samburu	-	-	1
Laikipia	-	-	11
Uasin-Gishu	-	-	86
Nandi	-	33	160
Kericho	7	77	230
Nakuru	-	-	39
Narok	1	5	7
Kajiado	-	2	4
Total:	8	189	728

Province/District	66/67	71/72	75/76
CENTRAL			
Nyandarua	-	7	57
Nyeri	2	51	59
Kirinyaga	6	59	36
Muranga	9	48	70
Kiambu	4	68	108
Total:	21	233	330
EASTERN			
Marsabit	-	-	-
Isiolo	-	-	1
Meru	-	61	62
Embu	-	29	60
Machakos	33	104	117
Kitui	2	54	70
Total:	35	248	310
COAST			
Tana River	-	-	1
Lamu	-	-	2
Taita	-	-	48
Kilifi	-	-	25
Kwale	-	-	15
Total:	0	0	91
NORTH-EASTERN			
Mandera	-	-	-
Wajir	-	-	-
Garissa	-	1	-
Total:	0	1	0
KENYA TOTAL:	104	1,171	2,541

Sources: Reports from Kenya Seed Co, Ltd. 1967, 1971/72 and 1975/76

of any particular interest for the present study. Anyone interested in these aspects are referred to the reports concerned with these matters, particularly KSC (1967).

It is of greater interest here to look at the way in which the programme developed from the commencement in 1966. Information on this is summarized in Table 5.4 and in Maps 5.1 and 5.2. Table 5.4 shows the rapid increase in the number of stockists from 1966/67 up to 1975/76. From the commencement in 1966 until 1976 the increase in the number of stockists was in absolute numbers 2,437, which gives an increase of 2,443 per cent in a nine- to ten-year period. A closer scrutiny of Table 5.4 indicates that the growth of the number of stockists includes two simultaneous processes. On the one hand there has been an expansion of the programme into new areas. In particular this has meant an expansion into districts adjacent to those already in-cluded in the first phase of the programme. If more con-tinuous data had been available it might have been possible

to see a diffusion process outwards from the initial core
areas.

On the other hand it is also obvious from Table 5.4,
that a great part of the expansion of the programme has
meant only an increase in the density of stockists in districts already served by a large number of stockists. Examples of this can be found in Bungoma and Kakamega Districts
in Western Province, in Nandi and Kericho Districts in Rift
Valley Province and in Kiambu District in Central Province.
The extraordinary growth in one or two districts is also
reflected in the provincial figures. Western and Rift Valley Provinces show a growth of 316 and 385 per cent respectively in the period from 1971/72 to 1975/76. With the exception of Coast Province, where no stockists existed until
the 1975/76 period, the growth in the remaining provinces
is much more modest.

The processes discussed above are also reflected in
Table 5.5 and in Map 5.3A-C, which will be discussed below.
Explanations of the two processes are easily found in the
light of the rationalities behind the breeding programme
and that for extending the use of improved seeds to also
include small-scale farmers. The explanations, of course,
are found in the successes of the breeding programme which
made improved seeds available to an increasing number of
areas with different ecological conditions. They are also
found in the fact that those farmers who did adopt hybrid
seed actually increased their yields (Hesselmark 1976) and,
thus, acted as 'change agents' and increased the demand for
seed. Hybrid Maize has also been very actively promoted
through the official extension service and this as well has
led to an increase in demand. The uneven growth of the number of stockists in different districts may then be due to
smaller variations in the suitability of certain seed for
local conditions, giving lower increases in yields. They
may also be due to variations in the functioning of the extension programme.

5.5.1 Spatial distribution of stockists

Statistics of the number of stockists in each district,
however, only give an average picture and fail to register
the great variations that may, and do, exist in the distribution of stockists. A comparison of Maps 5.1 and 5.2 with
the population distribution of Kenya (cf. i.a. RoK 1970a:
48-9) reveals, not surprisingly, the relationship of the
distribution of the population to the distribution of
stockists. At the same time the comparison shows that the

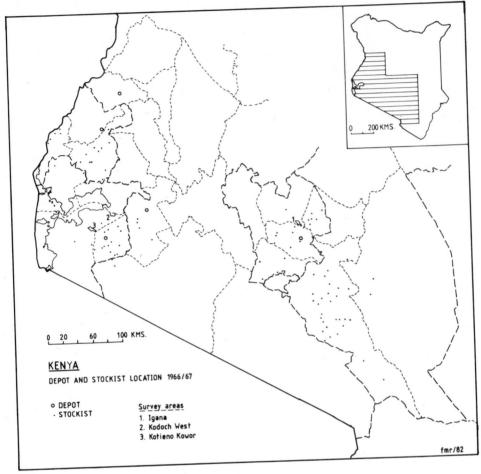

Map 5.1: Distribution of depots and stockists in 1966/67.

stockist distribution is not singularly related to the population distribution but that also other factors are relevant, primarily the transportation network (cf. i.a. RoK
1970a:69).

The distributional network of Hybrid Maize seed, as described above, is based on a number of depots located at
railway terminals and from these seed is either purchased
directly by stockists or distributed further down the chain
of supply nodes by lorry to sub-depots or to the stockists
directly. The structure of the supply network at levels
above the stockist-level can be seen on Map 5.4.

A closer scrutiny of Maps 5.1 and 5.2 shows the link between the transportation network and the location of stockists very clearly. In particular this link is obvious on

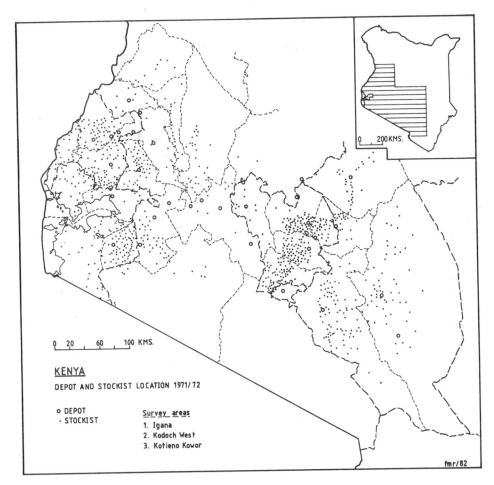

Map 5.2: Distribution of depots and stockists in 1971/72.

the map showing the location of stockists in the growing
season 1966/67 (Map 5.1). The map for 1966/67 also reveals
that only a limited number of districts had a significant
number of stockists, i.e. Kisii, Kakamega, Kirinyaga, Machakos and to some extent also Muranga, Kericho and Busia.
Apart from these districts the initial stage in establishing a distributional network to supply small-scale farmers,
consisted of a number of fairly isolated nodes that could
only have had a very local influence.

Map 5.2 shows clearly the dramatic expansion in the number of stockists which took place between 1966/67 and
1971/72. Several new districts have been added to those being served with Hybrid Maize seed. Also an increasing density of stockists is obvious in the districts already serv-

ed. The link between the transportation network and the
location of stockists is still apparent on closer scrutiny
of Map 5.2. What has happened is that the stockists have
come to be located closer to roads at lower levels in the
hierarchy of roads. To a great extent, however, stockists
are located along all-weather roads. If one choses to see
the expansion of the stockist programme as a diffusion process in itself, this is clearly an example of an infra-
structurally constrained innovation (cf. Brown 1981).

The emergent picture of the supply situation in 1971/72
(Map 5.2) is one of a fairly dense supply network with a
reasonably good coverage. At the same time it is obvious
that differences exist in accessibility to supply nodes and
that such differences occur not only between districts but
also within them. A walking distance of 5-8 miles, short
as it may seem, could be a barrier to the acquisition of
seed and other inputs related to the adoption of Hybrid
Maize as an innovation. In that perspective in 1971/72
large untapped areas exist which remain to be serviced.

Table 5.4 also gives information about the number of
stockists in the season 1975/76. This information has not
been mapped for two reasons. First, and this is the principal reason, the work involved in mapping the 2,541 stockists is more or less insurmountable. Moreover, judged in
relation to the potential value of such a map it was not
even tried. A map of stockist locations in 1971/72 existed
at KSC and this one forms the basis for Maps 5.1 and 5.2.
After having made some minor corrections of the 1971/72
KSC-map it was possible to trace the lines back to 1966/67.
To do this for 1975/76 is, however, very difficult.

The second reason for not attempting to draw a map of
the 1975/76 situation is the questionable value of such a
map. Table 5.4 shows clearly that there has been a continued increase in the number of stockists between 1971/72
and 1975/76. A map of the situation in 1975/76 would, of
course, reflect increase. At the same time, however, the
map would not be very different from the 1971/72 map. A map
of 1975/76 would show a great increase in the density of
stockists in some areas — particularly in some of the districts in Rift Valley and Western Provinces. It would also
show the continued expansion of the stockist programme into
new areas — primarily into some districts of Rift Valley
Province and into Coast Province as a whole. Such a map
would, however, not alter any of the conclusions drawn concerning the processes involved in the expansion of the
stockist programme.

It is clear that accessibility has been greatly improved for small-scale farmers in Kenya as a whole and for some districts in particular. In terms of the objectives of the stockist programme it seems as if several districts would have achieved access to the inputs within 'walking distance'. Some other districts — particularly those newly added and the more peripheral ones — are still a long way from the target.

A continued expansion of the programme will even out the differences in accessibility even more. To achieve complete equality will not be possible until every farmer has his stockist on the doorstep (cf. Smith 1979). Achieving this would call for a mobile distribution system to supplement the static system of stockists. Such a system has been tried successfully by the Ministry of Co-operatives in a limited number of areas (personal communication by Dr. Gyllström).

5.5.2 Coverage of stockists

In addition to a discussion about the pure locational aspects of the stockists and population, a combination of the two is of interest. In Table 5.5 and in Map 5.3A-C an attempt is made to combine the two factors in order to get a picture of 'coverage' of, or 'accessibility' to, stockists. What is attempted, is to give a per caput picture of the services provided by stockists in different districts. There are, however, some important drawbacks facing the approach. On the one hand a per capita calculation gives an average picture and local variations are evened out. Thus, the picture has to be contrasted with the actual location of stockists, as shown above, to get an understanding of the variations in the services provided.

On the other hand, no normative criteria exist on what is a good, or acceptable, service situation. Probably, however, there exist threshold values for the quality of the services provided and these do not take on one and the same value for every district in Kenya. Instead the threshold value has to be based on a number of local factors like population distribution, infrastructure, transport facilities, organization and production of the local agriculture etc. Combining a threshold value based on these factors with the actual location of the stockists, would provide a good picture of the service situation. This however, will not be possible to do here, and only tentative conclusions can be drawn with respect to what constitutes a good, or acceptable service standard.

Table 5.5: Population/stockist ratios at district level 1967, 1972 and 1976.

Province/District	Population/ Stockist 1967	Population/ Stockist 1972	Population/ Stockist 1976
WESTERN	59,148	6,458	2,296
Bungoma	322,685	4,347	1,373
Busia	26,723	7,153	5,970
Kakamega	56,335	7,964	2,703
NYANZA	104,460	8,650	6,589
Siaya	-	8,161	7,643
Kisumu	206,705	20,209	13,183
South Nyanza	39,459	12,764	14,459
Kisii	-	5,346	3,533
RIFT VALLEY	258,264	12,959	4,015
Turkana	-	-	-
West Pokot	-	6,993	5,111
Tranz-Nzoia	-	11,457	3,901
Elegoy-Marakwet	-	9,278	3,629
Baringo	-	6,415	2,829
Samburu	-	-	69,367
Laikipia	-	-	11,030
Uasin-Gishu	-	-	3,154
Nandi	64,002	7,022	1,687
Kericho	-	6,897	2,484
Nakuru	-	-	12,089
Narok	116,915	27,718	27,098
Kajiado	-	47,675	33,599
NAIROBI	-	70,958	-
CENTRAL	74,647	7,975	6,412
Nyandarua	-	28,035	3,692
Nyeri	168,825	7,848	7,437
Kirinyaga	33,827	4,078	7,302
Muranga	46,246	10,279	8,354
Kiambu	111,303	7,761	5,731
EASTERN	50,988	8,530	7,913
Marsabit	-	-	-
Isiolo	-	-	-
Meru	-	10,851	39,215
Embu	-	6,843	12,077
Machakos	20,038	7,557	3,956
Kitui	160,407	7,042	7,883
COAST	-	-	5,982
Mombasa	-	-	13,309
Tana River	-	-	83,340
Lamu	-	-	19,076
Taita	-	-	2,773
Kilifi	-	-	15,549
Kwale	-	-	17,339
NORTH-EASTERN	-	271,636	-
Mandera	-	-	-
Wajir	-	-	-
Garissa	-	-	-
KENYA TOTAL:	98,406	10,360	5,440

Sources: Reports from Kenya Seed Co. Ltd. 1967, 1971/72 and 1975/76; RoK 1974, RoK 1975 and RoK 1980

Furthermore, determining an acceptable service standard would also be dependent on the capacity of the stockists to serve a population of any size. The vast majority of stockists are small-scale traders owning a 'duka' in the rural areas. A 'duka' is a small shop and usually has limited capacity to keep large stocks of any commodity, not least of seed and fertilizers which are fairly bulky compared with the assortment usually sold (cf. KSC 1967). With the limited scale of operation the service capacity must be put at a farily low level. To quantify the level is difficult, but in using the classes on Map 5.3 a population/ stockist ratio of about 5,000 would probably be the maximum it is possible to serve from an ordinary 'duka'. It is not unlikely that such a ratio is on the high side.

Taking into consideration that in almost every district at least one stockist constitutes a co-operative union or society, which should have a greater capacity for storing inputs, a population/stockist ratio of 5,000 or less may signify a fairly equitable supply situation regarding the inputs needed. Some variation would still exist but, by and large, the inputs would be accessible without to great an effort for the potential consumer. Ratios in excess of 5,000 would then signify a less favourable accessibility situation, which also would involve greater and greater local variations the further one gets from the figure of 5,000. A detailed map of the situation would probably reveal and increasing number of isolated islands with good accessibility, surrounded by larger and larger areas with poor or no accessibility to Hybrid Maize seed, the further one went from the population/stockist ratio of 5,000.

Initially a short discussion on some methodological aspects is needed. The population component of the population/stockist ratio is not directly available and has to be calculated. Lacking a continuous population registry, Kenya relies on population censuses at 10 year-intervals, for its population statistics. The last two censuses in Kenya were taken in 1969 and 1979 and neither of these years fit in with the years for which information about the number of stockists is available. The figures from these two censuses have been used in calculating the population component in the ratios for 1967, 1972 and 1976. From a demographic point of view the method chosen could be seen as fairly crude. The purpose had not been to make a true population projection, but rather to arrive at a reasonable basis for comparison. Deviations from the true values may be found, but in all probability, the magnitude of these should not affect the overall results and the conclusions reached.

The method used is based on simple incrementation by discrete steps (cf. Rundquist 1982 and Woods 1982) — in other words simple interest calculations. The population figures for 1967 and 1972 have been calculated from the basis found in the 1969 Population Census in Kenya (RoK 1975) and the 1976 figures from the basis found in the 1979 Population Census (RoK 1980). In addition, an estimate on the population growth between the different years is needed. Here a simplifying assumption has been introduced and in each period one and the same figure for the population growth has been used for all districts. It would have been possible to calculate growth rates for individual districts between 1969 and 1979 but this has not been attempted in anticipation of an official analysis of the growth rates found. The figures used have been taken from the Development Plan 1974-78 (RoK 1974:99) in which figures for the population growth in different periods is presented. Here the figures are given as 3.4% per annum for 1962-69 and 3.5% per annum for 1969-74. The calculated national growth rate figure between 1969 and 1979 is slightly above 3.4% per annum which makes the used growth rate of 3.5% per annum for all the calculations credible.

It should be noted, however, that different estimates exist on the true extent of the population growth in Kenya in recent years. Mott & Mott (1980) puts the figure as high as 4% per annum in a study based on the 1977-78 Kenya Fertility Survey (ibid.:19). The figures presented by Mott & Mott are based on a sample survey with the possible biases produced by sampling errors. Similarly 'De Facto' Censuses in Africa, and elsewhere, are always facing the danger of mis-enumeration as well as sample errors for the more detailed information. An analysis of the possible sources of errors in the 1979 Kenyan Census, is what is needed in order to arrive at a reliable figure on the true population growth. What is clear, however, is that the present Kenyan population is growing at a very rapid rate, which probably is among the highest in the world (ibid.).

For the purposes of this study, it is not necessary to have the absolute exact figure, with the wide margins within which the population/stockist ratio is allowed to vary. Moreover, no very definite conclusions are drawn from the material. The more serious criticism that could be levelled at the calculations is the use of one and the same growth rate for all districts and provinces. The use of input data from different censuses, thus making the calculations 'forwards' and backwards' from the census years, reduces the risk of too great discrepancies in the material presented. It should also be mentioned, that the methodological deficiencies presented do not have a cumulative effect on the results. Thus, although not accurate in every detail, the information in Table 5.5 and Map 5.3 give a plausible and usable picture of the population/stockist relationships.

Turning to the implications from the material presented, it is immediately obvious that in the periods shown there has been a large increase in the overall 'accessibility' as measured by the population/stockist ratio. Looking at the Kenya Total row in Table 5.5, the national average has fallen from almost 100,000 to slightly more than 5,000 in period of nine years. Also, over the years the distributional differences between districts have been evened out. Of the 13 districts having stockists in 1967, the standard deviation in the population/stockist ratio is 85,601. For the 25 districts having stockists in 1972, the standard deviation is 15,052, while in 1976 the standard deviation has gone up sligthly to 18,034 for the 34 districts having stockists. This rise in the standard deviation is to a great extent dependent on the expansion of the stockist programme into some peripheral districts e.g. Isiolo, Samburu and Tana River. These districts are still in a building-up phase of the programme and have still a fairly low population/stockist ratio, which also affects the overall figures and raises the standard deviation.

Still, the fairly high standard deviations found in all three periods, with the exception of 1967 when the programme had just started, show that significant differences exist between districts in the population/stockist ratios. To some extent this is due to one or a couple of districts showing very high ratios. Disregarding the extreme cases, one still finds great differences. In 1972 the difference between Kirinyaga and Kajiado, the lowest and the second highest ratio, is as great as 43,597. Similarly, in 1976 the difference between Bungoma and Kajiado, the lowest and the fourth highest ratio, is as great as 32,226.

It should be noted, however, that the districts being compared do differ in many important respects, which naturally, also affects the stockist programme. In Kirinyaga and Bungoma the basis for the agricultural economy is permanent sedentary agriculture, while in Kajiado the agricultural economy is to a great extent based on pastoralism. Similarly, some other districts showing a high ratio have

an agricultural economy primarily based on pastoralism,
e.g. Garissa, Isiolo, Samburu and Tana River, in the areas
removed from the Tana River itself. Also in quite a number
of districts, the permanent sedentary agriculture occupies
distinct areas suited to such agriculture, while other
parts of the same district have an agricultural economy
based more on pastoralism. Examples of the latter type of
districts are West Pokot, Taita, Kitui and to some extent
Machakos, Kwale, Kilifi, Lamu Baringo and Laikipia — the
last two being something of special cases as they are also
part of what is referred to as the 'Highlands' which to a
large extent are large-scale farming areas.

The 'Highlands' deserve a special mention in a discussion about the expansion of the stockist programme. In the
'Highlands' — basically most of the Rift Valley districts
together with Nyandarua District in Central Province —
prior to 1976 stockists were almost non-existant, while in
1976 the area was one of the best serviced, i.e. having the
second lowest overall ratio. As already indicated the low
number of stockists in the 'Highlands' in the initial
phases of the programme is probably due to the structure
of agriculture being based on large farms, where the farmers could themselves transport the inputs needed from the
depots to their farms.

Between 1964 and 1969, however, a large number of
Settlement Schemes were established in the 'Highlands'.
Settlement Schemes are found over most of the 'Highlands',
but the majority of them are concentrated to Nyandarua, Kericho and Tranz-Nzoia Districts (cf. Rundquist 1977:105).
It is also these districts that have the lowest popula-
tion/stockist ratios — see Table 5.5 and Map 5.3. A comparison between Map 5.3 and the map presented in Rundquist
(1977) shows that the well serviced areas in the 'Highlands' to a great extent follow the distribution of Settlement Schemes, while other areas of the 'Highlands' have a
much higher population/stockist ratio, e.g. Nakuru District.

An interesting point in the expansion of the programme,
is the development in Coast Province, which is obvious in
a comparison between Maps 5.3A-C. To an extent it seems as
if the demands have been 'bottled up' and whith the release
of Coast Composite X-105 in 1973, a very rapid development
took place. Still most of the expansion has been in Taita
District and in the areas most suited for sedentary agriculture — Taita Hills. In the pure coastal districts the
population/stockist ratios are lower. It should be noticed,

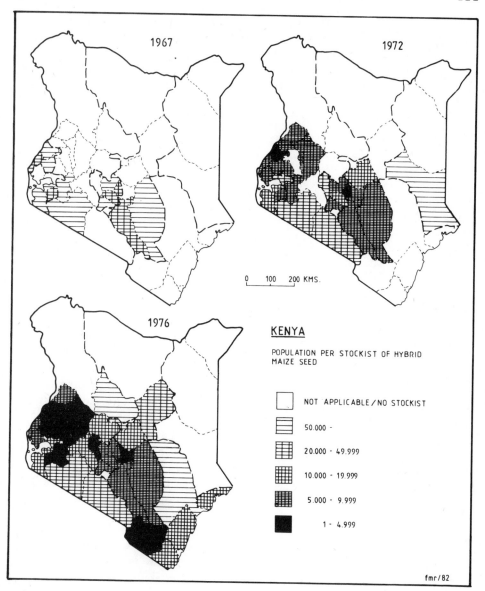

Map 5.3: Population/stockist ratios for 1967, 1972 and 1976.

however, that maize is not as important as a staple crop in the coastal areas as elsewhere in Kenya. Still, the expansion from a situation with no stockists in 1972 up to the situation in 1976 with 91 stockists in the region and stockists in each district, must be seen as a fairly rapid development.

The comments on Table 5.5 and Map 5.3 could be much more

detailed. This is probably not necessary as they, to a great extent, speak for themselves. A short technical note on the functioning of KSC and the supply networks is, however, called for. The entire programme is coordinated by KSC and they are very careful to only deliver certin types of seed to certain areas, i.e. the type of seed that has been specifically developed for the area in question. The KSC has its own field staff (in 1975/76 they were five, each member having his own transport) who operate over the whole of Kenya, where improved maize is sold and check the performances of the stockists. This, among other things, includes selling the right variety for the specific area (personal communication by Mr. Hazelden of KSC in 1976). Thus, although the discussion above has been kept general and focuses on the location of stockists, underneath this, also lie aspects of the functioning of the supply networks which may have implications for their accessibility.

5.6 Sales of Hybrid/Improved seed

The development of the sales of improved seed is shown in Figures 5.2 to 5.6 and in Table 5.6. Furthermore, Map 5.4 has been designed in order to show the structure of the upper layers of the supply networks. All information comes from a KSC report and, as discussed above, their statistical presentation do not fit in exactly with the administrative structure of Kenya. Thus, Map 5.4 is also an attempt to show the areas covered by KSC statistics. The breakdown of the figures is made at the convenience of the KSC. With the structure of the distribution system, even they find it difficult to make a more detailed breakdown of the figures than they already have. In a report on the 1974/75 sales figures they say:

"Further breakdown of sales figures may be possible by consulting the various K.F.A. Branches. However some of these figures would not be of any further assistance, since, if for example, seed is sold ex. Kisumu it is rather difficult to ascertain in which district it is to be planted." (KSC 1975)

The areas delimited on Map 5.4 should to a great extent cover the areas within which seed from the centres shown is sold, but it is also obvious that overlaps may occur and that it is difficult to state exactly where seed purchased at this level in the distributional network, will be planted later. By and large, with the farily high level of aggregation, the statistical areas delimited by KSC should

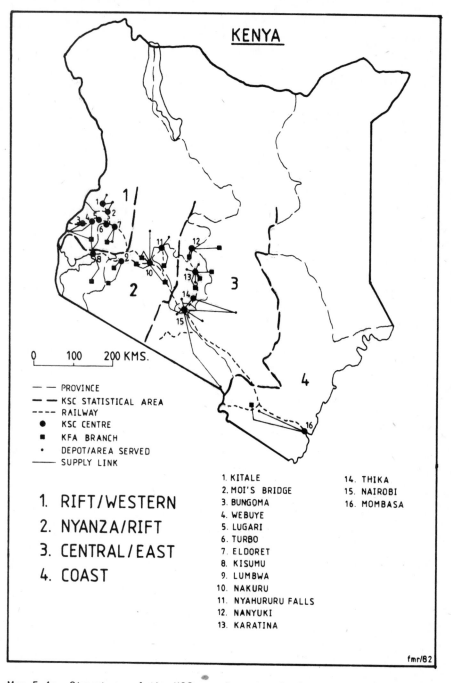

KENYA

0   100   200 KMS.

— — PROVINCE
▬ ▬ KSC STATISTICAL AREA
---- RAILWAY
● KSC CENTRE
■ KFA BRANCH
· DEPOT/AREA SERVED
— SUPPLY LINK

1. RIFT/WESTERN

2. NYANZA/RIFT

3. CENTRAL/EAST

4. COAST

1. KITALE
2. MOI'S BRIDGE
3. BUNGOMA
4. WEBUYE
5. LUGARI
6. TURBO
7. ELDORET
8. KISUMU
9. LUMBWA
10. NAKURU
11. NYAHURURU FALLS
12. NANYUKI
13. KARATINA

14. THIKA
15. NAIROBI
16. MOMBASA

fmr/82

Map 5.4: Structure of the KSC supply network above the stockist
level.

give an acceptable description of the development of sales
in the periods discussed here. Furthermore, the information
from KSC is given in tabular form and in great detail. Here
a diagramatic form is chosen for the presentation, as this
gives a better impression of both absolute and relative
differences in sales, without having to go into too many
details.

In view of the spectacular increase in the number of
stockists, it is not surprising that the sales figures, as
shown in Figure 5.2, show a very rapid increase. From the
start in 1966/67, when sales figures in each area are
around a few thousand 20 lb bags of seed (a package size
designed for the small scale farmer) and the national total
is just below 10,000 units, the figures rise steeply and
mostly for the Rift/Western and Nyanza/Rift areas. Progress
for the Central/East area is less rapid, but still shows
a substantial increase over the period being studied. The
sales in Coast Province are still at a very low level, although there is an indication of a rising curve in the last
two years. Moreover, the sales registered in Coast Province
before 1973 must have been seed bought elsewhere and being
tried out in Coast Province with probably only limited success. Not until the Coast Composite X-105 was made available in 1973, does the curve show a rising trend, if, however, not a very strong one.

The breakdown of the sales figures down to the level of
KSC centres (Figures 5.3 to 5.6) shows some interesting
features. Obviously large internal variations exist within
each statistical area. Figure 5.3 clearly shows that in
Rift/Western, four of the seven centres cater for the major
share of the sales, which may be attributed to the large
share of larger farms in the Rift Valley Province. The
centres, having the major share of the sales of seed to
small-scale farmers, are either servicing small-scale farming areas, i.e. Bungoma and Webuye, or lie in areas with
many Settlement Schemes, i.e. Kitale and Eldoret. The three
remaining centres lie in areas still dominated by large-
scale farming with a limited number of small Settlement
Schemes, i.e. Moi's Bridge, Turbo and Lugari.

Great internal differences exist within the other statistical areas as well and the differences are not as easily exlained as in Rift/Western. However, the same explanations partly applies. Nanyuki in Central/East and Nyahururu
in Nyanza/Rift are both towns which grew up as service
centres to parts of the 'Highlands' and although the ownership structure has changed somewhat around these towns,

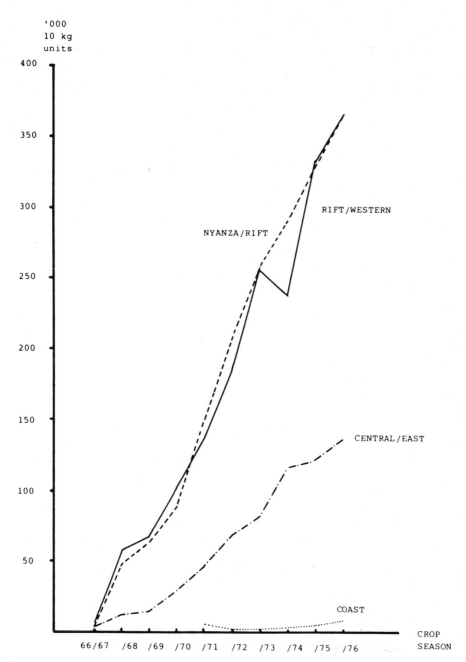

<u>Figure 5.2</u>: Sales of Hybrid Maize seed - small-scale farming sector,
10 kg units. Figures for KSC statistical areas. (Figures
for 1975/76 are predicted.)

there still exists a substantial element of large-scale
farming there and one would not expect a large sale of 20
lb units designed for the small-scale farming areas.

Disregarding the figures for Nanyuki, a closer look at
Central/East (Figure 5.4) still shows marked differences
between Karatina, on the one hand, and Nairobi and Thika,
on the other. The Karatina figures are only the ones expected, as the town lies in the middle of a densly populated
area dominated by small-scale farming. The Nairobi figures,
although lower than the Karatina ones, may be a bit surprising — Nairobi being the capital and a big city. It is,
however, situated in the middle of a small-scale farming
area. Furthermore, the structure of the transportation network may make it easier to take supplies from Nairobi rather than from somewhere else. This, i.e. the transport advantage, may also explain the fairly low figure for Thika.
The proximity to Nairobi may make potential buyers bypass
Thika and go to Nairobi for their supplies and combine the
purchasing trip with other errands which could not be carried out in e.g. Thika.

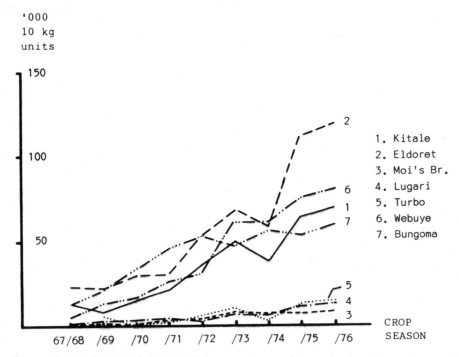

Figure 5.3: Sales of Hybrid Maize seed - small-scale farming sector,
10 kg units. Figures for Rift/Western KSC statistical area
at the level of KSC centres. (1975/76 predicted.)

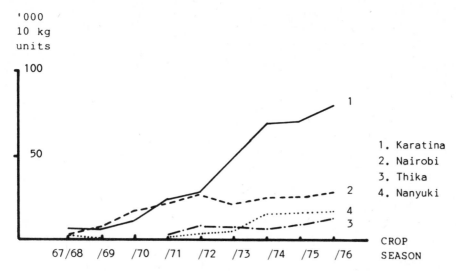

Figure 5.4: Sales of Hybrid Maize seed - small-scale farming sector, 10 kg units. Figures for Central/East KSC statistical area at the level of KSC centres. (1975/76 predicted.)

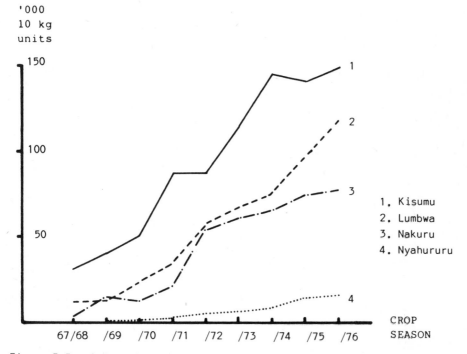

Figure 5.5: Sales of Hybrid Maize seed - small-scale farming sector, 10 kg units. Figures for Nyanza/Rift KSC statistical area at the level of KSC centres. (1975/76 predicted.)

In Nyanza/Rift (Figure 5.5), the differences between the centres, with the exception of Nyahururu, are less pronounced. The centre in Kisumu lies very strategically between two of the most densly populated areas in Kenya — Kisii and Kakamega Districts. Kisii is directly serviced by Kisumu, while Kakamega, according to Kenya Seed Company (KSC 1975:1), is mainly serviced from Webuye but also takes some supplies from Kisumu. It could be noted that the figures for Kisumu are the highest for all centres in the country. The other two centres in this area lie in the 'Highlands', but are located so that they service quite a number of large Settlement Schemes. In the case of Nakuru, for example, it is clear that a large portion of its sale of seed in 20 lb units, is sold to the large Settlement Schemes up on the Kinangop Plateau in Nyandarua District.

Finally, Figure 5.6 showing the sales of 25 kg units of seed which are intended for the large-scale farming areas, has been designed. The most striking feature of this diagram is its regularity. Over the whole of the period one can observe a slight upward trend in purchases. The season 1971/72 constitutes a peak, but in a few years' time 'order' is restored.

The figures showing sales of 10 kg (20 lb) and 25 kg units may be difficult to interpret unless they are translated into more familiar units. KSC (1975:2) assumes that 9 kg of seed is sufficient for the planting of one acre. Assuming no loss of seed during planting and that the re-

Table 5.6: Acreages under Hybrid/Improved Maize seed in the small- and large-scale farm sector 1967/68 - 1975/76.

Year	Small-scale	Large-scale	Total
1967/68	126,840	90,195	217,035
1968/69	158,864	97,605	256,369
1969/70	240,608	113,409	354,017
1970/71	370,316	157,613	527,929
1971/72	511,013	182,718	693,731
1972/73	654,073	131,877	785,950
1973/74	722,307	96,902	819,209
1974/75	869,922	125,271	995,193
1975/76[1]	874,000	125,000	1,086,400

Source: KSC (1975) - Tables I and II
Note 1: Figures for 1975/76 are predicted

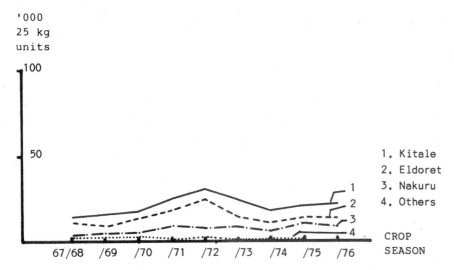

Figure 5.6: Sales of Hybrid Maize seed - large-scale farming sector, 25 kg units. Figures at the level of KSC centres. (1975/76 predicted.)

commended plant populations are retained, the sales figures can be turned into acreages (see Table 5.6). Naturally, it would have been possible to make the calculations for each centre, but in order to avoid to much detail only the aggregated figures for small- and large-scale farms are shown.

Table 5.6 can represent a summary of the discussions in this section. Some of the implications to be drawn from the table will be made in Section 5.7, where the overall adoption rates of improved maize seed as an innovation will be discussed. The only comment needed here, may be that it is obvious that the great increase in the total acreage under improved maize seed in Kenya, is mainly due to the adoption of seed by small-scale farmers, while the acreage for the large-scale farming sector has fluctuated around a figure of a 100,000 to 125,000 acres per year. The figure for 1972 is, of course, an exception to the rule.

5.7 Adoption and use of Hybrid Maize

It is not easy to obtain clear and unambiguous figures showing the adoption of Hybrid Maize in Kenya. The available information is usually limited to specific areas and to specific points in time (cf. i.a. Gerhart 1975 and RoK 1977). Presented with the problems of finding one individual set of data describing Hybrid Maize adoption in both

a spatial and temporal perspective, the approach chosen
here to describe the introduction of Hybrid Maize into
Kenyan agriculture, is to give information from several
different sources and to try to draw conclusions from the
combined impressions derived from these.

Table 5.7 gives information about adoption rates in Nyanza and Western Provinces and, in addition, information
about the adoption rates for some districts in Rift Valley
Province. The information for this table is found in a map
presented by Gerhart (1975). Unfortunately the information
taken from the map is not supplemented by any exact information in tabular form and, thus, only the class intervals
given on the map can be put into this table. Still it gives
a farily good picture of the development that has taken
place in the area. Moreover, it is the only piece of information that give a fairly consistent time sequence of the
development. As will be seen below all other sources provide information for discrete years only.

Table 5.7: Hybrid Maize use - percentage of farmers reporting as
having planted Hybrid Maize by district.

District	1964	1965	1967	1969	1971	1973
Bungoma	20- 50	20- 50	50- 80	80-100	80-100	80-100
Busia	0- 20	0- 20	0- 20	20- 50	20- 50	20- 50
Kakamega	0- 20	20- 50	20- 50	50- 80	50- 80	80-100
Tranz-Nzoia	20- 50	20- 50	50- 80	80-100	80-100	80-100
Uasin-Gishu	20- 50	20- 50	50- 80	80-100	80-100	80-100
Nandi	0- 20	0- 20	20- 50	20- 50	50- 80	80-100
Kericho	0- 20	0- 20	0- 20	20- 50	50- 80	80-100
Siaya	0- 20	0- 20	0- 20	0- 20	0- 20	0- 20
Kisumu	0- 20	0- 20	0- 20	0- 20	20- 50	20- 50
Kisii	0- 20	0- 20	20- 50	50- 80	80-100	80-100
South Nyanza	0- 20	0- 20	0- 20	0- 20	0- 20	0- 20

Source: Gerhart (1975:27, Map 4) - The map referred to is based on
the 1973 Kitale/CIMMYT Hybrid Maize Survey

The information provided in Table 5.7, gives a picture
of a fairly rapid adoption process for the majority of the
districts shown. The picture is one of a slow start in the
adoption process which rapidly gains momentum and in only
five years, districts like Bungoma, Tranz-Nzoia and Uasin-
Gishu are approaching the absolute saturation rate, viz.
almost a 100 per cent adoption. The process is continued

and in 1973 seven of the twelve districts in question have reached this level. The major exception to the rapid adoption processes is Nyanza — something which will be further emphasised in the tables presented below. Here Kisii District shows a very rapid adoption process, while the remaining districts have adoption rates of only up to 20 per cent in Siaya and South Nyanza and up to 50 per cent in Kisumu District.

The latter three districts belong to what Gerhart (1975) calls Zone III — a zone with lower than average rainfall probability than his other zones. In his study Gerhart explains the lower adoption rates for these districts in terms of risk factors, i.e. the farmers are less certain of a good crop and try to minimize the risks involved in agriculture. They do this by avoiding risky experiments like the purchasing of new seed. They rather try to minimize the risk by planting drought resistant crops like e.g. cassava. Gerhart finds a clear relationship between the growing of drought resistant crops and non-adoption of Hybrid Maize in his Zone III.

The information provided in Table 5.7, to a great extent falls in logically with the information and the discussions of the stockist programme and the development of sales. In looking at Maps 5.1 to 5.3 one sees a very clear relationship between the expansion of the stockist programme and the adoption rates in Table 5.7. The fact that the expansion of the stockist programme and the adoption rates run almost exactly parallel to each other, give an interesting perspective on the 'effective demand' concept being used as a rationale in the expansion of the stockist programme.

Table 5.8 gives a more general and comprehensive picture of the adoption of Hybrid Maize. Also the information supplied here supports the figures found in Table 5.7 — the areas covered in Table 5.7 are found here in categories 1 to 3. Besides information about adoption rates for specific areas, Table 5.8 gives information on the relationship between altitude/rainfall and adoption. Not surprisingly, the areas having the most favourable preconditions for permanent agriculture are the ones showing the highest adoption rates.

The overall impression is one of high adoption rates with the exception of category 3 and to some extent category 5. In the last category, rainfall and rain reliability should not constitute a problem but the high altitude may introduce an element of risk in the sense that the altitude affects the maturing time. Risk, however, should not be a

Table 5.8: Hybrid Maize use for altitude/rainfall zones and
districts - percentages.

Zones	1973	1974
1. More than 60 inches of rainfall - Kisii, Kakamega, Nandi, part of Kericho and Busia	92.8	100.0
2. Less than 60 inches of rainfall above 1,500 metres - Tranz-Nzoia, Bungoma, Uasin-Gishu, part of Nandi and Kericho	90.7	90.0
3. Less than 60 inches of rainfall below 1,500 metres - Kisumu, Siaya, South Nyanza, part of Busia	15.5	12.0
4. Central Province below 1,500 metres	--	60.0
5. Central Province above 1,500 metres	--	53.0

Source: KSC (1975, Table V)

major restricting factor in category 5, although it may
somewhat reduce adoption rates. In category 3 risk could
be a major restricting factor, as discussed earlier. Finally, the drop in the adoption rate for category 3 between
1973 and 1974 probably does not signify a trend, but is rather a random outcome of the data collection techniques
used in the different studies forming the basis for Table
5.8. This is also supported by the figures in Table 5.9.

The final table showing adoption rates, Table 5.9, is
based on the IRS 1975/75 (RoK 1977) and is perhaps the one
giving the most comprehensive picture of the adoption
rates. Its drawback, however, is that it only provides information for one agricultural year and, thus, it is not
possible to draw any conclusions from it with respect to
adoption processes.

Again the information provided in Table 5.9 is consistent with the information presented earlier. Some interesting differences exist, however, and they should be pointed
out. First, the overall adoption rate for Central Province
as a whole, lies above the figures given in Table 5.8. On
the one hand this may be due to differences in coverage and
methodology in the surveys on which this information is
based. On the other hand, this could be a sign of a con-

Table 5.9: Holdings with Hybrid Maize 1974/75 by province - percentages.

Province	1974/75
Central	66.6
Coast	19.1
Eastern	30.1
Nyanza	35.6
Rift Valley	91.5
Western	73.0

Source: IRS 1974/75 (RoK 1977:80, Table 9.3)

tinuous adoption process as there is a slight temporal difference between Tables 5.8 and 5.9, i.e. 1974 vs. 1974/75.

Second, the figure given for Nyanza Province as a whole is much higher that the figure given for category 3 in Table 5.8 — category 3 constituting the major part of Nyanza Province. Still, the difference between these two figures is difficult to interpret as the high adoption rate found in Kisii and also in parts of Kisumu districts (see Table 5.8), may be so high that they raise the provincial average to the level shown in Table 5.9. What is clear is that within Nyanza Province there are very great differences in adoption rates between districts. In the absence of additional information, which would give a clearer picture of the adoption rates in Nyanza Province, it seems as if the overall figure given, overshadows a lot of interesting information which could be revealing with respect to the differences in adoption rates for this particular province.

Concerning the figures for Western and Rift Valley Provinces they seem to be consistent with the information provided earlier. Finally, the figures for Coast and Eastern Provinces which have not appeared until in Table 5.9 and, thus, are not easy to comment on. The figures seem, however, to be a bit on the low side if one considers the expansion of the stockist programme and, not least, the fairly high population/stockist ratios found in parts of these provinces. As in the case of Nyanza Province, the overall adoption rate may overshadow great internal variations in the adoption rates. If district figures on the adoption rates would have been available, these differences would have come out in, presumably, a sharp relief. As it stands such differences can only be tentatively assumed and not qualified by any clear set of data.

The last set of tables, Tables 5.10 and 5.11, differ

Table 5.10:   Crop area under Hybrid Maize as percentage of total
maize acreage by province

Province	1969/70[1]	1974/75[2]
Central	5.1	28.1
Coast	0.0	8.0
Eastern	5.0	11.8
Nyanza	14.9	15.0
Rift Valley	41.3	80.7
Western	48.4	70.7
Total	14.8	29.5

Sources: 1. Statistical Abstracts 1975 (RoK 1975; Table 86 and 87).
Figures refer to small farms and Settlement Schemes only.
2. Statistical Abstracts 1980 (RoK 1980; Table 102). Figures
refer to small farms and exclude large farms and pastoral
areas.

from the earlier ones presented in the respect that they
focus on acreage under Hybrid Maize, rather than on the
number of farms that grow Hybrid Maize. Still they make up
a measure of adoption and it could be interesting to contrast the adoption rates based on acreage under Hybrid
Maize, with the rate based on the number of users of Hybrid
Maize.

Using Hybrid Maize does not necessarily imply that a
farmer plants only Hybrid Maize. Empirical investigations
into adoption behaviour, show clearly that it is customary
to try out an innovation on a limited scale before complete
adoption occurs. Involved in the adoption process are a
large number of factors which could make a difference between complete and partial adoption. These may include risk
minimization, i.e. the farmers are well acquainted with the
performance of Local Maize under different weather conditions, while they are less certain about the performance
of Hybrid Maize under, e.g. drought conditions. Thus, farmers may have a tendency to keep some of their acreage under
Local Maize rather than 'placing all their eggs in one
basket' and only planting Hybrid Maize. There may also exist preferences in favour of retaining some Local Maize —
although on face value Hybrid Maize should be the same
crop. Palatability has often been quoted as a major difficulty in the introduction of new crops — also when the
crops seem to be one and the same as is the case with Local
and Hybrid Maize in Kenya.

Table 5.11: Total area under Improved and Local Maize in 1969/79
and 1974/75 - '000 hectares.

Type of maize	1969/70	1974/75
Improved Maize	147.4	500.8
Unimproved Maize	848.3	1,194.8
Total	995.7	1,695.6

Sources: Statistical Abstract 1975 (RoK 1975; Table 86) and Statistical Abstract 1980 (RoK 1980; Table 102). Figures refer to
small farms only and exclude pastoral and large farm areas.

Turning to the actual contents of Tables 5.10 and 5.11,
it is obvious that direct comparisons between these and the
ones presented earlier are difficult. To an extent a direct
comparison would be similar to a comparison of 'apples and
pears'. Only very tentative comparisons are possible, first
due to the reasons given above concerning innovation behaviour, risk minimization and taste preferences. No information is available about how these factors would affect
the overall area planted with Hybrid Maize. Second, no information exists which indicates clearly the possible differences that may exist between farmers in different size
categories, regarding the proportion of their maize area
they would put under Hybrid Maize. Furthermore, there exists very little information that could be used to distinguish adoption behaviour between smaller and larger farms
even within the small-scale farming sector. It may be assumed, however, that the larger farms within this sector
are less risk minimizing and, from one point of view, more
economically rational, i.e. planting more of their area under Hybrid Maize benefitting from the higher yields.

Thus, in summary, only very tentative comparisons could
be made between the differnent data sets measuring the
adoption rates. It is obvious, however, that the two measures show considerable differences and these in themselves
are interesting. Only in Western and Rift Valley Provinces
do the two measures come close to each other. These two
provinces have the longest history of Hybrid Maize adoption
and, thus, the figures may indicate that with the passing
of time, farmers are putting more and more of their acreage
under Hybrid Maize. In all other provinces the figures
showing acreage are considerably below the figures showing
use, which may be an indication of a less complete adoption
in these areas.

What is seen directly from Table 5.10, however, is the large increase in maize acreage under Hybrid Maize in only a five year period. The extent of the increase is further emphasised if one also looks at Table 5.11 and notes the increased acreage under maize. The growht of almost 15 per cent in the relative figures (Table 5.10) is paralleled with an increase of about 340 per cent in acreage under Hybrid Maize in the five year period. In the same period the expansion of the area under local maize has been about 140 per cent and the total expansion of the maize acreage is close to 170 per cent. In absolute terms, no great difference exists between the expansion of acreage under improved and unimproved maize. The relative figures of the expansion show a much more striking difference, which underlines many of the figures showing the expansion of the breeding programme, the stockist programme and sales presented above.

One final comparison remains between the reported acreages under Hybrid Maize in Table 5.6 and the figures in Table 5.11. The figures in these tables have different origin and bases. Here, however, they refer to one and the same thing and, thus, a comparison should be possible. Originally the measurements differ between the two tables, in Table 5.12 they are measured in the same way. Comparisons, however, are only possible for two separate crop-seasons.

Table 5.12:   Comparison between acreage under Hybrid Maize (acres).

Year	From Table 5.6	From Table 5.11
1969/70	354,017	364,220
1974/75	995,193	1,237,460

Obviously the estimates provided by KSC (Table 5.6) are somewhat on the low side, even though the differences between the two sets of figures are not strikingly high. It is also stated in the KSC-report (1975) that their figures may be sligthly below the true figures. The KSC figures are, as mentioned, based on planting conditions, particularly with respect to plant populations per acre, that conform strictly to the recommendations given. In reality, one assumes that plant populations are kept slightly below the recommended numbers and, thus, the same amount of seed can be used for planting a somewhat greater acreage.

The relatively small differences between the KSC figures based on figures for the sale of seed and the figures based on various official statistics (Table 5.11), indicate that estimates on acreage under Hybrid Maize based on sales figures are fairly reliable. Thus, it should be possible to use these as estimates in analytical and/or planning undertakings where information on Hybrid Maize acreage is needed. Furthermore, these figures are available in continuous time series, which make them more useful for trend analyses than agricultural survey statistics collected at specific points in time.

5.8 Concluding remarks

The analyses of the present chapter have dealt with the most aggregated aspects of the analytical model introduced in Chapter III, viz. the underlying rationalities behind the creation and function of the supply networks for Hybrid Maize. Basically the analyses have been descriptive and, thus, confined to a recording of processes from the sixties up until the time of the survey. Still a clear relationship between the number of supply points and the development of sales has been found. Although the distribution network has been extended into having a fairly good general coverage of the most populated areas of Kenya, differences in densities between areas/regions clearly affect sales figures. It could be concluded that a very dense network of supply points is necessary in order to achieve a wide adoption of Hybrid Maize seed, rather than isolated islands of adoption around single supply points.

Also, in the latter part of the present chapter, an attempt is made to investigate the extent to which reported sales figures of Hybrid Maize seed from KSC reflect true adoption rates at a sub-national level. The purpose, of course, being to investigate the possibilities of utilizing sales figures which are easily available for descriptive and planning purposes referring to maize production. The conclusion from this part of the analysis, is that the sales figures reflect adoption rates fairly well and, thus, are useful as planning instruments. The advantage with these is that they are available on an annual basis and that their collection does not demand costly surveys.

VI. Adoption Patterns in the Survey Areas

6.1 Introduction

As indicated in Chapter II the analysis of Hybrid Maize adoption is made from two interrelated starting points and draws on the implications derived from what Brown (1981) calls the 'Market and Infrastructure Perspective'. Thus, once the preconditions for adoption have been established, the process moves into another phase, i.e. the linking up of the adopters to the specific nodes established. The analysis to follow deals with this particular interface between the distributing organizations and the individual adopters. The term interface is used because the approach combines two different 'perspectives' outlined by Brown (op.cit.) — the 'Market and Infrastructure' and the 'Adoption Perspective'. The first refers mainly to the actions, rationalities and constraints for the establishment of a marketing organization of an innovation, while the latter is concerned with individual behaviour in adopting innovations.

The two perspectives, however, are not exclusive and re-stricting factors for adoption, particularly infrastructural, are affecting adoption behaviour in both of these. Here the focus will be laid mainly on individual adoption behaviour, although factors related to the actual linking up with the distributional networks will be considered.

This chapter will also deal with more descriptive aspects of the diffusion of Hybrid Maize. The main emphasis will be on temporal and spatial diffusion patterns in the survey areas. In the two following chapters, VII and VIII, underlying factors of these patterns will be brought to the forefront of the analysis. The material used in Chapters VI-VIII is the information collected in the interviews described in Chapter IV. Thus, not only the analytical focus will change from this chapter onwards, but also the scale of the analysis is shifted from a macro- to a fairly extreme micro-analysis.

6.2 Description of survey areas and sample sizes

As described in Chapter III, the primary sampling unit was the sub-location. The sizes of different sub-locations vary quite substantially with respect to both area and population. Concerning the areal extent, it is not possible to set a definite limit. Populationwize the limits of the variation are clearer with a maximal size of about 10,000 persons down to a lower limit in the region of 1,000-1,500 persons. Even at the upper size limit it is obvious that the basic population from which to draw a sample is fairly small. This, in turn, affects the possibilities of making far reaching generalizations from the results arrived at, and may lead to a question on the rationalities behind this kind of analysis. The answer to the question has been hinted at in earlier sections, but it could be brought up and expanded upon here.

Underlying the innovation/diffusion waves, frequently identified in macro-studies, lie individual adoption decisions generating local adoption patterns that will not be visible on maps showing only a generalized pattern. Thus, the purpose of the micro-level analysis, is to try to penetrate beneath the surface of the innovation/diffusion wave typology and try to see the extent to which the macro-processes replicate themselves at local level. The logical hypothesis is that the patterns should be similar and that the possible differences in the resultant patterns should mainly be attributable to a scale factor. Still, it should be of interest to try to dig into diffusion patterns at local level, with the purpose of seeing how local factors, determinable only at this level, affect the diffusion processes and subsequently how the local patterns replicate or deviate from patterns determined at higher levels of aggregation.

Returning to the survey areas, it is time to define these more closely. Applying the sampling technique, described in Chapter III, resulted in three selected sub-locations — one in Nyeri District named Igana Sub-location and two in South Nyanza District named Kodoch West and Kotieno Kowor respectively. In these the number of farm units and the sizes of the samples drawn were distributed according to Table 6.1.

As evident from the table the criteria set up for the sampling, have been rather relaxed. Drawing somewhat smaller samples than postulated, in no way affects the statistical representability of the collected material. Actually the criteria as originally formulated, were a bit overambi-

Table 6.1: Sample sizes in the survey areas.

Sub-location	No. of farms	Sample size	Sample size in per cent
Igana	923	172	18.6
Kodoch West	795	186	23.4
Kotieno Kowor	929	189	20.3

tious and the gains in representability from increasing the
sample sizes, are negligible. From Table 6.1 it could also
be seen that in Kodoch West and in Kotieno Kowor, the size
of the samples reaches and even exceeds the 20 per cent limit, thus relaxing the criterion that the sample should
contain 200 farm units. In Igana the real size of the sample is low with respect to both criteria. Still, the size
of the sample in Igana is large enough to make it statistically representable.

The reason for the slightly lower sample fraction in
Igana, as opposed to the other sub-locations, is to be
found in two factors. First, the only clear refusal to being interviewed occurred in Igana. Second, in Igana, some
farms were lying fallow and it was not possible to locate
anyone in charge of the land. According to neighbours these
farms belonged to people who had migrated out of the area,
while they still retained ownership rights to the farms.
In some other cases the farms lying idle had recently been
sold and the new owner had not yet taken up residence. In
all, there were 30 farms in Igana, where it was not possible to conduct interviews due to the reasons mentioned.
From a locational point of view and with respect to their
size these farms are randomly distributed among the other
farms of Igana and should not have introduced any particular biases in the material.

Populationwise the survey areas are small, and this is
evident from Table 6.2 which gives the exact sizes. It also
shows some of their basic demographic characteristics in
comparison with the district populations and with Kenya as
a whole. The figures refer to the time of the 1969 Census
and are not completely accurate with respect to the time
of the present survey. Information from the 1979 Census for
sub-locations is not available at the time of writing and,
thus, it is not possible to measure or estimate a figure
for 1975/76. In view of the overall population trends in
Kenya, it can be assumed that the figures should be higher
on all counts, when they are given in absolute form. Dramatic changes in the relative figures, however, are less

Table 6.2: Population characteristics of the survey areas.

Distr./ Sub-loc.	Tot. Pop.	Pop./ km^2	/MALE %-age 0-14	%-age 15-	/ / FEMALE %-age 0-14	/ %-age 15-
NYERI	360,845	108	27	21	27	26
Igana	3,675	263	27	17	28	28
S. NYANZA	663,173	114	26	23	25	26
Kodoch W.	2,892	138	28	19	26	27
K. Kowor	3,387	121	27	24	24	25
KENYA	10,942,705	19	25	26 '	24	26

Source: Kenya Population Census 1969, Vol. I (RoK 1970b)

likely.

With the lack of data indicating changes in the relationships, there is no exact way to determine their possible direction. One can only tentatively assume the direction of these. Thus, it could be assumed that the percentage of children under 15 years of age should constitute
a slightly larger portion than they do in the 1969 figures.
It may also be assumed that the below-average figures for
males in productive ages, found in some of the survey
areas, have decreased further.

All three survey areas have population densities above
the district averages and the national average. This is
primarily a consequence of the fact that only about 14 per
cent of the total land area of Kenya can be classified as
suitable for crop-production (cf. ILO 1972 and ILO 1981).
Settlement patterns found in Kenya, are largely a reflection of these conditions, although also biased by historical forces (cf. Gyllström 1977b, ILO 1972:2 and Rundquist
1977).

The second point to be discussed in connection with
Table 6.2, concerns particularly the relative figures. Information concerning the available labour force can be derived from comparisons between national and district figures with the figures for the survey areas. One can note
that the relative figures show a high portion of children
below 15 years of age. For the districts and sub-locations
shown, this figure lies slightly above 50 per cent, while
the national figure lies slightly below 50 per cent. The
differences are not significantly large, however. On the
other hand the relative figures for males above 15 years
of age show some interesting features that could give a
picture of the available labour force.

The relative figures for males of 15 years and above lie below the national average for both the districts and the sub-locations. In two cases — Igana and Kodoch West — the figures are markedly below the national and district figures. In these two sub-locations it could be safely assumed that a fairly substantial number of the male population in economically active ages have left the areas in search of jobs or to pursue higher education and, thus, depleted the locally available labour force. The pattern is in line with modern migration theory and then particularly those parts referring to migration and urbanization patterns in the Third World. These often exhibit marked age- and sex-biases, indicating that certain strata of the population migrates to a larger extent than others — in Africa largely males in economically active ages (cf. White and Woods 1980). The net effect of this out-migration is difficult to determine, however.

The first and most obvious conclusion to be drawn, is that it has negative influence on the productivity in local agriculture and, furthermore, that it is a negative factor in the diffusion of agricultural innovations, which in many cases are more labour-demanding than production using traditional practices. On the other hand, out-migration may act as a positive factor in the diffusion of innovations particularly in two respects. First, it is possible that if the out-migrant has got a job and thus secured a regular income, he, through remittances back to his family, creates the financial basis necessary for adoption. Second out-migration as such may put the migrant in contact with new ideas and he may even be in a position to test some of these ideas under conditions that do not constitute a 'risk' for himself or his farming operations. The latter point coincides with the "Cosmopoliteness" discussion put forward in much of the literature on diffusion (cf. i.a. Rogers & Shoemaker 1971).

As regards the physical resource basis, the survey areas are far from homogenous — despite their relative 'smallness'. To a great extent, internal differences are determined by topographical differences which, in turn, cause differences in drainage patterns and subsequently affect soil formation in the micro-scale. The occurences of such differences are particularly evident in Central Province. Topographically large parts of Central Province are characterized by a series of parallel ridges running from the northwest in a southeasterly direction. In between these ridges one often find small streams.

This has had a distinct influence on settlement patterns, the structure of the transport network and on the
agricultural economy. Starting with the transport network
one can notice that roads often run on top of the ridges,
thus creating a situation where it is easier to travel
along the ridges than between them. Some smaller roads create links between the ridges, but they are not numerous and
often of an inferior quality to the ones on top of the ridges. Obviously the topography in connection with the transport network, channels movements in certain directions and
in the case of Central Province it would be incorrect to
talk of an isotropic transportation surface even in areas
as small as Igana Sub-location.

Settlements, with only few exceptions, lie along the top
of the ridges loosely connected to the main roads. From the
homesteads, the farms often stretch downwards along the
sides of the ridges towards the streams at the bottom of
the valleys. This has created a production system where
different crops are grown in specific combinations from the
top of the ridge to the valley floor. The differences in
altitude from top to bottom of the ridges are not very
large, but often large enough to create micro-climatic differences.

Kodoch West and Kotieno Kowor, both in South Nyanza
District, are from a topographical point of view quite different from Igana. The terrain in these does not generally
display the dramatic variation that can be found in Central
Province. The landscape is one of a gently undulating plain
broken off by lower ridges and heights of an 'inzelberg'
character. The road network is not as developed and dense
as in Central Province but, on the other hand, movement is
not restricted in the same sense as in Central Province.
In only considering foot-transport in the survey areas of
South Nyanza a, more or less, isotropic transport surface
is at hand. Settlement patterns also differ from Central
Province as they are not tied to specific topographical
features. The overall picture of the settlement pattern is
one of fairly evenly distributed homesteads over the area.

The agro-ecological classification of the survey areas
complies with that used by the IRS 1974/75 (RoK 1977),
where it was used as a criterion for stratification
(ibid.:8-9). The classification in the IRS was made by the
Farm Management Division of the Ministry of Agriculture.
The principal basis for the agro-ecological zoning was the
main cash-crop grown in the area. In areas where no predo-
minant cash-crop could be identified one used criteria

based on rainfall (ibid.).

The occurence of dominant cash-crops and, furthermore, the management practices associated with some cash-crops, could be important in understanding the adoption of Hybrid Maize. On the one hand, the cultivation of cash-crops may be a source of income that helps in adopting innovations. On the other hand, the growing of cash-crops may be an in- dication of a greater willingness to adopt innovations. The latter point could also have an informational aspect, i.e. the growing of cash-crops would probably involve some con- tacts with extension agents, or other informational sour- ces, and this could be a factor that positively affects the adoption of additional innovations.

The three sub-locations in this survey belong to diffe- rent agro-ecological zones. Igana lies in what is characte- rized as 'Coffee East of Rift Valley', while Kodoch West belong to the zone 'Coffee West of Rift Valley' and Kotieno Kowor to 'Upper Cotton West of Rift Valley'. The classifi- cation of Kodoch West is, however, somewhat debatable. In fact Kodoch West lies in the border area between 'Coffe West of Rift Valley' and 'Upper Cotton West of Rift Val- ley'. As it turns out both of these cash-crops are repre- sented in Kodoch West, although the number of farmers grow- ing cash-crops in the sample of both Kodoch West and Koti- eno Kowor is very limited. In the case of Kodoch West cof- fee is found on farms lying in the hills mentioned above, while cotton is grown at lower altitudes.

6.3 Adoption in a temporal perspective

Initially the description will deal only with the tempo- ral aspects of adoption, which to a large extent implies an analysis of the growth curves for the different innova- tions being studied. Tables 6.3-6.5 give a detailed de- scription of the adoption patterns in the three survey areas. The information in Tables 6.3-6.5 is also shown in graphical form in Figures 6.1-6.3.

It is clear that the adoption process of all the three innovations studied — Hybrid Maize seed, fertilizers and pest-/insecticides — starts much earlier in Igana than in the other two sub-locations. Second, the adoption process in Igana (Figs. 6.1-6.3) show the characteristic S-shape, which should indicate a diffusion process that has reached a saturation stage. As a 100 per cent adoption has not been reached in either of the survey areas for any of the inno- vations it is, of course, impossible to say that further adoption will not occur.

Table 6.3: Annual distribution of adopters in IGANA.

Year	Hybrid Maize Abs.	Cum.	%-tot.	%-ad.	Fertilizers Abs.	Cum.	%-tot.	%-ad.	Pest-/Insecticides Abs.	Cum.	%-tot.	%-ad.
1955	-	-	-	-	4	4	2.3	4.0	4	4	2.3	3.9
56	-	-	-	-	2	6	3.5	6.0	2	6	3.5	5.8
57	-	-	-	-	1	7	4.1	7.0	1	7	4.1	6.8
58	-	-	-	-	2	9	5.2	9.0	2	9	5.2	8.7
59	-	-	-	-	5	14	8.1	14.0	6	15	8.7	14.6
1960	-	-	-	-	6	20	11.6	20.0	6	21	12.2	20.4
61	-	-	-	-	7	27	15.7	27.0	6	27	15.7	26.2
62	-	-	-	-	4	31	18.0	31.0	4	31	18.0	30.1
63	-	-	-	-	9	40	23.3	40.0	10	41	23.8	39.8
64	2	2	1.2	3.4	10	50	29.1	50.0	10	51	29.7	49.5
65	2	4	2.3	6.9	7	57	33.1	57.0	7	58	33.7	56.3
66	3	7	4.1	12.1	6	63	36.6	63.0	7	65	37.8	63.1
67	-	7	4.1	12.1	7	70	40.7	70.0	9	74	43.0	71.8
68	2	9	5.2	15.5	17	87	50.6	87.0	19	93	54.1	90.3
69	2	11	6.4	19.0	3	90	52.3	90.0	3	96	55.8	93.2
1970	13	24	14.0	41.4	-	90	52.3	90.0	-	96	55.8	93.2
71	9	32	18.6	55.2	3	93	54.1	93.0	1	97	56.4	94.2
72	13	45	26.2	77.6	4	97	56.4	97.0	2	99	57.6	96.1
73	11	56	32.6	96.6	1	98	57.0	98.0	2	101	58.7	98.1
74	1	57	33.1	98.3	2	100	58.1	100.0	2	103	59.9	100.0
75	1	58	33.7	100.0	-	100	58.1	100.0	-	103	59.9	100.0

Apart from the fact that the adoption processes start later in the two survey areas in South Nyanza, the process of growth differs in other respects also. With the exception of Hybrid Maize adoption in Kodoch West, the general trend is that the adoption rates for these two lie markedly below the figures for Igana. In Kodoch West and Igana about a third of the farmers in the sample were using Hybrid Maize, while the figures for Kotieno Kowor was only about 10 per cent. The most marked differences in the adoption figures, however, are found in the adoption rates for fertilizers and pest-/insecticides. With respect to these, the figures for Igana come close to 60 per cent, while the comparable figures in Kodoch West are about 13 and 17 per cent and, finally, the figures for Kotieno Kowor are only about 7 and 3 per cent respectively.

The trends indicated by the growth curves (Figs. 6.1-6.3) also differ among the three areas. While the curves for Igana show the typical flattening out of the right-tail indicating a saturation stage, the curves for Kodoch West and Kotieno Kowor, with the exception of the curve for fertilizers in Kodoch West, indicate that the adoption process is still in its growth phase. Furthermore, the rates of growth differ among the areas. With respect to Hybrid Maize

136

Table 6.4: Annual distribution of adopters in KODOCH WEST.

Year	Hybrid Maize				Fertilizers				Pest-/Insecticides			
	Abs.	Cum.	%-tot.	%-ad.	Abs.	Cum.	%-tot.	%-ad.	Abs.	Cum.	%-tot.	%-ad.
1966	-	-	-	-	1	1	0.5	4.2	-	-	-	-
67	-	-	-	-	-	1	0.5	4.2	-	-	-	-
68	-	-	-	-	-	1	0.5	4.2	-	-	-	-
69	2	2	1.1	3.1	1	2	1.1	8.3	1	1	0.5	3.1
1970	4	4	3.2	9.4	4	6	3.2	25.0	3	4	2.2	12.5
71	9	15	8.1	23.4	4	10	5.3	41.7	2	6	3.2	18.8
72	5	20	10.8	31.3	3	13	7.0	54.2	2	8	4.3	25.0
73	13	33	17.7	51.6	8	21	11.3	87.5	7	15	8.1	46.9
74	13	46	24.7	71.9	3	24	12.9	100.0	7	22	11.8	68.8
75	18	64	34.4	100.0	-	24	12.9	100.0	10	32	17.2	100.0

Table 6.5: Annual distribution of adopters in KOTIENO KOWOR.

Year	Hybrid Maize				Fertilizers				Pest-/Insecticides			
	Abs.	Cum.	%-tot.	%-ad.	Abs.	Cum.	%-tot.	%-ad.	Abs.	Cum.	%-tot.	%-ad.
1959	-	-	-	-	1	1	0.5	7.1	2	2	1.1	40.0
1960	-	-	-	-	-	1	0.5	7.1	-	2	1.1	40.0
61	-	-	-	-	-	1	0.5	7.1	-	2	1.1	40.0
62	-	-	-	-	-	1	0.5	7.1	-	2	1.1	40.0
63	-	-	-	-	-	1	0.5	7.1	-	2	1.1	40.0
64	-	-	-	-	-	1	0.5	7.1	1	3	1.6	60.0
65	-	-	-	-	-	1	0.5	7.1	-	3	1.6	60.0
66	-	-	-	-	-	1	0.5	7.1	-	3	1.6	60.0
67	-	-	-	-	-	1	0.5	7.1	-	3	1.6	60.0
68	-	-	-	-	-	1	0.5	7.1	-	3	1.6	60.0
69	2	2	1.1	10.0	-	1	0.5	7.1	-	3	1.6	60.0
1970	1	3	1.6	15.0	1	2	1.1	14.3	-	3	1.6	60.0
71	2	5	2.6	25.0	2	4	2.1	28.6	-	3	1.6	60.0
72	-	5	2.6	25.0	-	4	2.1	28.6	-	3	1.6	60.0
73	2	7	3.7	35.0	3	7	3.7	50.0	1	4	2.1	80.0
74	4	11	5.8	55.0	3	10	5.3	71.4	-	4	2.1	80.0
75	9	20	10.6	100.0	4	14	7.4	100.0	1	5	2.6	100.0

and pest-/insecticides Kodoch West shows a higher growth rate than Kotieno Kowor.

From an analytical point of view, the differences in the adoption processes between the survey areas creates a small problem. The available material does not allow an estimate of what would be the levelling off, or saturation level for adoption in Kodoch West and Kotieno Kowor. In a breakdown into different adopter-categories along the time-axis, special caution would have to be exercised in analysing the adopters found in the growth phases of Kodoch West and Kotieno Kowor. Not knowing the saturation level, one does not know if the adopter-category being analysed covers all or most of the adopters in the growth phase, of if one only

covers some, and in that case the growth phase will continue for several years to come.

The problem lies in the amount of detail used in the
scale of measurement. In some studies on the diffusion of
innovations discussed in Chapter II, a very detailed division was made into adopter-categories at different phases
of the process (see Fig. 2.1). In the discussion by e.g.
Rogers & Shoemaker (1971) various characteristics are
ascribed to adopters in different phases of adoption. Lacking exact knowledge of the stages reached in seed and
pest-/insecticide adoption in Kodoch West and Kotieno Kowor, conclusions have to be reached with caution (see Section 8.2)

6.4 'Bundles of innovations'

In the discussion above the innovations have been looked
at individually — one by one. From Chapters II and V it
should be obvious that looking at the innovations studied
here as discrete entities may not give a true picture of
how they are presented to, perceived by and subsequently
adopted by small-holders in Kenya.

Hybrid Maize seed, the principal indicator used here,
is not presented as an individual innovation. KSC, in their
promotional policies, are deliberately trying to present
the seed as not just maize seed with an additional yield
capacity. Instead they are trying to present it as a new
crop which demands improved husbandry and additional inputs
in order to realize its full potential. One does not
directly refer to the seed as maize seed, instead one refers to the seed as 'HYBRID' — a name which is also painted
in bold letters on the cars used by KSC's own extension
staff.

In consequence one also tries to introduce the additional inputs and practices that have been tested at the Maize
Research Station in Kitale (see Ch.V for details). Thus,
the approach is to introuduce a 'bundle' of innovations rather than just one type of seed. Quite apart from the actual actions of KSC it should also be noted that only a few
innovations could be seen as single entities. Innovations
most often have to be 'linked' in different ways in order
to function, e.g. television as an innovation demands both
a transmission network as well as a system for electricity
distribution — to take by one simple example. Thus, the
question of 'bundles of innovations' is not limited to the
particular case being studied here. In the present study,
it is therefore important to look at the extent to which

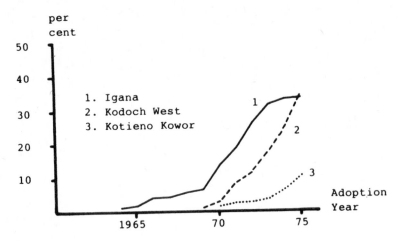

Figure 6.1:   ADY/ST - Adoption year for Hybrid Maize seed (see Appendix 32 for an explanation of the notation of the variables).

farmers adopt different combinations of the innovations
presented. It is possible that an analysis of this kind
could reveal more of the adoption process than what is
found from looking at the innovations as singular entities.

From Ch.V it was obvious that farmers could adopt the
package in full or chose parts of it. If proper husbandry
practices are maintained, better yields could be realized
through adopting Hybrid Maize only, while even higher
yields are possible if a larger part of the package is
adopted. In actual fact the farmers are put in a delicate
situation in which a large number of factors have to be
considered and evaluated one by one and in combination. In
making the choice the farmer will have to consider costs,
i.e. how much he could afford to spend on the innovations
— he will also have to consider labour availability and
ecological factors pertaining to his land.

One outcome of the choice process the farmer has to go
through, may of course be a 'staggered' adoption, viz. they
may start with one or two components and then gradually add
components if and when the outcome of the initial adoption
turns out to affect the yields positively. From a data processing point of view it is a bit difficult to handle a
'staggered' adoption for a large material. To analyse this
properly, one would have to go into individual cases at the
expense of the possible generality that could be found in
looking at a larger population. Initially, at least, the
analysis will restrict itself to the more general aspects
and concentrate on some typical combinations and the adop-

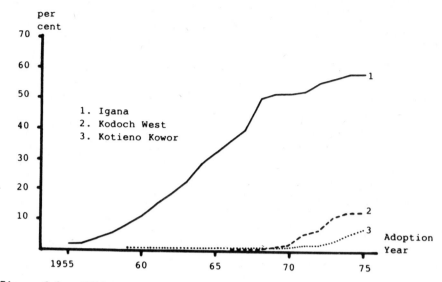

Figure 6.2: ADY/FT - Adoption year for fertilizers.

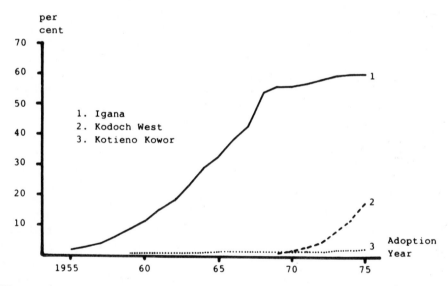

Fiugre 6.3: ADY/PT - Adoption yeas for pest-/insecticides.

tion patterns found in the survey material.

When penetrating an analysis of the different 'bundles',
it is necessary to make cuts in the empirical material
used. As it turns out, in going through the survey material, Kotieno Kowor constitutes an exception with respect
to adoption. The basic problem with the material for Koti-

eno Kowor is the very limited number of adopters of the innovations looked at. In Table 6.5 one sees that in Kotieno
Kowor only 20 farms have adopted Hybrid Maize, only 14 have
adopted fertilizers and only 5 have adopted pest-/insecti-
cides — out of a total of 186 farms. Although the prerequisites for adoption in Kotieno Kowor ought not be very different from the ones found in Kodoch West, the actual outcome is very different between the two areas.

On the surface the only initial clear difference that
exists between the two areas — situated in the same district and in more or less the same agro-ecological zone —
is one of 'remoteness'. Kotieno Kowor, although closer to
Kisii than Kodoch West, lies in a less well serviced area
with respect to roads. Moreover, the existing roads are
often of a low quality and, as a consequence of this, the
area is less well serviced by different kinds of public
transport — buses and 'matatus' (road taxis).

Furthermore, Table 6.5 shows that the adoption that has
taken place in Kotieno Kowor is to a large extent concentrated to the year of the survey or the year just preceding
it. Thus, 65 per cent of the adoption of seed occurred in
1974 and 1975. Similarly, 50 per cent of the adoption of
fertilizers takes place after 1973. The limited number of
adopters and the fact that most adoption is of such a recent origin, makes a proper analysis of spatial and temporal processes almost impossible in Kotieno Kowor. This, unfortunately, necessitates that Kotieno Kowor is left out
of the followig analyses. The data for Kotieno Kowor are
still interesting, as they refer to the time when the adoption curve starts to turn upwards. A further analysis of
the data for Kotieno Kowor will, however, not be made in
the present study.

Returning to the main theme of this section, the possible combinations — 'bundles' — and the number of farmers having adopted each combination was tabulated. The results
are shown in Tables 6.6 and 6.7 for Igana and Kodoch West
respectively. The results reveal quite a lot of the underlying processes involved in the adoption. The temporal
sequences in which the adoption takes place are shown in
Figures 6.4 to 6.6.

From the tables, it is obvious that certain specific
combinations totally dominate the adoption patterns. A comparison of the tables also reveals that the types of combinations chosen in the two areas are quite dissimilar. In
Igana, two particular combinations cater for more than 90
per cent of all adoption. The two combinations are Hybrid

Table 6.6:   IGANA - distribution of adoption-categories.

Adoption-cats.	No.	%-age of tot. adopters	%-age of tot. sample
Seed only	1	0.9	0.6
Fertilizer only	0	0.0	0.0
Pest-/Insecticides	4	3.7	2.3
Seed/Fert./Pest.	52	48.6	30.2
Seed/Fertilizer	3	2.8	1.7
Seed/Pest.	2	1.9	1.2
Fertilizer/Pest.	45	42.1	26.2
TOTAL	107	100.0	62.2

Table 6.7:   KODOCH WEST - distribution of adoption-categories.

Adoption-cats.	No.	%-age of tot. adopters	%-age of tot. sample
Seed only	23	35.9	12.4
Fertilizer only	0	0.0	0.0
Pest-/Insecticides only	0	0.0	0.0
Seed/Fert./Pest.	15	23.4	8.1
Seed/Fertilizer	9	14.1	4.8
Seed/Pest.	17	26.6	9.1
Fertilizer/Pest.	0	0.0	0.0
TOTAL	64	100.0	34.4

Maize seed, fertilizers and pest-/insecticides (ADY/SFP), i.e. the complete package, and fertilizers and pest-/insecticides (ADY/FP) separately.

The prevalence of these two combinations is clearly a reflection of what has been said above about the adoption in Igana. It was noted that the adoption curves (Figs. 6.1-6.3) in Igana all started earlier than the curves for the other survey areas. In addition to this, it could be that in Igana one obviously sees the effects of at least two diffusion processes. Looking at the curves for fertilizers and pest-/insecticides (Figs. 6.2-6.3), one sees that they start to level off in the right tail when the curve for seed adoption (Fig. 6.1) starts to turn upwards into the growth phase. Clearly then, adoption of fertilizers and pest-/insecticides in Igana is separated from the adoption of Hybrid Maize and this is instead related to the growing of coffee as a cash-crop in the areas. Hybrid Maize seed is then only added as one more innovation, by farmers who have already started to adopt innovations.

The end product in Igana then turns out to be one group that has adopted fertilizers/pesticides and adds Hybrid Maize seed as one additional innovation. The other major group in Igana consists of those farmers who adopted innovations related to coffee growing, but have not continued to adopt Hybrid Maize. A third group, of course, consists of the non-adopters, but these will be discussed in Chapter VIII. The predominance of the two sets of adoption combinations raises several questions concerning the the different characteristics possible, pertaining to the adopters of the different combinations. It must, for example, be quite common that farmers find themselves in a situation where they have started to adopt some innovations and are facing the problem of whether to continue adopting or not. At present, however, only the problem is outlined, while the discussion will be presented in later sections.

Kodoch West, on the other hand, has quite a different pattern of adoption. Table 6.7 shows that all adoption in one way or the other is related to the adoption of Hybrid Maize seed. In Kodoch West, seed is adopted in combination with other innovations out of the complete 'bundle' or by itself, which actually constitutes the largest group. Some instances of 'staggered' adoption do occur, but the time span between the first and later adoptions is generally only one or two crop seasons and, thus, distinctly different from the patterns found in Igana.

As in the case of Igana, the adoption-combinations emerging in Kodoch West could be understood in the light of what has been said about the sub-location in Section 6.2. In Kodoch West, a long and well established tradition of growing cash-crops does not exist, which in turn could have generated a familarity with some of the innovations being studied. Some cotton and coffee growing does exist in the area, but the number of farmers engaged in this is very limited. Thus, to a large extent Kodoch West is virgin land with respect to the adoption of the kind of innovations discussed here and one would only expect seed to be the primary innovation.

6.5 Temporal aspects of the adoption of the 'Bundles of Innovations'

In finding that the innovations studied are adopted in very specific 'bundles' the question of the usefulness of studying the adoption processes for each individual innovation is raised. Obviously, they are to a great extent, not perceived as singular innovations, nor adopted as such. To

Table 6.8: 'Bundles of Innovations' used in the analysis.

Var.|Var. No.	No.	Content of variable	Crit. var.	Used in
ADY/SFP; V157	52	Seed, Fert., Pest./ Insect.	Seed	Igana K. West
ADY/FP; V158	45	Fert., Pest./Insect.	Fert.	Igana
ADY/S, V161	23	Seed - only	Seed	K. West
ADY/SF; V162	9	Seed, Fert.	Seed	K. West
ADY/SP; V163	17	Seed, Pest./Insect.	Seed	K. West

Note: Explanation to the notation of the variables used is given in
      Appendix 32.

cope with this problem a new set of variables has been defined, based on the information from Tables 6.6 and 6.7.
The newly created variables, however, can only show adoption of a specific 'bundle' and then the time of adoption
for a specific 'criterion variable' chosen for each new
variable. It is not possible to create variables that could
cater for the occurences of 'staggered' adoption where such
adoption occurs and this, of course, is a drawback of the
newly created variables.

In creating the new variables it turns out that some
groups of adopters become fairly small, e.g. ADY/SF. This,
of course, creates some problems in drawing far reaching
conclusions and in obtaining statistically significant results from the analyses made. In trying to adapt the analysis to the empirical reality found in Tables 6.6 and 6.7,
there is no way of escaping the fact that some of the sub-
populations are becoming fairly small and the only way of
treating small populations in statistical analyses is to
be extremely careful when drawing broad conclusions and to
keep the size of the tested population constantly in mind
throughout the analysis.

Growth curves for the newly defined variables are shown
for Igana in Figures 6.4 and 6.5 and for Kodoch West in Figure 6.6A-D. In the case of Igana, the curves substantiates
what has been said above about the adoption sequences. In
the case of Kodoch West, however, the curves show some particular features that qualify some of the conclusions that
could be drawn from Figures 6.1 to 6.3.

Starting by commenting on the curves for Igana, it
should first be noted that both curves display the typical
shape of a 'completed' diffusion process, or one which has
reached a saturation stage. It should be noted, however,
that the two growth curves in Figures 6.4 and 6.5, should

144

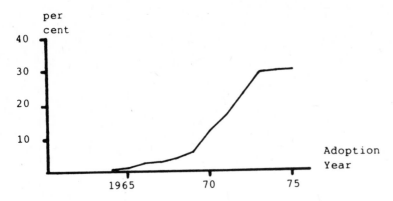

Figure 6.4:   ADY/SFP - Adoption year for Hybrid Maize, fertilizers and
              pest-/insecticides in IGANA.

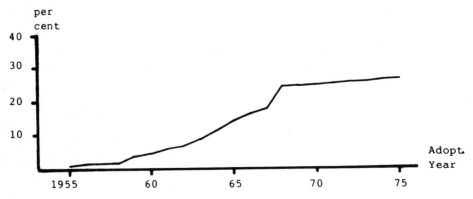

Figure 6.5:   ADY/FP - Adoption year for fertilizers and pest-/insecti-
              cides only in IGANA.

be compared to and, to an extent, also juxtaposed with the
Igana curve for ADY/FT in Figure 6.2, which gives a picture
of the overall adoption pattern out of which ADY/SFP and
ADY/FP constitute sub-sets. A comparison between ADY/FT and
ADY/FP reveals a much lower gradient of growth for ADY/FP
than what is seen for the overall adoption of fertilizers.
A tentative conclusion from this, is that the sub-groups
constituting the ADY/FP adopters, has a slightly higher re-
sistance to adoption and, thus, is also reluctant to continue with a further adoption of Hybrid Maize seed.

Otherwise, the curves seen in Figures 6.4 and 6.5 show
what was evident already in the earlier discussions, i.e.
Hybrid Maize adoption starts later and largely as an innovation being added to an earlier adoption of fertilizers

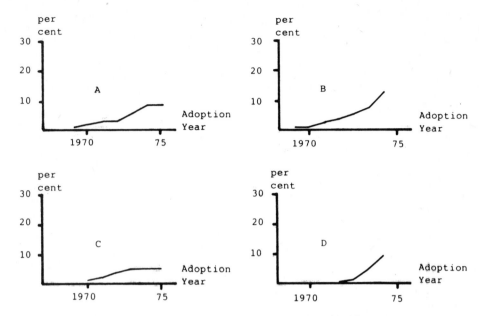

Figure 6.6: Adoption of 'bundles' in KODOCH WEST: A) ADY/SFP;
B) ADY/S; C) ADY/SF; D) ADY/SP.

and pest-/insecticides. It could also be noted that the
gradient of growth in the curve showing adoption of the
complete 'bundle' (ADY/SFP) is higher than the corresponding growth rate in the case of the adopters of fertilizers
and pest-/insecticides only (ADY/FP). This observation confirm the assumption that the two groups of adopters defined
for Igana, are different with respect to their readiness
to adopt. In consequence this leads to the further assumption that they may differ in other respects, a topic which
will be looked into further in the two following chapters.

Shifting the focus to the growth curves for the adoption
of 'bundles of innovations' in Kodoch West, one immediately
notes marked differences to the curves which were found in
Igana. Of course only one of the curves for each sub-location refers to the same set of innovations, still the differences in the overall patterns are obvious. The first
such difference concerns the time when the adoption processes start in the two sub-locations. Igana has a long tradition of accepting the innovations studied, while the adoption processes in Kodoch West do not start until the end
of the sixties and a significant growth in adoption is not
evident until the early seventies. In Igana it is only the
adoption of Hybrid Maize that shows significant growth in

the seventies.

The other striking thing with respect to Kodoch West, is the differences found in the adoption curves for the different 'bundles' which is interesting as the 'bundles' are all based on the same 'criterion variable' — i.e. the adoption year for Hybrid Maize seed. What is seen in the curves for Kodoch West is a changing pattern of adoption over a period, viz. different combinations of the 'bundles' are adopted at different times. The material is, of course, not very large and conclusions must be drawn with caution. There are, however, other pieces of data one may draw upon, that give some support for the changing composition of the 'bundles' over a period of time. What is particularly obvious is that fertilizers are not adopted very much in the later years of the period studied and this, of course, is related to the sharply rising prices of fertilizers after 1973.

A more detailed look at the curves for Kodoch West, shows that only for one type of 'bundle' does the curve resemble the typical S-shape of an adoption that has reached a 'saturation' stage. This is in Figure 6.6A (ADY/SFP), i.e. the adoption of the complete package. From the discussion above, it is obvious that the 'saturation' seen in this curve is the result of a decrease in the adoption of fertilizers. This is also obvious if one looks at the curve for the adoption of Hybrid Maize and fertilizers (ADY/SF). Although this curve does not display a distinct S-shape one may perceive the beginning of such a curve in 1970-72. Growth rapidly tails off after 1973 and the curve runs almost parallel to the x-axis. Again it seems obvious that the rising prices of fertilizers in 1973 cause a rapid decline in the adoption of any combination including fertilizers.

With the decline in adoption of some 'bundles', however, it seems as if other combinations gain momentum in the overall adoption pattern. This can be seen in the curves for adoption of Hybrid Maize seed separately (ADY/S) and the adoption of Hybrid Maize and pest-/insecticides (ADY/SP). Neither of these curves shows a tendency of approaching a stage of 'saturation'. Instead they indicate a rapidly increasing rate of adoption for the last few years investigated and to some extent this increase in adoption is most obvious in the years after 1973.

The overall picture of the adoption patterns found in Kodoch West, is one where the farmers act rationally in deciding the composition of the 'bundle' they are going to adopt. At this stage it is very difficult to draw definite conclusions concerning the motives behind certain types of behaviour. A tentative conclusion, however, is that the farmers are very much aware of and sensitive to the cost factors involved. This is inferred from the shift to combinations that do not include fertilizers, which may have become prohibitively expensive in relation to the expected yield increases.

Finally, a short note is needed concerning the changes in the composition of 'bundles' in Kodoch West in comparison to the trends found in Igana. A similar type of selectivity as was found in Kodoch West is not found in Igana. Table 6.6 clearly shows that two distinct combinations completely dominate the adoption patterns in Igana and both of these include fertilizers. Most of the adoption in Igana, however, was completed prior to the dramatic price increases of fertilizers and these, it seems, have not affected the patterns studied here. It may be assumed, however, that if the new prices affect the adoption it will be through a discontinuation of adoption and that this would occur after the survey period.

6.6 Spatial aspects of the adoption of the 'Bundles of Innovations'

Continuing along the lines of a more traditional analysis of the diffusion patterns found, attention should be turned to the spatial manifestations of these. From what has been said above on 'bundles of innovations' one realizes that an analysis of the individual innovation making up the 'bundles' may not be the most appropriate way of approaching this part of the analysis. With the exception of the adopters of Hybrid Maize seed separately (ADY/S) in Kodoch West, all other adoption-categories are a mixture of two or more of the individual innovations looked at. Thus, the focus should be on the adoption-categories described in Table 6.8. The spatial adoption patterns for some of the individual innovations will be shown, as they give a general/summary picture of the overall processes in which the 'bundles' form sub-sets.

With the micro-orientation of the study and the relative limited number of observations in some of the adoption-categories, no attempt will be made to construe any kinds of diffusion waves or trend surfaces. The analysis will restrict itself to an analysis of the point patterns as they emerge from the simple plotting of adopters in specific periods of time.

The basic hypothesis to be discussed, is whether the empirical generalizations on diffusion patterns made by geographers replicate themselves even in the extreme micro-scale. Although some of the results arrived at by Törnqvist (1967), among others, may point in other directions, it is difficult to make a case of an alternative hypothesis. At least in the early phases of the adoption process one may expect to find patterns that have been observed at higher levels of aggregation, i.e. initial agglomeration, radial expansion, secondary agglomerations etc. (cf. i.a. Gould 1969 and Hägerstrand 1953). The limited size of the survey areas may, however, lead to a fairly rapid spatial coverage in which distinct patterns are no longer discernible.

Thus, the most interesting parts of the diffusion patterns looked at should be the early phases of the processes, in order to try to identify the initial agglomerations if and, in that case, where they appear. Of interest in the analysis is also to try to identify obvious biases in the adoption patterns at this scale — biases that may not be possible to identify at higher levels of aggregation where they would be overshadowed by the general directions and trends found in the diffusion waves sweeping over the areas concerned.

Prior to the presentation of maps, a short methodological note may be necessary. The adoption sequences found on the maps are not based on any statistical criteria. In fact they are defined subjectively from an ocular inspection of maps drawn on a one year basis and the creation of the sequences is made with the intent of capturing critical phases in the overall processes. Particular emphasis has been placed on capturing the earlier phases of the processes to enable an analysis to be made of these. As already mentioned, the smallness of the survey areas led to a fairly rapid spatial coverage in which one is, more or less, only able to talk about an increasing density of adoption, rather than about distinct patterns or processes. In Chapter VIII more strict criteria for the definition of temporal adoption-catergories will be applied.

6.6.1 Adoption patterns in Igana

As a background to the discussions on spatial adoption patterns and in line with the theoretical approaches of the study, Maps 6.1 and 6.2 are shown. Map 6.1 places Igana in its setting of supply-nodes and transportation links (only motorable roads are shown). Map 6.2 gives a more detailed picture of the internal transportation network down to the

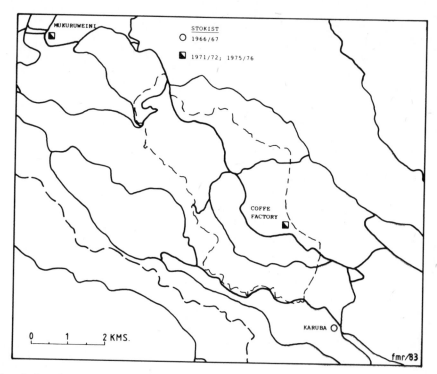

<u>Map 6.1</u>: Structure of the supply network in and around IGANA.

level of foot-paths. Although explicit references are not always made to these two maps in the discussions on the adoption patterns, the information contained in them, is naturally of importance for the understanding of the emerging adoption patterns.

The actual adoption patterns are presented in Maps 6.3 to 6.6 showing the adoption of Hybrid Maize seed separately (ADY/ST), adoption of fertilizers separately (ADY/FT), adoption of the complete package (ADY/SFP) and adoption of fertilizers and pest-/insecticides only (ADY/FP) respectively. In line with the temporal sequences found in the adoption processes in Igana, the discussion should start with the adoption of fertilizers (ADY/FT), which is shown on Map 6.4.

Here the first adopters appear in 1955 (methodological aspects of recall data of a duration of 20 years have been discussed in Chapter IV). The initial adoption forms a cluster in the north-west corner of Igana — in Hägerstand's (1953) terminology such clusters are referred to as "initial agglomerations". From the initial four adopters the adoption sequence is marked by an increasing number of

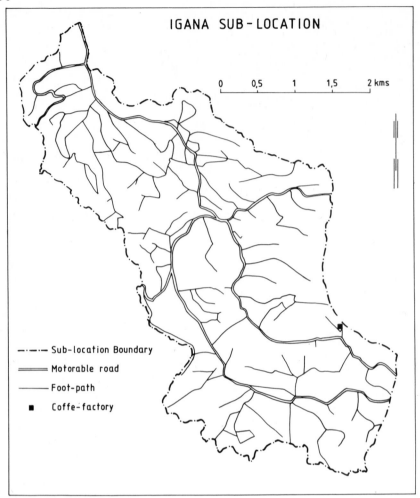

Map 6.2: Transportation network in IGANA.

adopters in the vicinity of the initial agglomeration (two
more in 1956) and the 'odd one out'. The latter, however,
appears in the last year of the sequence. At this stage it
is not necessary to try to explain the occurrence of individual adoptions, seemingly of a random character. It
should be noted, however, that the occurrences of such
adoptions, later leading to the formation of secondary
agglomerations, are well known from geographical studies
of the diffusion of innovations.

The next adoption sequence (1958-60) for ADY/FT, again
follows familiar patterns found in other studies, particularly in the so called developed world. Here we will not
attempt to go into the underlying causes for such similarities, but will only record the patterns as they emerge. A

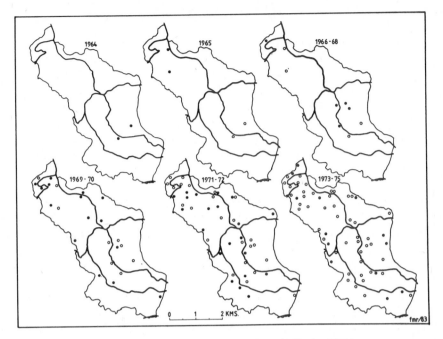

Map 6.3: Adoption of Hybrid Maize seed (ADY/ST) in IGANA.

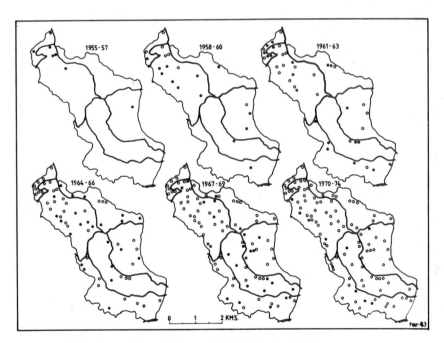

Map 6.4: Adoption of fertilizers (ADY/FT) in IGANA.

discussion on the similarities and their causes may otherwise be found in Rogers (1983:Ch.1-3).

The adoption sequence (1958-60) depicts familiar geographical traits. In the period the number of adopters has
trebled. The new adopters are, however, not randomly located in the area. The majority of the 'newcomers' are located in the north-west corner where the initial agglomeration was found. Using the established geographical terminology, the 'newcomers' are part of two distinct processes
that have been observed in connection with the development
of spatial diffusion patterns.

First, one notices a radial expansion of the initial
agglomeration and also an increasing internal density of
adoption in the initial agglomeration. Second, the forming
of a secondary agglomeration is seen in the eastern part
of Igana. This cluster, however is less distinct and much
more elongated than the initial one. The secondary agglomeration also displays more of a random process in its formation. Single, or pairs of, adopters appear for the different years and only in the last year of the sequence is the
'bridge' established with the adopter appearing here in
1957 — the 'odd one out'.

The third adoption sequence (1961-63), shows a continued
rapid growth in the number of adopters. In relative terms
it constitutes a doubling — the new adopters equal the
number of adopters found in the two preceding sequences.
It is possible to interpret the spatial diffusion pattern
in much the same terminology as has been used above. First,
a continued radial expansion from the established agglomerations is apparent. Secondly, an increasing internal density of adoption can be noted. To an extent the 'looser'
structure of the so called secondary agglomeration remains.
More important, however, is the fact that the two agglomerations, trough the gradual radial expansion, are nearing
a stage where they will merge, approaching a state of a
fairly complete coverage by the innovation. Coverage, of
course, here refers to the presence or non-presence of
adopters and is not related to possible saturation levels.

The remaining three adoption sequences need not be commented upon at length, as the patterns seen form a logical
continuation of the processes already discussed above.
First, in 1964-66 one notices the merging of the adoption
patterns from the two agglomerations identified. From 1966
onwards a fairly complete coverage of adopters of fertilizers is established in Igana. The period remaining up to
the time of the survey 1966-75, is mainly characterized by

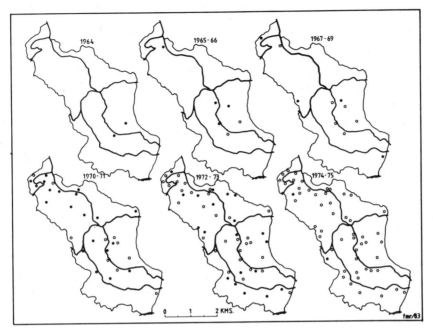

Map 6.5: Adoption of Hybrid Maize, fertilizers and pest-/insecticides (ADY/SFP) in IGANA.

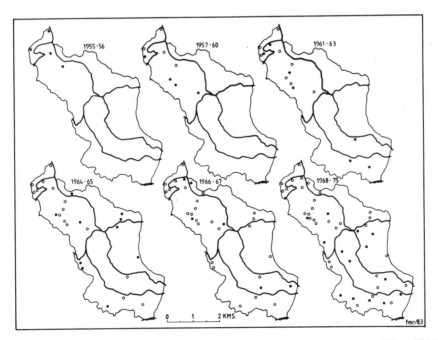

Map 6.6: Adoption of fertilizers and pest-/insecticides (ADY/FP), IGANA.

a gradual filling in of the 'empty' areas still remaining as pockets in the overall pattern. The period is also characterized by a gradually rising density of adoption throughout the sub-location. Finally, the rate of adoption decreases, which is also obvious from Figure 6.2.

The adoption found for fertilizers is directly related to the adoption of coffee as a cash-crop in the sub-location — as it was in Central Province as a whole from the mid 1950s up until the second half of the 1960s. The expansion of the coffee acreage in Central Province was mainly due to the Kenyan Government's following of the proposals presented in the Swynnerton Plan of 1954. The expansion was to some extent checked, but not halted, by the signing of the first International Coffee Agreement in 1962 (cf. i.a. Acland 1971:60). Thus, the underlying reasons for the adoption of fertilizers are in no way linked to the principal innovation studied here — Hybrid Maize.

Turning the attention to the adoption of Hybrid Maize as shown on Map 6.3, it is interesting to note that two adopters of this innovations did so two years before the seed was available anywhere near the sub-location — a first brand of Hybrid Maize was released in 1964 in Kitale. The actual distance from Igana to Kitale is not less than 300 kilometers, giving an interesting perspective on distance-decay functions and the effects of the friction of distance. The truth of the matter is, that both these adopters occupy fairly unique positions in both the informational- and economic-hierarchies of Igana. One had been an extension agent and the other is one of the wealthiest farmers of the sub-location. Thus, they may have had both information and supplies through channels of their own prior to the time when the innovation was generally available.

Also the two adopters in 1965 belong to a group of adopters that adopted before the innovation was available in the vicinity of Igana. The exact sources for the Hybrid Maize seed in the cases of these very early adopters is, unfortunately, not clear. The two latter adopters may have had their supplies from Embu, although this is not certain. It is obvious, however, that such early adoption must have included a major effort to aquire the seed.

Still, the main part of the adoption of seed took place between 1966 and the early 1970s. To an extent the adoption pattern for the adoption of Hybrid Maize differs from the one looked at for fertilizers. There, the initial agglomeration, or diffusion centre (see Brown 1981:21) was found in the north-west corner of the area. Here the diffusion centre is found in the central part of the sub-location. These differences should largely be due to the different sources for the innovations at the time they were introduced into the area (see Map 6.1).

The first stockist appearing in the vicinity of Igana is in Karuba Market, to the south-east of the sub-location. Four of the five 'newcomers' in the adoption sequence 1966-68 also live relatively near to this market, as well as to the first two adopters. Basically these four are also clustered along the main road leading to Karuba Market, thus giving a certain support to the assumptions in the 'Market and Infrastructure Perspective'.

In the cases of the adoption of fertilizers and pest-/insecticides, the principal outlets for the innovations are through co-operative unions and societies. In Igana the initial outlet for fertilizers and pest-/insecticides was found in Mukuruweini Co-operative Society and somewhat later also in the Coffee Factory situated within the sublocation. In the last year of the 1960s, Mukuruweini Cooperative Society started to supply Hybrid Maize seed as well, both in Mukuruweini and the Coffee Factory. This is reflected in the adoption sequence 1969-70 where, on the one hand, adoption gains momentum and, on the other hand, a shift of the centre of gravity in the adoption pattern towards the north-west corner of Igana is obvious. The importance of the co-operative movement in promoting the innovations studied, is reflected in the fact that 70 per cent of the population interviewed were co-operative members — a figure that increases to 91 per cent in the case of Hybrid Maize adopters.

In the last three adoption sequences one may identify three fairly loose clusters initially, i.e. the diffusion centre in the south-east; a secondary diffusion centre in the north-west and finally a loosely defined intermediate group in between the two mentioned. The last two sequences 1971-75 are characterized by a fairly rapid filling in process where the earlier defined clusters rapidly merge and disappear as identifiable entities. To an extent 'spatial coverage' is achieved much faster than in the case of fertilizers, which is not surprising as Hybrid Maize is entering an area and a social system that is already 'ripe' with respect to adoption. The total adoption of Hybrid Maize stops at a lower level than the other innovations. Still it is not possible to claim that this is a reflection of saturation in Igana. It is not unlikely that the adoption curve could turn upwards again, not least in the light of

156

the policies indicated in Sessional Paper No. 4, 1981 (RoK 1981b — see also section 5.2).

Turning to the adoption of specific 'bundles of innovations' in Igana, these are shown on Maps 6.5 and 6.6. As already mentioned, the two adoption combinations, ADY/SFP and ADY/FP, completely dominate adoption in Igana. The two groups comprise 97 out of a total adopting population of 107 farm units. In relative terms they comprise 67 per cent of the total population interviewed and almost 91 per cent of all adopters in the survey. Depending on the 'criterion variable' used in defining the adoption-category (see Table 6.8) the resultant adoption pattern almost invariably follows what has been seen for the individual innovations.

Due to the similarities in the adoption patterns found between the individual innovations used as 'criterion variables' and the 'bundles' it will not be necessary to comment at length on the patterns found in Maps 6.5 and 6.6. One observation could be made, however, although extreme caution should be exercised in interpreting the observation as a conclusion, even a _very_ tentative conclusion. To a degree the two adoption combinations shown are complementary to one another. A comparison between Maps 6.5 and 6.6 may lead to the observation that a slight locational difference exists between the two adoption-categories. One may infer that the adopters of the complete package have a slightly stronger tendency to being found along the main transport links than the adopters of fertilizers and pest-/insecticides only. If the observation is valid it could be interpreted as an additional support for the 'Market and Infrastructure Perspective'. Still it should be strongly underlined that the relative smallness of the survey area makes it difficult to draw any far reaching conclusion pertaining to distances. In absolute terms the locational differences referred to are made up of distance differences of one kilometer down to a couple of hundred metres. If distance-decay functions could be observed at such short distances, it may be a topic for discussion, at least observed differences at such short distances should be treated with utmost care in the drawing of conclusions. Still, the tendency observed will be of interest in the still more detailed analysis to follow in Chapter VIII.

6.6.2 Adoption patterns in Kodoch West

When the attention is turned to the spatial diffusion patterns found in Kodoch West some marked differences to the patterns found in Igana will become apparent. In the

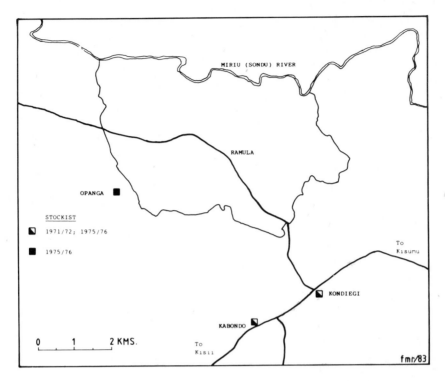

MIRIU (SONDU) RIVER

RAMULA

OPANGA

STOCKIST

1971/72; 1975/76

1975/76

To
Kisumu

KONDIEGI

KABONDO

0   1   2 KMS.

To
Kisii

fmr/83

Map 6.7: Structure of the supply network around KODOCH WEST.

case of Igana quite a lot of the discussions pertaining to
the adoption patterns of the individual innovations was applicable to the adoption patterns of the more complex
'bundles' as well. In Kodoch West it will be evident that
the adoption of the defined 'bundles' show distinctly different adoption patterns from the ones that could be inferred from the individual adoption of Hybrid Maize seed,
which is used as the 'criterion variable in the 'bundles'.

Part of the reason for the differences may be sought in
the differences in the temporal aspects of the adoption in
the two sub-locations as is evident from Figures 6.1 to
6.3. Linked to this are, of course, the temporal and spatial aspects of the supply network as shown in Map 6.7. To
completely understand the somewhat particular adoption patterns in Kodoch West it will not suffice to simply look at
temporal and spatial aspects, but also try to understand
some of the possible underlying structural aspects that may
influence the adoption patterns.

Concerning the individual innovations, in this case only
Hybrid Maize seed will be discussed, it is possible to li-

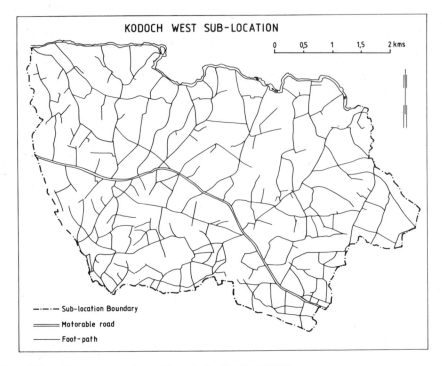

Map 6.8: Transportation network in KODOCH WEST.

mit the discussion to a couple of short observations — in light of what has been said on the adoption patterns for the 'bundles'. Looking at Map 6.9 it is obvious that the diffusion centre, or initial agglomeration, is found in the south-east part of the sub-location. In terms of the 'Market and Infrastructure Perspective' this is not surprising in comparison with Map 6.7.

The diffusion centre found for the total adoption of Hybrid Maize seed, of course, is related to the existence of stockists at Kabondo and Kondiego markets which lie along the main road between Kisumu and Kisii. Also the diffusion centre is to a degree related to the main road passing through Kodoch West linking up with the Kisumu-Kisii road at Kondiego. From this initial diffusion a radial expansion is obvious in the adoption sequence of 1971 (Map 6.9). Also a secondary agglomeration become apparent in 1971. In 1972 only an increased internal density of adoption is seen in the initial agglomeration. In 1973, however, a new cluster appears in the north-west part of the sub-location, while the processes of increasing internal density of adoption and radial expansion continues in the first two agglomera-

Map 6.9: Total adoption of Hybrid Maize seed (ADY/ST), KODOCH WEST.

tions. The latter is obvious in 1974 when a fourth cluster starts to emerge with the addition of two adopters in the south-west part of the area. Finally, in 1975 the fourth cluster becomes more marked and the first and second clusters more or less merge by a continued radial expansion. By 1975 a fairly complete spatial coverage has been achieved. Thus, the overall diffusion patterns found for the total adoption of Hybrid Maize conforms in all essential parts to the established theory on spatial diffusion.

Crucial concepts in the spatial diffusion theory are information and 'neighbourhood effect'. The impact of the latter has primarily been read into the initial clusterings of the adopters and in the radial expansion of early adoption centres. Here, due to the relative smallness of the

<u>Map 6.10</u>: Adoption of Hybrid Maize, fertilizers and pest-/insecticides
            (ADY/SFP) in KODOCH WEST.

survey areas and the subsequent rapid achievement of a spatial coverage, the influences of a 'neighbourhood effect'
are only visible in the initial phases of the adoption process. Still, in the discussion on the adoption patterns
found for the total adoption of Hybrid Maize seed (ADY/ST),
above, it is possible to infer a 'neighbourhood effect' in
the sense that early adopters transmit information to farmers in their vicinity, thus, causing both a radial expansion and an increasing internal density of adoption.

    Turning to the adoption of the particular adoption-cate-
gories defined, the emerging adoption patterns (Maps 6.10
to 6.13) will not, as in Igana, follow the patterns found
for total seed adoption but rather follow a logic of their

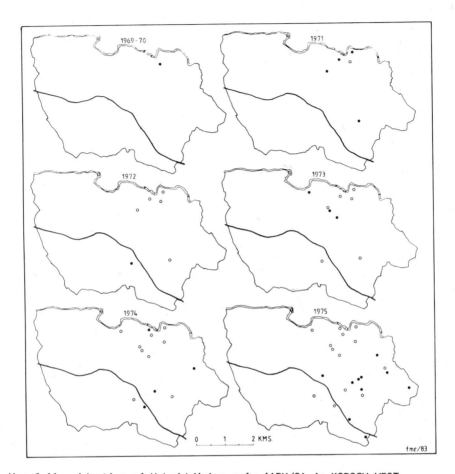

Map 6.11: Adoption of Hybrid Maize only (ADY/S) in KODOCH WEST.

own. The most notable feature of these adoption patterns
is a stronger tendency to clustering than that found in
Igana. In fact it is possible to infer that certain adoption-categories are found in specific parts of the sub-
location. Minor overlaps occur but basically it could be
inferred that the 'neighbourhood effects' in Kodoch West
are of such a nature that they form very closely knit spatial structures.

The data available in this study do not allow a detailed
analysis of the underlying causes of this. Possible explanations can be found in, for example, the social organization of kinship groups and extended families. It may be assumed that these groupings have a relatively free flow of
informal informational contacts and that the clustering is

<u>Map 6.12</u>: Adoption of Hybrid Maize and fertilizers (ADY/SF) in
KODOCH WEST.

a manifestation of the location of such groups within the
sub-location. Explanations can also be sought in, for example, local agro-ecological conditions, pressure on the
available land, crop production patterns, co-operative membership, differences in socio-economic status etc. In sum,
the assumption is that a number of basic structural factors
pertaining to the area may generate closely knit locally
defined groupings, which within themselves adopt specific
combinations of the innovations studied. Still, the factors
referred to may not be exhaustive and should rather be seen
as parts of the underlying factors explaining a particular
adoption pattern. Differences within groups can still be
large and may be important as steering factors in deciding

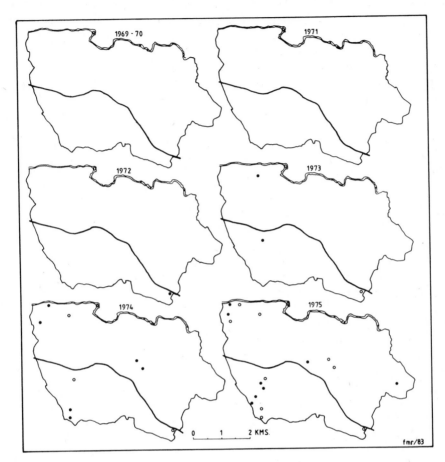

Map 6.13: Adoption of Hybrid Maize and pest-/insecticides (ADY/SP) in KODOCH WEST.

adoption or non-adoption as the integration into an informal information network. In Chapter VIII, attempts will be made to penetrate more deaply into the validity of some of the above mentioned factors in explaining the specific adoption combinations.

Returning to the concrete physical manifestations of the adoption patterns, it is at this stage, difficult to give definite explanations to the patterns as they emerge. Roughly, a broad division of the sub-location into four quadrants of a system of co-ordinates with the origin set in the middle of the area and the axes following a north/south and an east/west direction, specifies the main clusters for the different adoption-categories.

Starting with the adopters of the complete package (ADY/SFP), Map 6.10, a tendency to a clustering in the south-east quadrant close to the origin is evident throughout the adoption process. From 1973 onwards some adoption, however, takes place in the north-west quadrant forming what could be labelled a secondary agglomeration. Both adoption-categories including fertilizers in Kodoch West show a stagnating or, at least, a markedly reduced adoption rate after 1973. Thus, it is difficult to foresee the future development of the adoption of the complete package.

The final result is one of two fairly distinct clusters — one in the south-east and one in the north-west quadrant. Concerning the first of these it may be possible to explain its establishment in terms of the 'Market and Infrastructure Perspective', viz. proximity to stockists/markets and to major links in the transportation network. The latter cluster is more difficult to explain in the same simple and rather normative terminology. In fact the north-west quadrant does contain a fairly large concentration of the more wealthy farmers of the sub-location in terms of land-ownership and in terms of annual income/turn-over (INC/ATO). Thus, the explanation of the secondary cluster may be found in basic structural variables rather than in simple locational factors. In that perspective it is interesting to note the 'delay' before this group is brought into the adoption process.

The dominant adoption-category in Kodoch West, in terms of the number of adopters, is the one pertaining to adoption of Hybrid Maize seed only, which is shown on Map 6.11. As in the case of the adopters of the total package these adopters form a distinct cluster, but this time in the north-east quadrant of the area. In terms of the normative explanations that could be derived from the 'Market and Infrastructure Perspective', these adopters display a slightly 'deviant' behaviour. In search for such explanations one would immediately look for the supply point relatively near to the adopters and none such is found. Also the Sondu River which forms the northern boundary of the sub-location, is not bridged close to Kodoch West and there are no fords in the vicinity. Moreover, even if it were possible to cross the river no stockists would be found close by on the other side. Thus, the adopters of seed found in the north-east quadrant have been dependent on the stockists found in Kabondo and Kondiego for their supply of the innovation. Obviously, then, it is not possible to apply an explanation, phrased in purely spatial terms, to the adoption patterns found for ADY/S, at least in its early phases. Also, although a large part of the discussion on adoption patterns is in spatial terms, too strong a dependence on such explanations is felt to be too simple and unrealistic. Instead, as indicated, explanations will have to be sought for in the formation of formal and informal networks, as well as in the position of the adopters on the basic structural parameters examined in the present study.

To briefly summarize the course of the adoption of ADY/ S, it should first be noted that adoption starts in a 'remote' part of the sub-location. With the exception of two adopters, in 1971 and 1972 in a more southerly location, adoption up until 1974 is concentrated in the northern part of the sub-location. In 1974 a couple of adopters close to the main road form an embryo to a secondary agglomeration — if, however, not very distinct. Finally, in 1975 adoption continues in what could be interpreted as a radial expansion, linking the two clusters and also forming a fairly complete spatial coverage in the north-east quadrant. In an overall perspective, the most noteworthy aspect of the ADY/S adoption in Kodoch West is its concentration to a portion of the sub-location.

Next, the adoption-category of the adopters of Hybrid Maize and fertilizers ADY/SF should be discussed (Map 6.12). Among the different adoption-categories defined, this is the one which shows the clearest clustering. The nine adopters found in this category are almost exclusively concentrated to the south-east quadrant and closer to the boundary of the sub-location, than the cluster found for the adopters of the complete package, which was also located in the south-east quadrant. In fact the adopters of ADY/SF are situated nearest to the supply points in Kabondo and Kondiego. It should be noted here, however, that up until the time of the survey fertilizers were not available at the above mentioned markets and had to be acquired from Kisii and transported to the area. This, of course, is made possible, when private means of transportation are not available, by utilizing public transport in the form of buses and 'matatus'. This option, however, would not be open to everyone and it could be assumed that adoption of a combination including fertilizers would be related to the economic status of the adopters.

Economic status, however, will not suffice as singular explanations of the patterns found. In the case of the adopters of the complete package, it was also noted that a secondary cluster appeared in the north-west quadrant and, furthermore, that some of the more wealthy farmers are found in that quadrant. Generally, however, there exist a fairly strong concentration of adopters adopting combinations including fertilizers in the south-east quadrant, nearest to the supply points and the main transport artery to Kisii. Thus, a 'friction of distance' notion seem to be applicable as an explanation as well as purely economic and structural variables.

Here it could be noticed that, while seed and pest-/insecticides are sold in small packages of no more than 10 kg, fertilizers are sold in 50 kg bags and thus are quite difficult to transport for longer distances without additional means of transport. It could also be noted that carrying burdens on the head is the dominant means of transportation in the area — as reported by 73 per cent of the sample. Heavy burdens such as a bag of fertilizers could not be carried very far by means of head porterage. Thus, we are faced with a set of explanations of the patterns found, which lie between purely economic and purely spatial ones. Again, this will be a topic of interest in the more detailed analyses to be pursued in the following chapters.

The last adoption-category defined for Kodoch West is the one describing adoption of Hybrid Maize seed and pest-/insecticides (ADY/SP). The adoption pattern of this combination, the second most important in Kodoch West, is shown on Map 6.13. As an adoption-category, it is of course possible, but not one of the more expected ones. From a yield point of view, one would expect, in cases where the complete package is not adopted, a combination of seed and fertilizers. Individual adoption of seed is also expected for groups that may not have the financial means of adopting more than a single component out of the package. The category at hand, however, gives the impression of being a compromise between an adoption of either ADY/SFP or ADY/SF in view of the rising prices of fertilizers. To an extent this is reflected in the relatively late apperance of the combination, which coincides with the price increase of fertilizers, i.e. 1973.

The adoption pattern for ADY/SP is a bit unusual also in its spatial manifestations, in the sense that the initial phases are marked by a high degree of randomness. Not until the year of the survey (1975/76) does any kind of pattern emerge. In terms of clusters and the quadrants discussed, three small clusters can be inferred in 1974 — one in the south-west, one in the north-west and one close to the origin in the south-west quadrant. In light of the fur-

ther development, the cluster in the south-west is the most
interesting. In the survey material all respondents give
the markets in Kabondo and Kondiego as the sources for the
innovations. In fact, a stockist was established in Opanga
in 1974 (see Map 6.7), which seems to be reflected in the
relatively large number of new adopters in the south-west
quadrant close to Opanga in 1975.

Again it would be easy to assume a simple normative spatial explanation for at least, the south-western cluster.
A complication is that the stockist in Opanga in 1974/75
only sold Hybrid Maize seed and, thus, the adopters were
still dependent on other stockists for their supplies of
pest-/insecticides. As already mentioned the information
provided in all interviews points to Kabondo and Kondiego
as the sources for the innovations and, thus, the conclusions concerning the influence of Opanga in the later phase
of the adoption, lack support in the available data. Still,
the information provided in Map 6.13 strongly points to the
conclusion that Opanga does play a role in the adoption
processes found.

Of the four quadrants identified adopters of very specific combinations have been ascribed to three of them. The
north-west quadrant, however, has not been commented upon
at any great length yet. First, one should notice that a
relatively limited number of adopters are found here, which
may fall in line with the relative 'remoteness' of the
quadrant and adhere to a more normative spatial explanation. Second, of the adopters found in the quadrant, a majority accepted the complete package and the remainder
adopted a combination of seed and pest-/insecticides, which
may seem to contravene the normative explanations based on
a notion of the friction of distance. It has been asserted,
however, that to some extent, the quadrant contains a
larger number of more wealthy farmers. Thus, the underlying
reasons for the adoption found here must, again, be sought
in the more complex functional, social and economic aspects
referred to as basic structural variables.

6.7 Concluding remarks

To briefly summarize the discussions on the adoption
patterns found for the individual adoption-categories a reference to the hypothesis concerning the extent to which
macro-processes replicate themselves at the micro-scale
could be made initially. Basically it has been found that
the well known features of 'initial agglomerations', 'radial expansion', 'increasing internal density of adoption'

and the occurrences of 'secondary agglomerations' displaying much the same characteristics as the initial ones in
promoting adoption, are found also at the scale of investigation used in the present study. In addition, the relevance of the 'Market and Infrastructure Perspective' has
been identified, although no very formal testing of hypotheses to this end has been made. Thus, as an overall conclusion, it may be stated that aggregated diffusion processes are made up of a number of cyclical adoption processes
identifiable at several levels of aggregation where the
difference between layers may be the speed at which the
process progresses.

At the same time it is obvious that the diffusion patterns at the micro-level display a fair amount of randomness that is more difficult to explain. Concerning diffusion processes at a micro-scale Brown (1981:43) writes,
however — "...although more difficult to discern, order may
be present in apparently random patterns of diffusion". The
key to an identification of this order, may lie in what has
been called the basic structural variables. Thus, it is
possible that the "opportunity set" discussed by Brown is
to be found in the position of adopters and non-adopters
in the hierarchies defined in terms of social- and economic-position, together with positions in informational and
functional hierarchies that reaches beyond the immediate
survey areas.

VII. 'Correlation-Analysis'

7.1 Introduction

In the light of some of the discussions presented in Chapter IV concerning the data available for the present study, and not least the causality problems, it may seem strange to approach the more detailed analyses by means of a 'correlation analysis'. This, however, is not made with the intention of establishing causal relationships between adoption and a number of 'independent variables'. Rather the analysis is made in order to determine relationships, in a statistical sense, that exist between the different variables used and the directions of these relationships. Implicit in the analysis is, of course, the desire to establish the relationships postulated in the more general hypothesis hinted at in the preceding chapter, i.e. adoption and non-adoption are related to the position in social-, economic- and informational-hierarchies. Regarding the causality problem, an established relationship will not be taken as a causal one, however, in the sense that the position in one or several of the indicated hierarchies is taken as a reason for adoption, or non-adoption. As discussed in Chapter IV such a position could very well be the outcome of adoption and not its cause.

The Pearson Correlation Coefficients have been tabulated in matrix form for both Igana and Kodoch West and are presented in Tables 7.1 and 7.2 respectively. Although quite a large number of 'significant relationships' exist among the correlation coefficients, these have not been marked in any way. The overall impression from the matrixes, is one of a large number of fairly low correlation coefficients and it turns out that the occurrences of significant relationships are more dependent on the large populations on which the coefficients have been calculated, than on the strength of the relationships between the variables. Moreover, an analysis of non-adoption is not made in connection with the correlation matrixes. The question of non-adoption will, however, be dealt with in Chapter VIII.

7.2 Correlation matrix — adoption in Igana

Starting with the correlation coefficients found for Igana, the first thing to notice are the strong correlations found between the time of adoption for fertilizers, ADY/FT and pest-/insecticides, ADY/PT. The correlations between these and adoption of Hybrid Maize seed, ASY/ST are much lower. Again this underlines what has already been concluded concerning the sequences of the overall adoption processes in Igana, and what has been shown in Chapter VI.

Other strong correlations found in Table 7.1 could be referred to as 'autocorrelations'. As evident from the list of variables (Appendix 32) some of the variables summarize sets of other variables, e.g. LO/LOT is the sum of LO/LR and LO/ADL. Similar cases are found with respect to INC/ATO and VAL/CAT. Moreover, the variables with the PC/ prefix have been calculated as ratios from other variables. Thus, some of the relationships found are only to be expected and are not the outcome of the variables being related to adoption.

Still, some interesting relationships are found. First, one notices, that the adoption of innovations, i.e. time of adoption, is negatively related to the relative use of Hybrid Maize (cf. PC/HMTA; PC/MTA; PC/HMMA; ARE/HM and ARE/M vs adoption variables). It could be assumed that the relative profitability of adopting this innovation would have led to the planting of relatively large areas with Hybrid Maize once the utility of the innovation had been established. This, however, seems not to be the case, while at the same time one can notice positive correlations between the relative share of land used for cash-crops and adoption. Together these findings underline the general notion of the adoption processes in Igana. They also point out the dual role played by Hybrid Maize as an innovation — on the one hand as a land saving innovation and, on the other, as a cash-crop.

The adoption process in Igana has been interpreted as consisting of an initial adoption related to cash-crop production into which, at a later date, the seed component is added. Not all initial adopters continue with the adoption of seed as well, and one may start looking for a motive behind the taking up of the additional innovation or not. Part of the explanation may be found in the land saving quality of Hybrid Maize seed as an innovation and this may be reflected in the low negative correlations for Hybrid Maize seed use and the positive correlations with cash-crop acreage.

Table 7.1: Correlation matrix for IGANA.

	ADY/FT	ADY/PT	ADY/SFP	ADY/SF	VAL/LS	VAL/BH	VAL/CA	EXP/LA	EXP/HO	INC/ATO	VAL/CAT	LO/LR	LO/ADL	LO/LOT	LAB/HP	LAB/HT	DIST/SO	DIST/MA	EXT/FQ	LAB/EQ	PC/HMTA	PC/MTA	PC/CCTA	PC/HMMA	ARE/HM	ARET/M	ARE/CC	ADY/CC
ADY/ST	.22	.23	1.00	--	.24	.26	.08	.36	.12	.23	.19	.13	.19	.22	.38	-.02	-.29	.05	.22	.03	-.15	-.15	.05	-.10	-.15	-.13	.19	.03
ADY/FT		.98	.19	1.00	.15	.11	.14	.18	-.02	.12	.15	.11	.26	.25	.19	.07	-.09	-.09	.10	.16	-.08	-.08	.09	.00	.06	-.01	.27	.92
ADY/PT			.19	.97	.22	.14	.13	.17	-.01	.11	.19	.08	.28	.26	.17	.06	-.04	-.32	.12	.14	-.05	-.21	.06	.01	.06	.02	.25	.93
ADY/SFP				--	.27	.27	.06	.38	.13	.23	.18	.16	.20	.25	.41	-.04	-.35	.07	.23	-.15	-.29	-.28	.08	-.10	-.18	-.15	.22	-.01
ADY/SF					.05	.12	-.01	-.02	-.01	.08	.09	.04	.31	-.22	-.01	-.14	-.06		.19	.13		-.31	.17	.13		-.17	.40	.97
VAL/LS						.34	.27	.52	.25	.47	.74	.32	.24	.37	.50	.44	-.06	-.11	.25	.31	.22	-.19	.05	.39	.43	.17	.34	.31
VAL/BH							.31	.48	.28	.50	.65	.04	.30	.25	.48	.41	-.05	.02	.11	.10	.15	-.18	-.04	.21	.24	.09	.21	.33
VAL/CA								.54	.23	.72	.75	.01	.35	.27	.49	.30	-.04	-.12	.05	.15	.10	-.15	-.05	.24	.24	.04	.30	.19
EXP/LA									.30	.84	.65	.19	.38	.40	.97	.58	-.14	-.07	.19	.03	.07	-.26	-.02	.32	.34	.05	.34	.25
EXP/HO										.52	.38	-.06	.17	.09	.23	.31	-.07	-.08	.07	.15	-.02	-.07	-.08	.02	.09	.02	.19	.01
INC/ATO											.77	.07	.44	.37	.76	.46	-.04	-.00	.08	.20	.05	-.20	-.00	.22	.28	.11	.37	.21
VAL/CAT												.15	.10	.66	.61	.31	-.01	-.17	.31	.37	-.05	-.07	.02	.37	.38	.27	.37	.34
LO/LR														.81	.22	.23	-.18	-.17	.20	.04	-.20	-.20	-.17	.07	.16	.14	.25	.25
LO/ADL															.30	.21	-.13	-.08	.16	.14	-.02	-.27	-.08	.13	.27	.25	.52	.13
LO/LOT															.36	.29	-.20	-.20	.19	.03	-.04	-.32	-.16	.32	.29	.41	.54	.35
LAB/HP																.52	-.14	.01	.52	.03	.20	-.02	.01	.39	.29	.29	.28	.34
LAB/HT																	-.08	-.04	.16	.13	.09	-.19	.13	.03	.44	-.00	.27	.25
DIST/SO																		-.08	.07	-.03	-.06	.22	-.07	-.04	.01	.08	-.03	-.14
DIST/MA																			-.02	.07	.13	.09	-.08	-.08	-.07	-.07	-.05	-.23
EXT/FQ																				-.02	-.18	-.03	.29	.26	.16	.16	.31	.10
LAB/EQ																					.06	-.03	.05	.01	.06	.06	.18	.12
PC/HMTA																						-.13	.02	-.15	.76	.27	.07	.11
PC/MTA																							.13	-.05	.08	.08	.51	-.22
PC/CCTA																									.02	-.18	.58	-.12
PC/HMMA																									.78	-.04	.23	.24
ARE/HM																										.31	.29	.19
ARET/M																											.23	.10
ARE/CC																												.29
ADY/CC																												

NOTE: The population basis on which the correlation coefficients have been calculated is 172 farms with the exception of the following variables:
ADY/ST n=58; ADY/FT n=100; ADY/PT n=52; ADY/SFP n=103; ADY/SF n=45; ADY/CC n=130.

Tentatively one can assume that with successful adoption of cash-crops, it can be in the interest of an adopting unit to expand on that part of the total farming activities, while at the same time trying to reduce costs, land- and labour-use in the subsistence part of the activities. Hybrid Maize, properly managed could achieve these results and make possible the production of the same amount of food in a smaller area and, thus, save on at least two of the above mentioned components. Assuming that some of the income from the cash-crop production is used for such an additional investment, the cost may not be prohibitive and may, furthermore, lead to a raising of the overall profits. To an extent, this line of reasoning is corroborated by the fact that the strongest negative correlations are found for PC/MTA and that the correlations between ADY/SFP and the list of variables above, are clearly negative. The results of such actions would be to release land and labour which could then be used for a further intensification of the cash-crop part of the total activities.

This line of reasoning, however, lacks credibility if it is not related to the population aspect, i.e. the number of people living on the farms and to be fed by their production. This could, to an extent, be inferred from the matrix by looking at LAB/EQ and its relationships to the variables discussed above. First it should be noted that LAB/EQ does not measure the total population on each farm but is a weighted variable giving a measure of the labour available. In some respects it may also be a 'better' variable on which to measure food needs as the weights are constructed to refer to 'labour capacity', being based on age and sex criteria, which could also be used as a rough proxy on caloric needs.

Generally speaking, no striking relationships are found for LAB/EQ and the variables indicated — most of the correlations are close to zero. Two interesting exceptions exist, however. First, a positive, but low, correlation between LAB/EQ and ARE/M indicating a relationship between the total area under maize and the labour availability measure. Second, a relationship is seen between the area under cash-crop and the 'labour' variable — ARE/CC and LAB/EQ. Neither of the correlations are strong and they must be treated with great caution when drawing far reaching conclusions. To a degree, however, they lend support to the discussion on the possible action taken by adopters when adding the seed-componenet and, furthermore, to the possible deliberate use of the land-saving quality of Hybrid

Maize by some of these adopters.

The frequency of extension contacts, EXT/FQ, is used here as a measure of the position in the informational-hierarchy. Again the correlation coefficients found for this variable are fairly low. Some positive, but low, correlations could be pointed out however. On the one hand, such correlations are found with ADY/ST and ADY/SFP, indicating that a higher frequency of extension contacts may have been instrumental in promoting further adoption of Hybrid Maize seed. On the other hand, such correlations are also found with respect to PC/HMMA, PC/CCTA, and ARE/CC, indicating a relationship between the farm economy, its commercialization, and the frequency of extension contacts.

The analysis of the correlation matrix for Igana, could be continued along similar lines by going into more and more specific aspects of the correlations shown. Taking into account, that the majority of the correlations are fairly low, such an excercise would not be very rewarding. Of greater interest would be to identify systematic trends over a number of variables. Such trends are found with respect to some of the 'economic' variables and the hiring of labour. Largely, however, these relationships are to be expected and do not add very much to an understanding of the processes. Thus, with one exception, further analyses of the matrix for Igana will be left to the reader. The one exception is the relationship found between adoption and the distance variables, which will be of interest in the continued analysis.

In Chapter VI, adoption in relation to distances to sources of the innovations and to different markets was discussed, but then only from a locational point of view. Here the distances have been quantified (in practice the shortest route from each farm in the sample, to the nodes discussed have been recorded). The distance-decay functions inferred in the earlier analysis is substantiated here in the negative correlations found between DIST/SO and DIST/MA with the different adoption combinations.

Again the values of the coefficients are not very strong, but the direction of the overall trend is consistent with the assumption of an outward moving diffusion wave over the period being studied. Interesting, however, is the break that exist between the two distance variables with respect to the different adoption combinations. ADY/ST and SDY/SFP show negative correlations with DIST/SO, while the other adoption categories show negative correlations with DIST/MA.

These findings are consistent with the description of
the course of adoption in Igana, presented earlier. Supply
nodes in the initial phases of the adoption processes, were
the markets surrounding Igana when it came to the adoption
of fertilizers and pest-/insecticides. Later, when seed was
introduced, the set of distributional nodes had changed
and, thus, a different accessibility surface had developed.
Furthermore, the findings could be interpreted as additional support for the 'Market and Infrastructure Perspective'
on adoption (cf. Brown 1981). Most innovations are not ubi-
quious and their adoption is affected and directed by the
structure and locational characteristics of the supply and
transport networks available to gain access to them.

7.3 Correlation matrix — adoption in Kodoch West

The correlation matrix for Kodoch West (Table 7.2) has
many traits in common with the one for Igana. The overall
picture is one of fairly low correlation coefficients. The
exceptions are, as in the case of Igana, 'autocorrelations', i.e. high correlations between variables measuring
different aspects of the same pehnomenon or between summary
variables and the variables making up the parts of the
sums.

In Igana, a discussion on the relationship between adoption and absolute and relative acreages of Hybrid Maize and
cash-crops was presented. Similar relationships could be
inferred for Kodoch West, but the trends are less distinct
and it is difficult to draw similar conclusions to those
drawn for Igana. In Kodoch West these relationships differ
very much between the adoption-categories — particularly
evident in the case of PC/HMMA. To a degree PC/HMMA can be
seen as a measure of the rate of adoption and in this light
the different trends may be a bit a surprising in their
lack of consistency.

Frequently, adoption behaviour includes a trial period
in which the innovations are being tested on a limited
scale, later leading to an increasing rate of adoption (cf.
Rogers 1962 and 1983). Thus, implicit in the reasoning on
the adoption rates (PC/HMMA) for both Igana and Kodoch
West, lies the assumption that these should display a positive correlation with an increasing length of adoption
period. This is not the case in Igana, which has been explained by the possible role of Hybrid Maize in the total
farm economy. In the case of Kodoch West the divergent
trends found, make the picture even more difficult to interpret.

Table 7.2: Correlation matrix for KODCH WEST.

	ADY/ST	ADY/FT	ADY/PT	ADY/SFP	ADY/S	ADY/SF	ADY/SP	VAL/LS	VAL/BH	VAL/CA	EXP/LA	EXP/HO	INC/ATO	VAL/CAT	LO/LR	LO/ADL	LO/LOT	LAB/HP	LAB/HT	DIST/SO	DIST/MA	EXT/FQ	LAB/EQ	PC/HMTA	PC/MTA	PC/CCTA	PC/RCTA	PC/HMMA	ARE/HM	ARE/M	ARE/CC	ADY/CC	ARE/RC
ADY/ST	-	.63	.98	1.00	1.00	1.00	1.00	.28	-.12	.17	.04	-.03	.17	.17	-.02	.16	.04	-.04	.10	-.25	-.08	-.05	.03	.06	-.06	.14	-.17	.51	.14	.02	.13	--	-.13
ADY/FT		-	.74	.63	--	--	--	.28	-.12	-.14	-.02	.05	.35	-.14	-.28	.45	-.08	.08	-.05	-.40	-.09	-.03	-.07	.06	-.17	.17	.04	-.12	-.16	.13	.27	--	-.10
ADY/PT			-	.98	--	--	.96	.17	-.11	-.14	-.14	-.31	.46	.08	-.06	-.06	-.01	-.11	.11	-.44	-.28	-.21	-.02	-.20	-.33	.13	.05	.45	-.13	-.17	.13	--	-.04
ADY/SFP				-	--	--	--	.04	-.11	-.10	.24	-.12	.64	.00	-.16	-.25	-.28	-.11	-.39	-.34	.06	-.12	-.01	-.37	-.20	-.15	.39	-.17	-.33	-.17	.15	--	-.04
ADY/S					-	--	--	.52	.33	.09	.18	-.04	.04	.43	.21	.34	.35	.17	-.04	.43	.38	-.03	.14	.11	-.06	.25	-.44	.30	.38	.27	--	--	-.29
ADY/SF						-	--	-.30	-.37	.18	-.16	-.16	.39	-.27	-.18	.18	-.03	.17	-.18	.08	-.31	.41	.34	-.41	-.17	-.05	-.37	-.35	-.30	-.35	.25	--	-.21
ADY/SP							-	.56	--	-.37	-.18	-.16	.39	.02	.07	.18	.03	-.23	-.18	-.39	-.01	-.09	.28	-.16	-.18	--	.12	.06	.33	.33	--	--	.28
VAL/LS								-	.37	.51	.05	-.09	.21	.90	.35	.12	.38	.03	.22	.18	-.01	-.01	.52	.07	.07	-.05	-.01	.07	.22	.37	-.01	.00	.23
VAL/BH									-	.47	.13	-.03	.13	.60	.22	.03	.23	.13	.14	.30	.11	.03	.29	.00	-.02	-.05	.08	.12	.16	.24	-.07	.39	.21
VAL/CA										-	.13	-.08	.63	.67	.28	.00	.29	.94	.07	.16	.16	.22	.29	.17	.07	-.07	.03	.17	.31	.00	.00	.33	.21
EXP/LA											-	.57	.63	.08	.28	.02	.29	.58	.07	.16	.14	.22	-.01	.11	.07	-.01	-.16	.08	.09	.00	-.02	.30	-.09
EXP/HO												-	.76	-.09	.01	.12	.03	-.09	-.01	-.01	.03	.11	-.12	.17	.02	-.05	-.07	-.05	.13	-.02	-.05	.30	.08
INC/ATO													-	.21	.21	.13	.16	.60	.13	.26	.02	.15	.22	.11	.01	-.05	-.07	.06	.11	.37	-.03	.30	.08
VAL/CAT														-	.37	.07	.12	.16	.60	.28	.01	.02	.57	.05	.01	-.05	-.09	.01	.32	.76	-.03	-.03	.27
LO/LR															-	-.10	.97	.13	.13	.28	.11	.07	.28	.05	-.03	-.03	-.09	.01	.26	.12	.08	-.30	.71
LO/ADL																-	.13	.19	.09	-.26	.21	.01	-.02	.00	.14	-.02	-.02	.05	.12	.09	.10	.28	-.02
LO/LOT																	-	.78	.04	.38	.12	.02	.27	.05	-.03	-.05	-.05	.05	.38	.10	-.05	-.21	.70
LAB/HP																		-	.23	.10	.05	.26	.29	.14	.08	-.05	.03	.15	.26	.12	.18	--	.15
LAB/HT																			-	.14	.05	-.08	.13	.13	-.00	.00	.20	.19	.19	.13	.13	--	.17
DIST/SO																				-	.19	.26	-.10	-.11	-.10	.03	.03	-.10	.05	.13	-.03	-.12	.15
DIST/MA																					-	-.08	.14	.11	.15	-.16	.15	.15	.26	.05	-.03	-.21	.13
EXT/FQ																						-	.12	-.13	-.10	-.05	.02	.17	.17	.17	-.03	-.12	.07
LAB/EQ																							-	.14	.03	-.02	-.06	.01	.08	.26	.08	-.43	.08
PC/HMTA																								-	.06	.01	.09	.79	.01	.08	.08	.28	.27
PC/MTA																									-	.63	.49	.23	.79	.52	.04	.21	-.04
PC/CCTA																										-	.07	.01	.23	.02	.02	.26	-.00
PC/RCTA																											-	-.01	.49	.86	.04	.21	-.04
PC/HMMA																												-	.66	.15	.06	.60	.01
ARE/HM																													-	.63	-.01	.64	.27
ARE/M																														-	.10	-.06	.58
ARE/CC																															-	.03	.10
ADY/CC																																-	-.13
ARE/RC																																	-

NOTE: The population basis on which the correlation coefficients have been calculated is 186 farms with the exception of the following variables:
ADY/ST n=64; ADY/FT n=24; ADY/PT n=32; ADY/SFP n=15; ADY/S n=15; ADY/SF n=9; ADY/SP n=17; ADY/CC n=15.

In Kodoch West, Hybrid Maize can not be seen as an additional innovation in an adoption sequence that has started with other rationalities. Also, although some of the correlation coefficients in Kodoch West may indicate similar trends to the ones found in Igana, it is doubtful if these could be interpreted as indicating the land saving quality of Hybrid Maize as an innovation. A more likely role of Hybrid Maize in Kodoch West, is a combination of the land saving qualities with the role of being a cash-crop. This could be gathered from the fact that in Kodoch West 67 per cent of the farmers interviewed indicate that they sell maize, while the corresponding figure for Igana is only about 9 per cent. In comparison one may notice that only about 3 per cent of the farmers in Kodoch West sell more commercially oriented cash-crops, e.g. coffee, tea, cotton, sisal etc., in comparison with about 65 per cent of the farmers in Igana selling such cash-crops.

Even in this light, however, the correlation coefficients are not clear. The difficulty with interpretation in Kodoch West, is the relatively short duration of the adoption process and the fact that this process can not be regarded as complete. Thus, some of the assumed effects of an adoption may not be seen as yet. Furthermore, and this will be an all-pervading problem in the following analyses, the number of adopters are fairly limited in some adoption-categories, making it difficult to draw far reaching conclusions.

In two spheres, the correlation coefficients show interesting results that point to some of the underlying processes behind adoption. First, the economic variables are correlated with the adoption variables. Particularly this is applicable to INC/ATO and the adoption variables. INC/ATO should be used with caution as a singular explanatory variable as discussed in Section 4.5. Still it gives a fairly good description of the general economic status of individual farms.

Generally a positive relationship between adoption and the economic status of the adopters is assumed. In Igana no very clear such relationships were found, while in Kodoch West some fairly strong such relationships can be seen. Naturally, we are facing a causality problem in determining whether the relationships are the results of or the causes to adoption (cf. Section 4.6). Still, the correlations are obvious and of significance in interpreting the processes under study. In particular the correlation between ADY/SFP and INC/ATO is interesting. The adoption of the complete package is correlated positively to economic status. This could also be inferred in Igana, but the strength of the correlation was much lower there. In spite of definitional and causality problems, the correlation coefficients indicate a clear relationship which supports the general hypotheses on diffusion and adoption of innovations.

Concerning the informational variable, however, it is more difficult to find indications that give clear support to the relationship between adoption and the intensity of information. It will be evident in Chapter VIII that the frequencies of extension contacts in Kodoch West are generally very low and the majority of the farmers, adopters and non-adopters alike, have had no contact with the extension service. The large number of low but negative correlations with the adoption variables is surprising and contradicts what generally may be assumed. This, however, may be due to the overall incidence of extension contacts. Only in the case of ADY/SF does one find a positive correlation pointing in the direction expected. Although the correlations found for EXT/FQ are not very conclusive, some of these can be pointed out. First, the correlations with the economic variables show a consistent trend of positive correlations. Second, a slight but positive relationship is seen between EXT/FQ and the variables dealing with the acreage under Hybrid Maize — PC/HMMA and ARE/HM.

The second sphere of interesting relationships concerns the correlations between the distance variables and adoption, which was also discussed in the case of Igana. In Kodoch West, however, a much more consistent picture emerges and the distance decay functions assumed with respect to adoption is evident on one variable only — DIST/SO. ADY/ST constitutes an exception to the trend. This adoption, however, was discussed extensively in the preceding chapter. Generally speaking the trend in Kodoch West is consistent and in the analyses to follow it will suffice to look at one distance variable only.

Some additional comments on the correlation matrix for Kodoch West are warranted. First, and in line with what was done with Igana, it is of interest to look at some of the correlations found for LAB/EQ — particularly the ones between LAB/EQ and ARE/M; ARE/CC and ARE/RC. Risk-crop in the latter variable is mainly defined as cassava, which may be somewhat ambigious as cassava is also a popular part of the staple diet in large parts of Western Kenya. Still, its main function is as a risk-crop and it is also basically percived as such.

Starting with the correlation between LAB/EQ and ARE/M a similar trend to the one found in Igana is seen. Largely, such a relationship between maize acreage and the available labour force is to be expected. A positive correlation is also found between LAB/EQ and ARE/RC, which, again, is to be expected and falls in line with the correlation for ARE/M. In Kodoch West, however, no relationship is found between the available labour force and cash-crop production, as was found in Igana. With the low number of farmers growing cash-crops in Kodoch West this may only be expected.

Second, some interesting correlations are seen between LAB/EQ and the variables measuring economic and socio-economic status. In particular LAB/EQ shows fairly high correlations with VAL/LS; VAL/CA and VAL/CAT. Only in the case of the value of livestock (VAL/LS), was a similar trend found in Igana and then the correlation was significantly lower. The direction and strength of these correlations may be taken to inidicate basic structural differences between the two areas with respect ot the orientation of the agricultural economy. In particular the differences manifest themselves in the commercialization of the agricultural economy where South Nyanza, and thus Kodoch West, show more traits of traditional subsistence agriculture (cf. i.a. RoK 1977:Section 8 and ILO 1981). It should be remembered, however, that great variations exist within the different farming communities and that generalizations of this kind should be used with caution and not be pushed to far. Still, they could be of value in indicating analytical courses to follow in the later analysis of adoption and non-adoption.

7.4 General comments on the correlation matrix analysis

In an overall perspective, the analytical value of the conclusions drawn from the correlation matrixes for Igana and Kodoch West is limited. To a degree the analysis may be compared with an attempt to get blood out of a stone. As indicated repeatedly, the correlation coefficients found are not very strong and the possible relationships are not very surprising — basically they fall within the sphere of the 'established knowledge' concerning the diffuison of innovations. Thus, the reasons for the inclusion of this part of the analysis may be questioned.

Still, its inclusion could be justified from two points. First, the analysis of the processes being studied is arranged in a way that it is gradually funnelled into more and more micro-oriented aspects of the processes. In traditional geographical terminology it may be compared with the gradual moving down the Cones of Resolution (cf. Gould 1969). The analysis of the matrixes may, thus, be seen as a step in this direction. Moreover, the macro-oriented analysis implied in the use of correlation matrixes as an analytical tool, is very much in line with an established research tradition in the field of diffusion studies. A part of the purpose of the present study is to see how and to what extent the 'established knowledge' is applicable to the problem at hand.

Second, the macro-oriented approach is also used in determining fields of particular interest for continued analysis. Partly, then, the analysis of the correlation matrixes is used in pointing out directions for the final part of the study. In the light of the overall plan for the study, the latter purpose of the 'correlation analysis' is the most important.

In sum, however, the 'correlation analysis' has not contributed significantly towards a deeper understanding of the processes. To an extent the so called 'established knowledge' is confirmed in the matrixes by reading across sets of correlations. The large number of low correlations and the occurrences of correlation coefficients that run counter to what should be expected, limits the analytical value and actually make it more confounding than enlightening.

VIII. Micro-Analysis; Consequences of Adoption

8.1 Introduction

The analyses presented so far, points in one and the same direction, i.e. that a further breakdown is necessary — breakdown in the sense that the material should be analysed at lower and lower levels of aggregation. Beneath such an approach lies, of course, the implicit assumption that important and relevant relationships for the understanding of the adoption processes are obscured by the level of analysis. The problem with the analysis at a high level of aggregation, is the heterogenous nature of the groups with respect to the factors being investigated and, thus, the subsequent high variances in the material. Thus, the continued analysis should aim at creating fairly homogenous groups that could be analysed both independently and in comparison with other similar groups.

8.2 Analytical steps in the micro-analysis

To pursue the analysis in the direction indicated a couple of decisions will have to be made. First, it will be necessary to decide on the criteria that should be used in the breakdowns. Second, the methods of analysis will have to be defined. A continued sub-division of the material into increasingly smaller categories makes it difficult to apply standard statistical tests, e.g. inferential statistics where the limited sizes of the defined subgroups will make it difficult to establish significant relationships.

Starting with the latter point, the analytical approach will be one of using basic and simple descriptive statistics. More complex statistical methods have been applied, but have been abandoned. The results arrived at have been surrounded by such a large number of questionmarks of a statistical/technical nature, that they have been difficult to use. Moreover, the use of sophisticated techniques always run the risk of giving an impression of a much greater exactness in the quality of the conclusions drawn, than is warranted by the quality of the data. Also, in line with

the general debate on the use of quantitative techniques
in the social sciences, there is always the question whether the methods are not obscuring more than they reveal (cf.
i.a. Gould 1979 and Widberg 1979). The author would not
wish to take a dogmatic stand on that question. Quantitative methods may be useful in revealing hidden relationships, but should be used with care. Unfortunately this has
not always been the case in the social sciences and, thus,   .
the anti-quantification pendulum may have swung a bit to
far in the opposite direction.

In summary, only simple descriptive statistics will be
used in the analysis, basically means and medians. A continued breakdown of the population and the use of descriptive statistics does, however, not solve the problem of
high variances — in fact the problem may be even further
emphasised. With increasingly smaller sub-populations, the
effects of extreme values will be felt much stronger. In
particular this will be the case when the analysis is based
on mean values only. In some instances, the extreme values
are tied to particular strata of the sub-populations and
are, thus, of a particular analytical interest. Generally,
to solve some of these problems, both the means and medians
for the defined sub-populations will be presented and discussed.

To return to the criteria to be used for the continued
breakdown of the total sample populations into sub-populations, it is obvious that a very large number of such criteria could be applied. Regarding the problem at hand, two
principal criterion variables could be defined, i.e. time
and space. The choice should be seen in the light of the
fact that the diffusion of innovations is a temporal process which manifests itself on the surface of a defined
area. The defining of criteria, or 'criterion variables',
does, however, not solve the additional problem of finding
logical breaking points in these for the creation of sub-
populations.

From the existing literature, it is obvious that great
efforts have been put into the defining of adopter-categories in a temporal perspective (cf. i.a. Rogers 1983:Ch.7;
see also Rogers 1962 and 1971). Usually the categorization
is made from the S-curve — the cumulated curve of the normal distribution of adoption frequencies (see Fig. 2.1),
by means of the means and standard deviations. It has been
well established that significant differences exist between
adopters at different times in the overall diffusion processes and, thus, it should be possible to use a similar

approach for the criterion variable <u>time</u> used here.

Two problems are faced when doing this, however. First, the temporal adoption patterns differ between different adoption-categories (see Ch.VI). On the one hand, adoption of the different adoption-categories starts and ends at different times and, on the other, some of the adoption processes are not 'completed'. In the latter case the creation of sub-groups creates a definitional problem, i.e. the extent to which the sub-groups truly describe qualitatively different adopter-categories. In the first case the problem lies in the comparability of the created sub-groups.

In addition, the number of adopters of some adoption-categories is not very large and does not allow a detailed sub-division of the mother population. In most instances it is only possible to define three sub-groups and sometimes it is not possible to go beyond a division into early and late adopters. In combination, the factors pointed at create a problem of clearly understanding the nature of the sub-groups defined — particularly whether they should be related to the more 'Ideal Types' of adopter-categories as discussed above (cf. Rogers 1983:247-51). In this light it would be tempting to try to find a more 'natural' way of defining the sub-groups by the use of, e.g. obvious inflexion points in the adoption curves. Again, however, this would not completely solve the problems pointed out. Thus, with the lack of an unambigious and logical base for the sub-division of the mother population a pragmatic approach is chosen, i.e. to use the population parameters as they stand. This means that the sub-division will be made by use of the means and standard deviations for each adoption-category, but also considering the limitations set by the sometimes limited sizes of the mother population. In the overall perspective, this approach would not generate any major analytical difficulties for the within group comparisons, while the between group comparisons will have to be treated with some caution.

Similarly in the sub-division on the criterion variable <u>space</u>, a number of problems are encountered and may actually be even further accentuated. The variables used to measure 'space' here are DIST/SO and DIST/MA both of which are given in kilometers. To define the space dimension, for example, by using discrete steps defined as even kilometers, would give space an absolute quality that it most probably does not have. Space must be given a much wider meaning than just an entity where relationships manifest themselves in the form of patterns characterized by shape and distances to given points (cf. Josefsson & Lindström 1979 and Hansen 1979 — see also Section 8.3). The critical point is the explanatory power that is given to spatial factors, viz. if they are given an explanatory power in their own right, or if they are seen as factors that mould and direct processes that manifest themselves spatially, but are basically the outcome of more fundamental societal changes.

Again, it is obvious that no 'natural' method exist for making the sub-division on the space criterion. In the creation of the supply networks, however, the underlying rationalities were phrased in terms of increasing the physical access to the supplies needed for adoption. Here the intrinsic logic in the establishment of the nodes could be used for the sub-division of the space variable. This is achieved by an analogy with what was made in the time-dimension, i.e. the population parameters for the distance variables are used. In practice the division is made relative to the mean distance to markets and/or supply nodes. From a practical point of view it should be remembered that once made, the spatial sub-division does not change with different adoption-categories, as was the case with the temporal variables.

It is now possible to describe the analytical course that will be followed throughout the remainder of this chapter. The steps are described in Figure 8.1 and, hopefully, this figure should be largely self-explanatory. From Figure 8.1, it should be obvious that the sub-divisions, or the breakdowns (BRKDW in the figure), start from the total sample population and are gradually developed into finer and finer sub-categories. The 'criterion variables' are used for a breakdown into sub-groups, within which the mean and median values for the 'independent variables' used in the study are calculated. These values have been tabulated and are presented in Appendices 1-30. In addition, some of the tabulated values will be shown graphically in connection with the discussions on the results from the breakdowns.

The different breakdowns made, are specified in the figure by first indicating the 'criterion variable' used and second the number of sub-groups created. The latter is shown by the parentheses (1,3) and (1,2) indicating a sub-division into respectively three and/or two sub-groups. A sub-division into three sub-groups is based on a deviation of ± 1/2 standard deviation from the mean for both 'criterion variables' used, while the division into two sub-groups is based on above or below the mean for the 'crite-

184

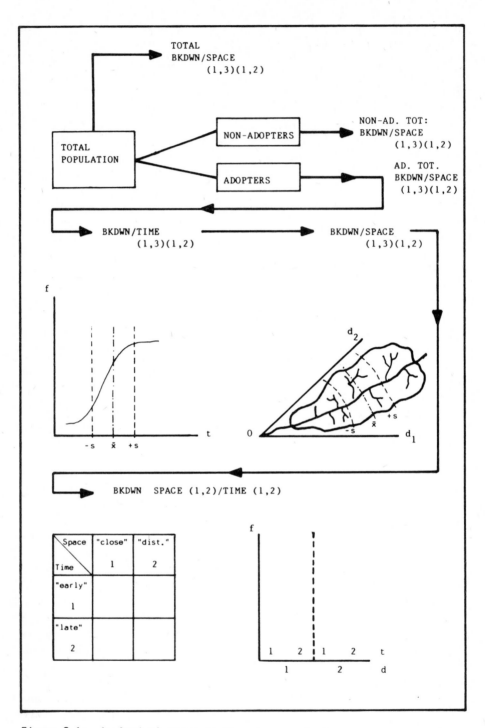

<u>Figure 8.1</u>: Analytical steps in the micro-analysis.

rion variables'. As it turned out, for purely practical reasons, it was necessary to choose + 1/2 standard deviation as the breaking point in the sub-divisions. Having used + 1 standard deviation would have rendered too small sub-populations in the 'tails' to enable meaningful comparisons between these. Also, quite naturally, a breakdown of the time variable has only been made for the group of adopters of any combination of the innovations, while all groups have been broken down on the space variable.

As evident from Figure 8.1, the adopters are the ones subjected to the most elaborate breakdown into sub-groups. This is initially made for the two 'criterion variables' separately, after which a combination is made in a further breakdown called Space/Time. In this step the temporal aspects of adoption are looked at within fixed distance categories. For practical reasons it is only possible to use two categories for each of the 'criterion variables'. As indicated in the figure, the results from the latter breakdown can be thought of and presented as a four-way matrix. It is, however, also possible to present the results graphically, which probably is a better way of grasping the relationships emerging from this breakdown.

8.3 The role of the Spatial Dimension in the analysis

As the spatial dimension is frequently referred to as an active component in the steering and shaping of the actual adoption patterns, it may be necessary to clarify some points concerning the role of 'space' as an explanatory and/or descriptive category. Initially some distinctions concerning different possible perceptions of space should be made. According to Harvey (1973) space may be perceived in an "absolute sense" as "relative space" or as "relational space". Mabogunje (1980:52), drawing heavily on Harvey's discussions, describes the latter two categories as:

"...relative space which emphasises relationships between objects and which exists only because those objects exist and are related to each other. ...relational space in which space is perceived as containing and representing within itself other types of relationships which exist between the objects."

And somewhat later on the same page:

"The location of objects and the perception and social evaluation both of the objects and their location, do influence the pattern of behaviour of members of a given society."

In an explanatory capacity, space is often discussed in terms of distance-decay functions. Here this would imply a decreasing number of adopters with an increasing distance from the supply nodes. It could be assumed, however, that not only are there fewer adopters at greater distances, but also that qualitative differences may exist between similar adoption-categories in different locations.

The perspective on the adoption processes applied here, implies that certain relationships have to be established between adopters and critical nodes in supply and diffusion supporting networks. The media for these relationships may, for example, be the infrastructural links but also economic (monetary) transactions. In the first case the relationships could be described, and analysed, in terms of a 'relative space', while in the latter case the so called basic structural aspects will influence the processes and their spatial manifestations.

It is possible to hypothesise a 'compensational effect' as part of an explanation of some aspects of the adoption patterns studied. The occurrence of such an effect would be based on the notion that adopters in more distant locations may belong to the higher strata of the economic- and informational-hierarchies used here. Discussing in terms of a 'compensational effect' indicates a 'relative space' concept where adopters 'compensate' themselves for an otherwise less favourable location (cf. Harvey 1973:13-14). Here the basic meaning of the concept is that it may have a stratifying effect, in the sense that the relatively 'better off' farmers are in a position to compensate themselves for the negative effects of a less favourable location.

Added to this are the 'functional aspects' discussed briefly at the end of Chapter VI. These are here primarily thought of as — links/relationships with a 'reach' that goes beyond the immediate surroundings of the potential adopters, e.g. co-operative membership, transfers of income from family members working outside the farm, formalized information through the extension service and courses at FTC:s, incomes from non-farming activities, credits etc. The 'functional aspects' define a kind of 'relational space' concept and must be seen as supplementary to the pure locational factors. These may contribute to, and even strengthen, the stratifying effects discussed with resepect to the locational factors through a selective process in their being established. Thus, it is not possible to separate one from the other in the analysis.

To an extent the 'functional aspect' used here coincides, if not completely, with the functional perspective
used by Brown (1981:40-45) — see Section 2.3. In particular
the concepts are related with respect to what Brown calls
the "innovation establishment interface", i.e. aspects of
how an innovation is introduced and promoted into an area.
The kind of relationships thought of can be exemplified by
a couple of quotations, which also serve the purpose of
concretizing the need felt to go beyond 'pure spatial' ex-
plantions and the attempt to define relationships pertaining to a 'relational space' concept.

> "...it is still a difficult matter to decide how much a pattern of
> adoption is due to information variables and how much to structural
> variables, e.g. size of farm, availability of liquid capital, access
> to credit, ability to take risks, etc." (Blaikie 1978:273)

and

> "When social access to the means of production is restricted, the
> diffusion of entrepreneurial innovation at one level of economic so-
> ciety is often accompanied by a complementary process of 'nondiffu-
> sion' at another level." (Yapa 1977:350)

Yapa also writes in the same paper:

> "...nondiffusion is not to be equated with the passive state of lack
> of adoption due to low levels of awareness, apathy, or resistance. It
> is an active state arising out of the structural arrangements of the
> economic society." (ibid.:359)

8.4 Basic structural differences between adopters and non-adopters

A large part of the following discussion will deal with
aspects of the consequences of adoption. Largely this discussion will be phrased in terms of stratification, or in
terms of possible stratifying effects of diffusion. Regarding the causality problem, however, the exact nature of the
stratifying effects can only be tentatively inferred from
the results. Stratification as an outcome of the diffusion
process is two-sided and these individually or in combination, could cause the differences found between adopters
and non-adopters and between adopters of different combinations of the innovations. These sides could be labelled
pre- and post-stratification. The first indicates the possibility that the actions of the 'propagators' are such

that they single out adopters with particular structural characteristics, while the latter refers to the economic benefits that may accrue from an adoption. Some of these benefits could be thought of as "windfall profits" (cf. i.a. Brown 1981; Griffin 1972; Rogers 1983 and Yapa 1977).

Initially it is possible to study the existence of basic structural differences by looking at the confidence intervals for some adopter-categories and variables. Naturally, it should be possible to calculate confidence intervals for all 'independent variables' used, but this would not contribute significantly in clarifying the processes studied. Here the analysis limits itself to the calculation of confidence intervals with a 95% probability for four principal 'independent variables', i.e. INC/ATO, VAL/CAT, LO/LOT and EXT/FQ, summarizing aspects of the hierarchies discussed here. For each of these variables confidence intervals have been calculated for the total population, adopters and non-adopters.

The results are summarized in Figure 8.2 showing the intervals for each variable and the adopter-categories for the two sub-locations studied. Also in the figure, a standard scale for each variable is shown. Thus, the figure allows the study of stratification at two levels. First, within area differences between the groups presented. Second, between area comparisons for the different variables studied. It should be noted that the confidence interval for the total population does not in itself reveal the full magnitude of the internal stratification, but is presented as a measure against which to gauge the values for adopters and non-adopters.

Largely the patterns appearing in Figure 8.2 are similar for all four variables shown. Differences do exist, but these are more of degree than of kind. Starting with the means ($\bar{x}$) the same pattern appears for each variable, group and sub-location, viz. the adopters generally have a higher mean value than the non-adopters — in some instances the differences in the mean values are strikingly large. In the light of established diffusion theory, these findings are not surprising and may only confirm what is expected (cf. i.a. Rogers 1962, 1971 and 1983). The confidence intervals in Figure 8.2 could, however, also be discussed in terms of stratification. Thus it is obvious that basic differences exist between adopters and non-adopters and that these differences, at least, show an initial stratification (pre-stratification) but also, most probably, a growing stratification related to the adoption of certain agricul-

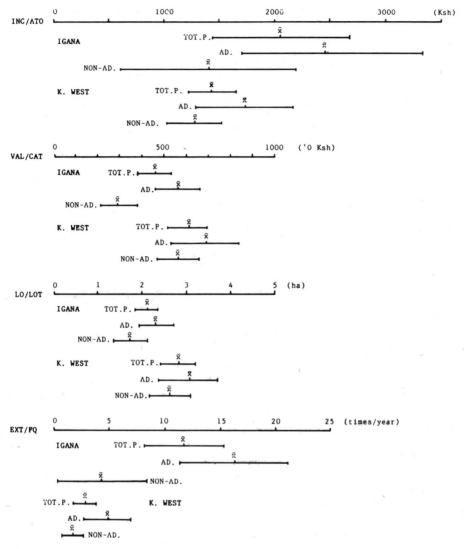

<u>Figure 8.2</u>: Confidence intervals (95%) for Total Population, Adopters and Non-Adopters on four selected 'independent-variables'.

tural innovations (post-stratification).

A second point that should be noted concerning the confidence intervals, is the width of some of the intervals. Following this observation is the fact that the adopter-categories are not mutually exclusive and that the intervals, with few exceptions, overlap each other. A further observation is that the confidence intervals for the adopters have a tendency to cover a wider area than the one for non-adopters — indicating a greater variance in the data for the variable. Taken together, these observations on the one hand, underline the notion of stratification, but also the fact that the intervals can not be taken normatively due to the overlaps between groups.

On the other hand, and this is a very tentative conclusion, the greater width of the intervals for the adopters, could be taken to indicate that adoption further increases an initial stratification. It could be assumed that the earlier adopters are to be found on the right of the intervals, raising the means and increasing the width of the intervals. Relatively later adopters would not have had the opportunity — as yet — to draw the same amount of benefits from their adoption. Still this conclusion, if true, does not preclude the possibility of an initial selection process based on the already existing structural differences in the areas studied.

Figure 8.2 also allows some tentative conclusions concerning basic structural differences between the two areas studied. Such conclusions could be drawn from the relative position of the intervals for the different variables for each area. It is noticable that the intervals for INC/ATO and EXT/FQ, in the case of Igana, have a tendency to be markedly higher than the corresponding intervals for Kodoch West. This may be interpreted in terms of the fact that Igana (particularly the adopters there) are more integrated into the formal (monetarized) economy as well as being linked more to the established administrative/bureaucratic structure (through the extension contacts which have their base in this structure).

Kodoch West, on the other hand, shows higher figures for the two variables that could be identified with status and economic position in a more 'traditional' setting, viz. VAL/CAT and LO/LOT. Naturally, such a generalization should not be taken normatively — the same variables would also indicate status in Igana. The variables could also be taken to indicate less pressure on the available land resources, thus allowing larger farms and enabling the farmers to keep larger herds of livestock (livestock are included in VAL/CAT and constitute in the case of Kodoch West a substantial part of the total value of VAL/CAT). The point will not pushed further here. It may suffice to mention that the notion, which seems to be embraced by several researchers on Kenya as well as many Kenyans themselves, could clarify some of the differences found in the adoption patterns between the two sub-locations.

Finally, a couple of more specific comments can be made

on the intervals shown. First, one could notice that the
overlaps in the confidence intervals for adopters and non-
adopters in Kodoch West, tend to be larger than in Igana.
This may be explained by the relative shorter adoption history in Kodoch West (cf. Ch.VI), viz. the post-stratification effects are not as visible in Kodoch West as they are
in Igana. Still, it should be noted that a stratification
exists between adopters and non-adopters.

Second, in light of the importance ascribed to the informational variables in the existing diffusion theories,
it is interesting to note some features of the confidence
intervals for EXT/FQ. Although these basically show similar
traits to those of the other confidence intervals, the differences between adopters and non-adopters seem to be more
pronounced. Also, the differences between Igana and Kodoch
West are more pronounced, which may indicate a general difference in the intensity of supporting activities to promote diffusion in the two areas. Of still greater importance is the fact that while adopters seem to receive information with a certain amount of regularity, the non-
adopters are severely handicapped in this respect. Considering the nature of the confidence intervals, it is obvious from the figure that a large number of the non-adopters do not receive any information through formal channels. Thus, again the intervals shown give indications of
a stratification which may explain parts of the resultant
adoption patterns found.

8.5 Adopters and non-adopters in a spatial perspective

It will also be of some interest to look at the spatial
distribution of the mean values for adopters and non-adopters. These are shown in Figures 8.3-8.5 where the 'independent variables' are broken down on DIST/SO (Igana and
Kodoch West) and DIST/MA (Igana). As discussed in Section
8.2, the population of adopters and non-adopters has been
subdivided into three classes based on the mean and the
standard deviation of the distances measured.

To a large extent the figures speak for themselves and
do not call for a lengthy commentary. The marked differences between adopters and non-adopters already seen in Section 8.4 are found again here and may be accentuated even
further. With isolated exceptions, the diagrams shown follow a similar pattern, i.e. the mean values for the group
of adopters on the 'independent variables', lie above the
corresponding values for non-adopters.

Again we are facing a picture indicating the existence

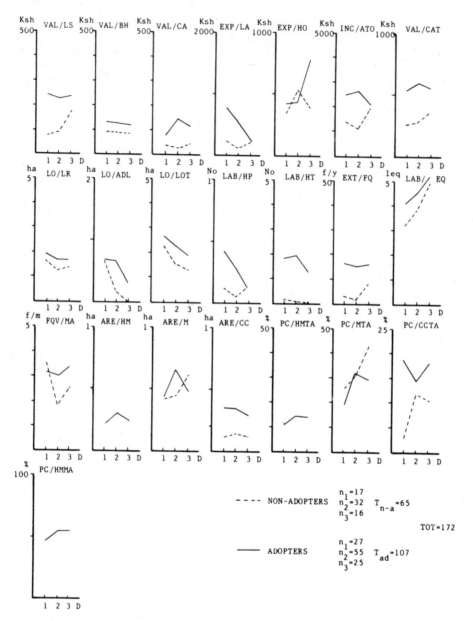

Figure 8.3: Comparison between Adopters and Non-Adopters - IGANA.
'Criterion variable' for the space dimension - DIST/SO.

of a marked stratification between these two groups. The diagrams, however, also allows some tentative conclusions to be reached in terms of the underlying processes that they may show. In some instances the lines run almost pa-

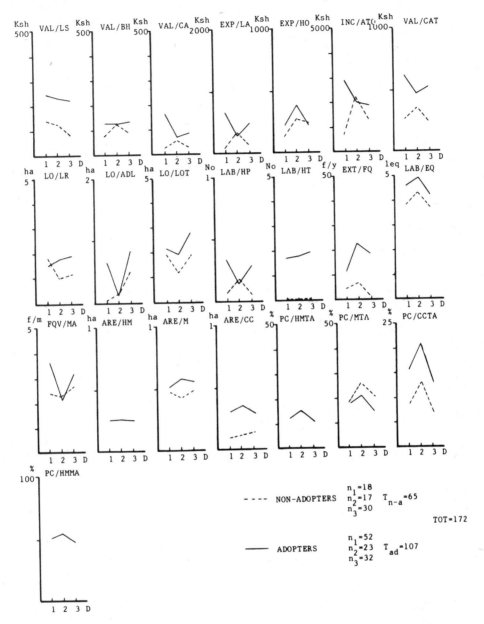

Figure 8.4: Comparison between Adopters and Non-Adopters - IGANA.
'Criterion variable' for the space dimension - DIST/MA.

rallel to one another, which could be interpreted in terms
of a pre-stratification. The implication is that the underlying cause for adoption is to be found in the existing
'status' differences, but that these are basically left un-

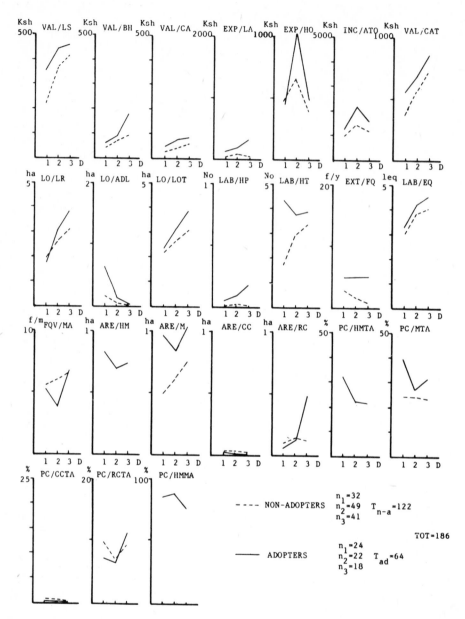

Figure 8.5: Comparison between Adopters and Non-Adopters - KODOCH WEST.
'Criterion variable' for the space dimension - DIST/SO.

altered by the adoption. It should be remembered here that
adoption generally moves from 'close' to more 'distant' locations — with some exceptions in Kodoch West (see Ch. VI).
More frequent cases, however, are the ones where there

are marked differences between adopters and non-adopters, and in which strong tendencies of converging or diverging over the space grouping are seen. This could be taken to indicate a post-stratification and, thus, point in the direction that adoption not only reflects basic structural differences by also affects these initial differences. Still, it should be noted that the conclusions drawn are tentative and only give rough indications of possible relationships.

While the group of non-adopters do not present any definition problems, it should be noted that the group of adopters used here, in itself, forms quite a heterogenous group consisting of adopters from all the different adoption-categories. Similar presentations for individual categories could deviate quite substantially from the aggregated picture presented. In view of this, a discussion of the detailed aspects of individual variables would not contribute significantly to an overall understanding of the separate adoption processes. Figures 8.3-8.5 should, thus, be seen as a further specification only, in a spatial perspective, of the stratifying effects discussed in Section 8.4.

8.6 Analysis of single adoption-categories in Igana and Kodoch West
8.6.1 Introduction, methodological comments

In the remainder of this chapter the focus will be on the different adoption-categories (Table 6.8). Although the analytical approach has been described in Section 8.2, some particular methodological comments will be necessary below. First, however, a couple of more general comments on the analyses to be presented will be made.

In view of the methodological discussion in Chapter IV — particularly those pertaining to 'one-shot' interviews and the causality problem — it should again be emphasised that it is only possible to draw very tentative conclusions from the material presented below. Also the analysis to be presented is based on an elaborate series of breakdowns of the original material. This leads to fairly frequent occurrences of very small sub-groups, making it difficult to draw firm conclusions. Given this background, the drawing of very definite conclusions from the material would lead to a discussion of a hair-splitting nature, which could be likened to attempts to get blood out of a stone. Thus, the commentaries accompaning the material presented below will be restricted and only attempt to point out the broad trends which can be inferred.

Basically the analysis will rest on a number of diagramatic presentations giving information on a number of 'principal independent variables'. Over and above these, information will be given in a large number of appendicies (Appendicies 1-30). In these, both mean and median values are given for each of the defined sub-groups as well as for the total population, adopters and non-adopters. Basically the conclusions which will be drawn, will rest on the over-all impressions from the large set of figures presented in the appendicies, combined with trends that can be seen in the diagramatic presentations. In principle the analysis below should be seen as a furhter specification of the earlier analyses dealing with the effects of adoption.

The diagrams used will follow a standard layout for each individual adoption-category. In their basic format the figures will contain six subsets of diagrams (A-F). The first two will show the diffusion process in its spatio-/temporal-dimension. In the A-diagram the mean adoption year will be put on the y-axis, while the x-axis will show the defined space-categories. The B-diagrams will show the mean adoption years, on the y-axis, for early/late adopters on the one hand, versus their location into close/distant space-categories (both these are shown on the x-axis) on the other. The latter diagram is identical in construction to the Space/Time breakdown described in Figure 8.1.

Diagrams C-F give information on the values for four different 'independent variables' after having been 'broken down' on the space and time criterion variables, according to the principles described in Section 8.2. Three diagrams are presented for each 'independent variable' showing, in turn, the mean values for the sub-groups defined on the time, space and space/time criteria. In all the adoption-categories discussed the four 'principal independent variables' shown are VAL/CAT, INC/ATO, LO/LOT and EXT/FQ. Although a number of other variables may have analytical interest, it has been asserted that the four presented give a fairly good summary picture of the socio-economic and informational-hierarchies referred to frequently. Also, the chosen variables in themselves, with the exception of EXT/FQ, are summary variables of a number of more detailed variables.

Finally, in some of the figures a couple of additional diagrams (G-H) are presented. This is done when the information on some additional 'independent variables' is deemed relevant for a deeper understanding of the processes studied. Also, throughout the diagrams C-H, the corresponding

information for the group of non-adopters in the area studied is shown with broken lines whereever possible — i.e.
in the space breakdowns.

8.6.2 Adoption of seed, fertilizers, pesticides (/SFP) and fertilizers, pesticides (/FP) in Igana

Placing, initially, the two adoption-categories into
perspective, it is first noted from Appendices 1-3 that the
adopters of /SFP and /FP generally show higher values of
the 'independent variables' than do both the total population and, in particular, the non-adopters. In some instances these differences are marked. It can also be noted
(App. 2), however, that a difference exists between the two
adoption-categories, in the sense that the adopters of the
complete package (/SFP) generally depict higher values than
the adopters of /FP. It has been assumed earlier in the
text that Hybrid Maize in Igana is an innovation which is
added to a previous adoption and primarily among the more
successful previous adopters. The overall differences in
the values of the 'independent variables' for the two adoption-categories can be taken to support this assumption.

The diagramatic presentations for the /SFP- and /FP-
adopters are given in Figures 8.6 and 8.7 respectively.
Starting with Figure 8.6 one first notices the outward
spread of adoption (Fig. 8.6A), which largely synthesizes
what could be inferred from Map 6.5. In the more elaborate
breakdown (Fig. 8.6B) it is seen, however, that fairly
large differences exist within the overall group of adopters if one also considers the relative earliness/lateness
of adoption together with their location — close/distant.
Early adopters close to the sources are, indeed, earlier
than their namesakes in the more distant categories. The
differences are obvious and, moreover, give support for the
wave-analogies used in spatial diffusion theory. A similar,
but less pronounced, trend may be inferred for the later
adopters. Largely, however, what is observed for this group
could be taken to signify a filling in process — again a
concept frequently used in spatial diffusion theory (cf.
i.a. Brown 1981; Gould 1969 and Hägerstrand 1953).

Shifting the attention to Figure 8.6C-F indicates that
other factors than the neighbourhood effect alone may have
a bearing on the outcome. By first looking at the temporal
aspect, it is obvious that a similar declining trend as was
seen in Fig. 8.6A exists also for the four 'independent
variables'. Although variations exist in the trends, the
overall impression is that the relatively earlier adopters

198

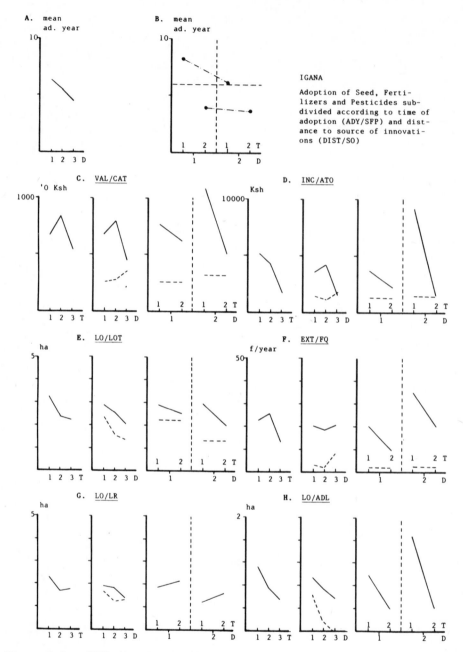

IGANA

Adoption of Seed, Ferti-
lizers and Pesticides subdivided according to time of
adoption (ADY/SFP) and distance to source of innovations (DIST/SO)

Figure 8.6: /SFP-adoption in IGANA.

show higher values on these than do the later adopters. Similar trends are also found for the spatial dimension, with
the exception of EXT/FQ which indicates a fairly evenly di-

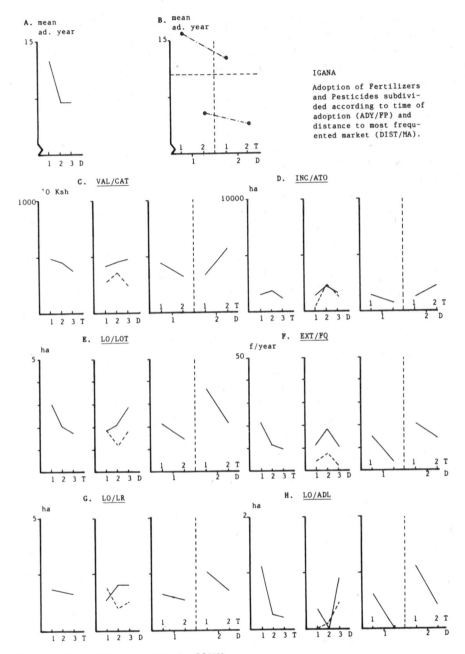

Figure 8.7: /FP-adoption in IGANA.

stributed access to formalized information over the area. Concerning the latter variable, however, it should be noted that a fairly clear trend is seen in the temporal dimension.

In sum, the discussion on the diagrams for the spatio-/
temporal-dimensions, indicates an initial stratification
in the sense that the more wealthy, again, are the first
to adopt and furthermore are the ones that receive a major
share of the more formalized information disseminated in
the area. Of particular interest are the trends found for
the spatial-dimension, and also the correspondence between
the spatial and temporal trends as there is nothing inherent in the spatial dimension as such that would cause
these. Instead an explanation of the similarities should
have to be sought in the socio-economic organization of the
area and the activities by promotional agents for the innovations. Brown (1981:284), for example, writes:

"...we can account for a great deal of variance in the spatial patterns and temporal rates of diffusion by looking at institutional,
rather than individual, behaviour, and the relevant institutional
behaviour, in this instance, pertains to the supply side of diffusion
and its impacts."

Concerning the activities by promotional agents, a spatial segmentation is possible if the change agents work
their way out from the supply nodes by means of the established transportation network (cf. Brown ibid.:121-26 —
particularly Fig. 4.7). Empirical findings supporting this
notion are found in Blaikie (1975:73-78) discussing the actions of Family Planning Extension Agents in India. Second,
a segmentation/stratification may be caused by what has
been termed pre-stratification. The latter, of course, refers to the change agents' tendency to focus attention on
the more innovative farmers, which often also means the
more wealthy. As this seems to be the case in Igana as
well, the combination of the two factors pointed out could
explain the similarities in the trends between the temporal
and spatial diffusion processes.

To continue with the space/time diagrams in Figure
8.6C-F it turns out, with some exception for LO/LOT, that
the four adopter-categories defined show distinctly different values of the 'independent variables'. Within each
space category, the relationship is one of distinctly negatively sloping trends between earlier and later adopters,
but also that the earlier adopters in the more distant
space category, show markedly higher values compared to
their namesakes in the 'close' one.

The latter observation may underline some interesting

aspects of the initial adoptions. It can be assumed that certain threshold values exist, defined in socio-economic and informational terms, which have to be surpassed before adoption takes place. Accepting this notion, it can also be assumed that locational factors may affect the actual level of these values. This, in turn, leads back to a reasoning in terms of a 'compensational effect' (see Section 8.3), viz. that early adopters in less favourable locations, lie even higher in the hierarchies defined here, than the early adopters in more favourable locations. This line of reasoning is, to a degree, in agreement with the discussion on "innovation penetration boundaries" and how these may change over a period of time (Brown 1981:239-44). Moreover, it can be assumed that a supply system gradually refines its techniques in reaching potential adopters and, thus, the importance of the threshold values may be lessened at later stages in the adoption process.

Finally, in the discussion on the /SFP-adopters some additional comments are needed. First, the diagrams shown in Figure 8.6G-H are presented in order to further clarify the role of land-ownership in the adoption process. It should be noted that the negatively sloping trends seen for LO/LOT are not primarily the outcome of initial land-ownership, LO/LR, but rather the result of what is seen for additional land — LO/ADL. To an extent, this may indicate that post-stratification effects are also revealed in the material — although acquisition of additional land is found among the non-adopters as well (Fig. 8.6H).

From the discussion concerning the /SFP-adopters, attention should be turned to the adoption of fertilizers and pesticides, /FP, in Igana. Although this adoption-category does not contain Hybrid Maize, it is still of interest as it could qualify some of the notions concerning the adoption history assumed for Igana. The /FP-adopters then, constitutes the potential adopters that did not continue with additional innovations after their first adoption.

Starting with the aggregated figures in Appendix 2, it is obvious that the /FP-adopters almost invariably lie below the /SFP-adopters both for the mean and median values. The overall impression from the appendix is one of less success with the first adoption and this may have caused them to refrain from additional adoption. In comparison with the non-adopters the /FP-adopters show higher values, while in the comparison with the /SFP-adopters it can be assumed that they have not surpassed the threshold which could have led to further adoption of Hybrid Maize.

Some of the information for the /FP-adopters has been summarized in Figure 8.7, which is identical in its format to Figure 8.6. Focusing, initially, on the purely temporal aspects of the adoption (Fig. 8.7A-B), similar trends to those found for the /SFP-adopters are seen. Concerning the diagrams in Figure 8.7C-H, however, the emerging relationships differ in some respects from those found for the /SFP-adopters. The first observation, in line with the discussion above, is that the curves shown for the /FP-adopters lie much lower than the corresponding curves for the /SFP-adopters. Furthermore, the diagrams show less clear trends, particular in the spatial and the space/time dimensions, than was the case in Fig. 8.6. In the temporal dimension, it is possible to infer similar trends to those found for the /SFP-adopters, but they are not as pronounced as they were for the adopters of the complete package. Also the discussion on the possible occurrences of 'compensational effects' finds little support in Fig. 8.7, with a possible exception for the diagrams showing land-ownership variables (Fig. 8.7G-H).

It should be noted, however, that a different criterion variable is used for the space dimension in the case of the /FP-adopters as compared to the /SFP-adopters — DIST/MA instead of DIST/SO. This, of course, could partly explain the differences found in the trends. Still the correlation matrix for Igana presented in Table 7.1, quite clearly indicated different spatial relationships for the different adoption-categories and, thus, this could not be taken to completely explain the differences found here between the two adoption-categories.

An explanation should rather be looked for in the assumed differences in the outcome of the initial adoption between the two categories. Thus, although the /FP-adopters in the temporal dimension seem to have followed much the same course of adoption as those later becoming /SFP-adopters, they have not had the success which could generate additional adoptions. Also, although they seem to have been affected by similar segmentational activities on behalf of the change agents (indicated by the temporal diagrams in Fig. 8.7C-H), this has not led to a similar post-stratification effect (indicated by the generally smaller differences between adopters and non-adopters in the spatial diagrams of Fig. 8.7C-H) as was the case for the /SFP-adopters.

In sum, the /SFP- and /FP-adopters differ in many important respects and this could explain why some of the initial adopters of fertilizers and pesticides did, and some did not, continue with the additional adoption of Hybrid Maize seed. In Section 8.7 the concept of 'Functional Aspects' of the adoption will be introduced and some of the differences found between the two adoption-categories will, hopefully, be put in an enlightning perspective.

8.6.3 Adoption of seed, fertilizers, pesticides (/SFP); seed-only (/S); seed, fertilizers (/SF) and seed, pesticides (/SP) in Kodoch West

In all essential parts, the analysis of the adoption-categories found in Kodoch West (Table 6.8) will follow similar analytical lines to those followed in the case of Igana. A larger number of adoption-categories will be looked at in Kodoch West, as the adoption there is found in a greater number of combinations (Table 6.7) than in Igana. The latter will not affect the analytical approach, however. A minor methodological difference exists in the analyses for the two sub-locations though. To retain as much variance as possible in the succesions of breakdowns, an attempt has been made to present as many sub-groups as possible. In the case of Kodoch West, however, some of the sub-groups created contain only 1-3 observations, giving individual extreme values an undue strong influence in the diagrams in Figures 8.8-8.11. The latter is particularly obvious with respect to the temporal dimension in Kodoch West and, thus, for this dimension the breakdown has been made into two sub-groups only.

By first taking a general view of the adoption-categories found in Kodoch West, Appendices 16-18, interesting differences from those found in Igana are immediately seen. Apart from the lower values for some of the 'independent variables', it is seen that contrary to Igana, no clear hierarchy exist between the adoption-categories. The /SFP-adopters do not stand out here as a group that lies significantly above the other groups of adopters. If anything the /SP-adopters should be regarded as the more wealthy, at least on the 'principal independent variables', judging from the fact that they have a larger number of 'high scorings' than the others (App. 17). Still, in a comparison between the adoption-categories and the group of non-adopters, similar differences are found, as in Igana. The latter differences here are, however, less distinct and actually some overlaps occur (App. 17-18).

A possible explanation to the lack of a very clear hierarchization among the adoption-categories and the less marked differences between these and the non-adopters, may be looked for in the adoption history in Kodoch West. As opposed to the stepwise adoption inferred in Igana, all adoption-categories defined in Kodoch West, centres around Hybrid Maize as the principal innovation and thus they are in priciple, all reflections of one and the same process. In spite of this, marked differences are found between the categories with respect to the mean adoption year for each (Table 8.1).

Table 8.1: Mean adoption year for the Adoption-categories in Kodoch West.

Adoption-cat.	Mean ad. year
ADY/SFP	3.93
ADY/S	2.52
ADY/SF	4.33
ADY/SP	1.77

Note: Mean adotpion year is calculated backwards from the time of the Survey 1975/76, viz. adoption 1975=1; 1974=2 etc.

The table largely summarizes what can be inferred from Maps 6.9-6.13, i.e. a shift from more expensive and more complex combinations towards less complex and less expensive ones. In particular the fertilizer component seems to be critical and the one which has fallen out of the combinations with a lower mean adoption year. This shift should have been caused by the rising price of fertilizers after 1973. A second, more tentative, reason may be agronomic findings (Allen 1969) emphasising more the managerial aspects rather than the use of fertilizers, which in turn may have affected the advice given by extension agents. In combination, these two points may have caused a lowering of the threshold values which have to be surpassed in order to adopt. In the process, the underlying basis of potential adopters may have been broadened and subsequently caused a wider variation in the aggregated values of the 'independent variables'.

Turning to the detailed diagramatic descriptions of the adoption-categories in Kodoch West (Figs. 8.8-8.11), it should first be noted that these are more difficult to draw conclusions from, than the ones shown for Igana. The combination of a smaller number of overall adopters and the larger number of adoption-categories, means that each adoption-category contains relatively few cases. Thus, the

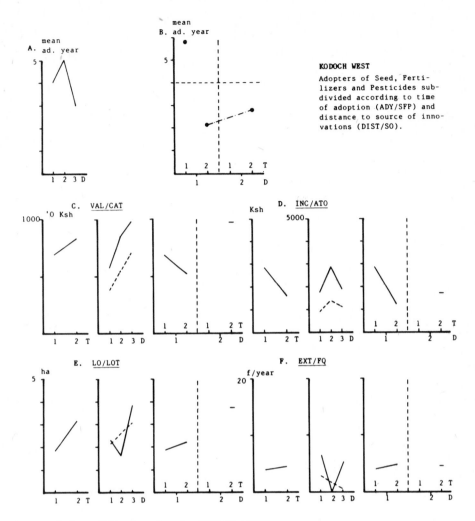

Figure 8.8: /SFP-adoption in KODOCH WEST.

sub-groups created are often small, and isolated more or less extreme values may have a strong influence on the results. In this light the commentaries to the figures for Kodoch West will be even more restricted than the ones for Igana and limit themselves to noting only very broad trends. Appendices 16-30 do, however, contain details for each adoption-category and for all 'independent variables' used and, thus, it is possible for the interested reader to draw his own conclusions.

Starting with the A- and B-diagrams of Figures 8.7-8.11, it is possible to infer an outward moving diffusion process from the sources of the innovations for the /SFP- and /SP-

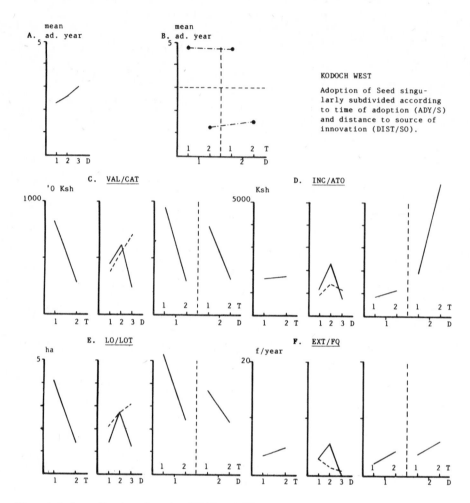

Figure 8.9: /S-adoption in KODOCH WEST.

adopters. The /SF-adopters, however, are a limited number
that form a distinct cluster from which no such conclusions
could be inferred (see Map 6.12), and the /S-adopters display an adoption process that is almost a reversal of the
hypothesised trends (see Map 6.11 and the discussion in Ch.
VI). Although differences are found between the different
adoption-categories, it is possible to conclude that, basically, the adoption patterns follow similar processes to
those seen in Igana and also with more general theoretical
premisses. When structural aspects and their spatial distribution are added to the exlanations, the differences
seen are explicable as will be shown below.

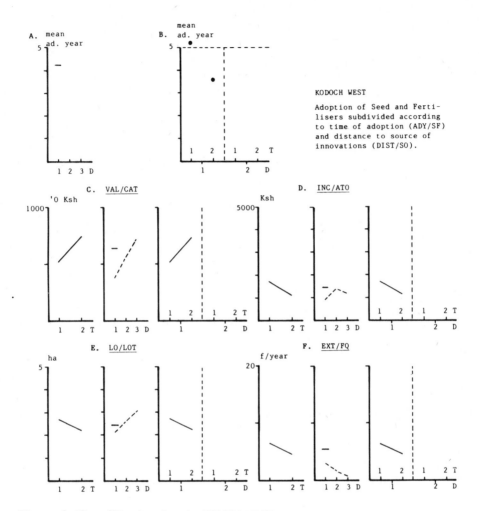

Figure 8.10: /SF-adoption in KODOCH WEST.

Turning to the more detailed presentations found in the
C-F diagrams in Figures 8.8-8.11, a cursory examination of
these may give a very fragmented picture from which no
clear implications can be drawn. In two instances, basic
similarities with the diagrams for Igana are seen — for the
/S- and /SP-adopters. In these cases similar explanations
to those put forward in the case of Igana should apply. A
close inspection of the diagrams presented reveals, however, that the most basic differences between the ones for
Kodoch West and the ones for Igana, is to be found in the
diagrams showing the spatial dimension.

Referring back to Figure 8.5, it can be seen that the

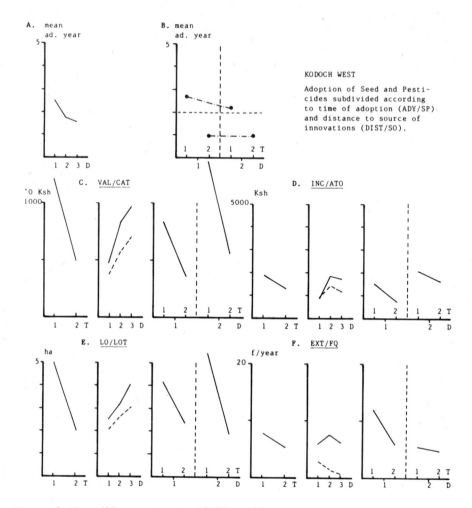

Figure 8.11: /SP-adoption in KODOCH WEST.

'reversal of trends' in Kodoch West is a reflection of basic structural differences with very clear spatial expres-
sions. Given the definition of the spatial dimension, i.e.
the use of DIST/SO as a criterion variable, it can be seen
that several of the 'independent variables' show a clear
positive trend concerning increasing distances. This is obvious for, for example, VAL/LS, VAL/CAT, LO/LR, LO/LOT etc.
In other words, Kodoch West displays a much stronger spatial stratification, i.e. the larger and more wealthy farms
are found in the more peripheral/distant parts of the sub-
location, than was the case in Igana (compare Figures
8.3-8.5).

In the light of this spatial stratification, to which should be added the fairly short overall adoption history in Kodoch West implying that the differences between early and late adopters are not very great, the diagrams become more comprehensible. Generally, the adoption processes in Kodoch West, with an exception for seed-only, are a combination of a spatially determined such process based on proximity to the sources of the innovations in the initial phases, with a hierarchical diffusion process based on structural aspects, primarily economic in a latter phase. In, for example, the case of /SFP-adoption, this is quite obvious (see Map 6.10). From an initial adoption cluster in the south-east of the area, a secondary cluster is established farily rapidly among the more wealthy farms in the north-west. Thus, in principle similar explanations could be applied to the adoption in both Kodoch West and Igana, viz. spatial and structural aspects interact in forming the actual diffusion patterns. Also, at this level of aggregation, the structural aspects to a degree gain the upper hand, causing a fair amount of 'randomness', or deviations, in the resultant adoption patterns — as compared to the expected theoretical norms.

A second similarity between the diagrams for Kodoch West and Igana, which should be noticed before the attention is turned to the so called 'Functional Aspects', is the within group differences. As was the case in Igana, it is obvious in the diagrams for Kodoch West that great differences are found between early and late adopters within one adoption-category. This is particularly obvious in the space/time diagrams. It is difficult in Kodoch West to draw conclusions concerning early/late adopters in different locations and to talk about, e.g. 'compensational effects', as was done for Igana. Although exceptions exist, the general impression for Kodoch West coincides with the findings for Igana, i.e. early adopters have a tendency to have higher values of the 'independent variables' than do the relatively late adopters. Again it is possible to think in terms of initial threshold values which have to be surpassed prior to adoption and the fact that these are gradually lowered as an innovation become established in an area.

8.7 'Functional Aspects' of the adoption in Igana and Kodoch West

8.7.1 Introduction

To an extent the discussion in Section 8.6 has centred on 'place bound' farm characteristics as explanations of particular aspects of adoption behaviour. In much of the sociological literature, however, it has been noted that adoption is related to the degree of "Cosmopoliteness" of the adopters (cf. i.a. Rogers 1962, 1971 and 1983). Rogers (1983:258) writes:

> "...Earlier adopters are more cosmopolite than later adopters, the innovators' networks are more likely to be outside, rather than with-in, their social system. They travel widely and are involved in matters beyond the boundaries of their local system."

Such a perspective will have to be introduced here as well, in order to deepen the understanding of the processes underlying adoption. Conceptwise, however, this will be re-ferred to as the 'Functional Aspects' of adoption rather than 'Cosmopoliteness' as the present analysis will contain a slightly wider and more formalized approach to the dimen-sion than seems to be the case when sociologists used it. The concept is defined as — links that go beyond the imme-diate surroundings of the potential adopters, i.e. links of a non-local character that tie the potential adopters to networks operating at national-, regional- and/or dist-rict-level.

Operationalizing the 'functional aspects' is not an easy task and the variables used can only be seen as indicating the dimension. It should be noted that the variables used — AT/FTC, AT/AGS, COOP/M, TR/INC and CRED — are all dicho-tomous (Yes/No), thus, not giving any qualitative indica-tion of the content/extent of the participation. To clarify the 'functional aspects' it will be necessary to briefly outline the variables used in describing it.

Attending courses at a Farmers' Training Centre (AT/FTC) is based on a selection of particular farmers with the in-tention that these should become 'opinion leaders' in their respective communities. The selection is often made by ex-tension agents and it is possible to imagine biases in this selection of a similar kind to the one discussed in terms of pre-stratification above (cf. Rogers 1983:Ch.9).

Attending Agricultural Shows (AT/AGS) indicates an ac-tive interest on behalf of the farmers in acquiring infor-mation on agricultural matters. Such shows are often used by different companies and organizations for displaying agricultural innovations.

Co-operative membership (COOP/M) is in many instances a prerequisite for the adoption of many innovations, e.g. coffee and pyrethrum. Co-operatives are frequently used in promoting agricultural innovations and their factories and Godowns are often used as supply nodes for Hybrid Maize, fertilizers etc. Moreover, co-operative societies and unions are directly linked to the Ministry of Co-operative Development and, thus, the links to higher levels and to national development priorities are clear.

Transfers of Income (TR/INC) indicates the fact that incomes derived from purely agricultural activities are supplemented from external sources. These may be family members working elsewhere (often in urban areas), or rural industrial and/or service activities. Thus, over and above purely monetary aspects, the variable implies a link with activities and nodes outside the farm and its immediate surroundings.

Finally, Credits (CRED) a variable which is strongly linked to COOP/M. Although other sources for credits do exist, e.g. Commercial Banks; co-operative societies and unions turn out to be the most important sources for credits. The reception of credit from other formal sources often involves quite strict demands for collaterals, e.g. 'Title-Deeds', as well as demands for, for example, a minimum acreage. Extension agents often play an important role in the giving of credits in that their opinion on the applicant is frequently requested. In addition, informal channels for credits may be used — 'Moneylenders'. The material for the two survey areas, however, indicates that such sources do not play an important role there. Where such sources are used, it is mainly restricted to minor amounts in the form of hand-loans.

The data for the 'functional aspects' is presented in Appendices 7-11 and 22-26. The presentation in the appendices is made at a very detailed level, showing a three-way breakdown including the spatial and temporal dimensions as well as participation or not. In the discussion below, the basis will be aggregated figures from Appendices 7 and 22. The other indicated appendices have been included as they form a background to the more general conclusions drawn, and also enable the reader to draw his own conclusions.

8.7.2 'Functional Aspects' of adoption in Igana

Table 8.2 summarizes the 'functional aspects' at an aggregate level for Igana. The most obvious feature of the table is the clear difference between adopters and non-adopters. With the exception of TR/INC the figures all imply a 'positive' bias towards the adopters. The relationships between Yes- and No-answers for the total population

Table 8.2: 'Functional Aspects' of adoption in Igana

		AT/FTC		AT/AGS		COOP/M		TR/INC		CRED	
		N	%	N	%	N	%	N	%	N	%
Total	YES	40	23	37	22	121	70	108	63	92	54
population	NO	132	77	135	78	51	30	64	37	80	46
	TOT.	172	100	172	100	172	100	172	100	172	100
Adopters	YES	31	29	21	29	102	95	68	64	84	79
	NO	76	71	76	71	5	5	39	36	23	21
	TOT.	107	100	107	100	107	100	107	100	107	100
Non-	YES	9	14	6	9	19	29	40	62	8	12
adopters	NO	56	86	59	91	46	71	25	38	57	88
	TOT.	65	100	65	100	65	100	65	100	65	100

are generally strengthened for the group of adopters, while they are weakened or reversed for the non-adopters.

On looking a bit more closely at the figures in the table, it is obvious that the majority of those indicating 'participation' on AT/FTC and AT/AGS are to be found among the adopters, which clearly points out a relationship with adoption. COOP/M and CRED both show a reversal of trends between adopters and non-adopters. The importance of COOP/M in the adoption processes in Igana is clearly seen, and this also underlines the role of cash-crop production in inducing and encouraging further adoption there. The figures in the table also makes it possible to infer a link between COOP/M and CRED. Finally, TR/INC where the lack of clear trends may cause doubt about its use as a description on the 'functional aspect'.

It is worth noting, however, that more than 60 per cent of the population supplement their incomes from agriculture by means of remittances — a figure which is substantiated by the IRS (RoK 1977:56 — Table 8.8), where it is seen that about 50 per cent of the household incomes in Central Province are derived from sources other than farming. Thus, generally speaking, transfers of incomes play a very important role in Central Province and Igana. Here, however, the lack of a qualitative/quantitative measure on TR/INC may be the reason why no relationship with adoption is found. It can be assumed, but not verified, that the adopters receive larger amounts than the non-adopters. If this is the case, TR/INC should have an influence on adoption even though it cannot be seen from Table 8.2.

Lastly, when looking at some details of the 'functional aspects' for the two adoption-categories analysed in Igana

Table 8.3: Percentages of 'YES-answers' on the 'Functional Aspects'
of the Adoption-categories in Igana.

Adoption-category	No.	AT/FTC	AT/AGS	COOP/M	TR/INC	CRED
/SFP	52	48	44	96	62	71
/FP	45	11	16	100	62	96

(Table 8.3) some interesting points can be noted. Comparing
the figures for the two adoption-categories with each other
and also with the corresponding figures for the adopters
in Table 8.2 shows, initially, that no very significant
differences exist with respect to COOP/M, TR/INC and CRED.
The only one worth mentioning is the one found for CRED.
Here the slightly higher figure for the /FP-adopters compared to the /SFP-adopters in Table 8.3, could be taken to
reflect the assumed adoption history in Igana. The implication would be that the /FP-adopters have not been able to
rid themselves of some of their needs for credits in order
to keep up their initial adoption and are thus, not in a
position to continue with additional adoptions.

More significant differences in the figure are found,
however, for AT/FTC and AT/AGS. Here the /SFP-adopters show
markedly higher figures than the general group of adopters,
while the /FP-adopters show markedly lower figures. This
indicates a much stronger integration of the /SFP-adopters
into wider networks, not least such networks through which
they will have easier access to information on innovations,
than is the case for the /FP-adopters. The two variables,
but particularly AT/FTC, may also be taken as reflecting
a pre-stratification process in that extension agents are
active in the selection of farmers to attend FTC:s. If the
latter notion is accepted, the figures in Table 8.3 again
underline the fact that the /SFP-adopters are generally
found in a more favourable position than are the /FP-adop-
ters.

8.7.3 'Functional Aspects' of adoption in Kodoch West

The analysis of the 'functional aspects' in Kodoch West
is made against the same backkground and follows similar
lines as in Igana. Aggregated data for Kodoch West is presented in Table 8.4 and this table should inititally be
compared to Table 8.2 for Igana. In this the most obvious
differences between the two sub-locations are found for
COOP/M and CRED. Obviously the co-operative movement is
much weaker in Kodoch West, which probably also affects the

Table 8.4:   'Functional Aspects' of adoption in Kodoch West.

		AT/FTC		AT/AGS		COOP/M		TR/INC		CRED	
		N	%	N	%	N	%	N	%	N	%
Total	YES	52	28	97	52	4	2	121	65	7	4
population	NO	134	72	89	48	182	98	65	35	179	96
	TOT.	186	100	186	100	186	100	186	100	186	100
Adopters	YES	18	29	37	58	4	6	45	70	7	11
	NO	46	72	27	42	60	94	19	30	57	89
	TOT.	64	100	64	100	64	100	64	100	64	100
Non-	YES	34	28	60	49	0	0	76	62	0	0
adopters	NO	88	72	62	51	122	100	46	38	122	100
	TOT.	122	100	122	100	122	100	122	100	122	100

credit possibilities. Tentatively it could, also, be assumed that this difference could explain parts of the relatively lower overall adoption rates in Kodoch West compared to Igana (see Tables 6.3 and 6.4). A second, somewhat surprising, difference is found for AT/FTC. In Kodoch West no differences are found between adopters and non-adopters for this variable, as may have been expected from the findings in Igana. For AT/AGS a slight, but very much less marked difference than in Igana, is seen. Finally, TR/INC differ from the findings in Igana in the sense that the adopters lie more markedly above the non-adopters. Still, it is not possible to draw far reaching conclusions concerning the role of the transfer of incomes in the adoption process in Kodoch West. Generally speaking, however, the information in Table 8.4 gives no clear indcation of the relationships between the 'functional aspects' and the adoption processes in Kodoch West.

When the attention is turned to the distribution of Yes-answers for the individual adoption-categories in Kodoch West, however, the role and relevance of the 'functional aspect' is more clearly seen (Table 8.5). Although it should be pointed out that the base for the presented percentages in the table is generally low, even a cursory look at it reveals significant differences between the different adoption-categories.

The first point to notice from Table 8.5 is the hierarchization that is seen between the /SFP- and /SF-adopters, on the one hand, and the /S- and /SP-adopters, on the other. The two former adoption-categories clearly display a greater integration/participation in the wider networks defined by the 'functional aspects'. It can also be noted,

Table 8.5: Percentages of 'YES-answers' on the 'Functional Aspects' of the Adoption-categories in Kodoch West.

Adoption-category	No.	AT/FTC	AT/AGS	COOP/M	TR/INC	CRED
/SFP	15	87	93	13	60	7
/S	23	9	30	0	74	0
/SF	9	33	78	22	67	22
/SP	17	0	53	0	76	6

in a comparison with Table 8.1, that the two adoption-categories showing the largest integration are also those with the highest mean adoption years. It is, thus, possible to interpret the figures in Table 8.5 as a reflection of a pre-stratification effect, not least as the actions taken by the various change agents may influence the outcome of some of the variables used in the describing the 'functional aspects'. Additional support for the latter conclusion may be taken from the fact that the /SFP-adopters lie above the /SF-adopters, while both these, in turn, lie above the /S- and /SP-adopters.

Disregarding the figures for COOP/M and CRED, which are actually based on a limited number of observations, the only variable for which the /S- and /SP-adopters lie above the other two is TR/INC. Althought the figures lack a qualitative indication, as commented upon for Igana, they could still be used for tentative conclusions. The slightly higher figures on TR/INC for the adopters of the less complex and expensive combinations, may indicate that these belong to the lower layers of the assumed hierarchies and, thus, are in the position that they cannot adopt without additional financial support. It can also be noted, in a comparison with Table 8.1, that as a group they generally belong to the later adopters in the sub-location. Thus, it can be assumed that they belong to a group that does not adopt until the innovations have been fairly well established in the area. The latter may be due to their generally lower integration into the wider networks, or due to financial constraints as, perhaps, indicated by TR/INC.

8.8 Concluding remarks

The main conclusion to be drawn from the analyses presented in this chapter, is that the adoption of the innovations looked at is clearly linked to a stratification process. This is reflected in the facts that the adopters generally show much higher values on the 'independent variables' studied than do the non-adopters. The stratification is further reflected within the group of adopters as well as within singular adoption-categories — i.e. adopters of more complex/expensive combinations and early adopters within adoption-categories, tend to lie above the other groups. Given the 'causality problem' the available data does not allow a clear conclusion as to whether this is a cause or an effect of the adoption (pre- or post-stratification). Basically, however, the data seem to indicate a pre-stratification to which is linked a stronger integration into the wider networks, defined here as 'functional aspects' as a major cause of early adoption. Moreover, it seems as if both pre-stratification and the 'functional aspects' are positively related to preferential treatment on the part of various change agents.

IX. Summary; Conclusions & Outlook

9.1 Introduction

This concluding chapter will be divided into two separate, but interlinked parts. First, a summary of the main findings from the study will be made. The summary will follow the general disposition of the work as outlined in Section 1.4 — i.e. from a discussion of the theoretical basis for the study, the empirical material has been presented from an initially high level of aggregation down towards gradually more and more disaggregated levels. The presentation in Section 1.4 gives, however, a broad outline of the content of individual chapters and, hence, the summary presented below could focus more on the direct results and implications that can be drawn from the material presented.

Second, from the analysis which has gone into more and more micro-oriented aspects of the diffusion processes studied, it will be necessary to try to generalize from the results arrived at. In the first instance, the attempted generalization will be made in a Kenyan perspective, which in view of the framework of the study should be the most important level of aggregation. In addition, to the extent it is possible, an attempt will also be made to generalize from the findings, up to the level of a more general debate on development issues, as well as trying to draw implications from the results for rural development approaches in the Third World as such.

9.2 Summary

The theoretical foundation for the study is basically derived from two academic fields, out of the many within which the diffusion of innovations have been studied, i.e. Sociology/Rural Sociology and Geography. Developments of theory formulation within these academic fields, and some others, have been summarized in Chapter II. In this chapter an attempt is first made to summarize and present parts of the available theoretical discussions that are relevant to the present study. From the discussion, two more recent developments in the discussion on the diffusion of innovations are brought forward as the principal theoretical basis for the study.

First, the "Market and Infrastructure Perspective" presented by Brown in several publications during the 1970s and summarized in Brown (1981). Second, the 'Consequences of Innovations' are brought forward as being of principal interest for the study. The discussion here is based very much on the works by Griffin (1972) and Yapa (1977), but also on Brown (1981) and Rogers (1983). Thus, having set the scene, the discussion goes into the more concrete aspects of the present study by way of a discussion on the basic problem formulation.

Chapter III presents an analytical model which attempts to conceptualize the problem formulations. These formulations follow the theoretical presentation very closely and then also give the general layout of the study. With the addition of policy aspects on the diffusion of Hybrid Maize in Kenya (Ch. V), the analysis is initially set out in conventional terms concerning geographical diffusion studies, viz. an analysis of temporal and spatial diffusion patterns is first made. From these pieces of analysis the focus is more on the 'Consequences of the Innovations'. The analytical model then refers primarily to the first two steps of the analysis.

Chapter IV focuses on the different methodological problems faced in carrying out the type of study intended. The issues raised concern problems of questionaire design, selection of study areas, validity and reliability of the data collected among other things. The most important part of this chapter deals with 'The problem of causality' (Section 4.6) and this deserve a short comment here. The issue is the extent to which causal relationships can be determined from interview data collected in a 'one-shot' interview, where information on the dependent variables (here adoption) is collected by means of retrospective questions. The problem lies in the fact that the value of the dependent variable may have influenced the value of the 'independent variables'. In the case of the diffusion of innovations, this is almost taken for granted for economic and socio-economic variables.

The conclusion drawn with respect to this problem is that it is unavoidable, considering the way in which the data has been collected. Hence, it will not be possible to establish any definite causal relationships, in the sense that the values found on the 'independent variables' are directly used as explanations of adoption behaviour. In practice, this implies that the results arrived at cannot be used for any types of normative or categorical conclusions. Rather a qualitative approach is used in interpreting the results and conclusions which are drawn as implications from a fairly large set of 'independent variables'. Another consequence has been that simple statistical methods have been used, in preference to attempting to establish significant relationships from sophisticated methods.

In Chapter V and the three following chapters, the analysis of the available material is pursued and the results are presented. Following the general layout of the study, viz. the study could be likened to a funnel going from a high level of aggregation into more and more micro-oriented aspects of the problems at hand. Chapter V deals with the aggregated aspects of the diffusion processes studied. Initially, the discussion in the chapter focuses on the role of maize in Kenyan agriculture, characteristics of the innovations being studied and how these affect, among other things, established managerial practices in producing maize. From this the discussion continues, looking into the underlying policy aspects in the creation of a supply network for the innovations. In this context analyses are made of the actual creation of the supply network over a period of time, the extent of coverage in terms of population/ stockist ratios (Map 5.3) and the development of sales of Hybrid Maize; the latter being presented at regional levels. Finally, the available statistics on sales of Hybrid Maize are used in an evaluation of the extent to which these figures could be used as proxys for the rate of adoption at national and regional levels.

The purpose of the discussions in Chapter V is largely to define the 'Market and Infrastructure Perspective' which more directly will form the basis for the analyses to follow in the next few chapters. In terms of the main conclusions, the results clearly indicate relationships between diffusion and the developments within the breeding programme for Hybrid Maize, i.e the extent of and the rate at which improved seed varieties are made available in new parts of the country. Linked to this, of course, is also the expansion of the supply network, making the new seeds available to the farmers in a larger number of areas. It could be noted, however, that in spite of the phenomenal growth in sales found not least in Figure 5.1, marked regional differences exist in the use of Hybrid Maize (Table 5.9). In one respect this seems to be related to the number of stockists (Table 5.4), but also to the fact that the regions showing a high proportion of use are also the ones where improved seed was available first.

Beginning in Chapter VI the level of aggregation is brought down to the micro-level, which implies here that the analysis is carried out at a sub-locational level. Initially some basic characteristics of the selected sub-locations are discussed, from which the analysis goes into the more conventional aspects of diffusion studies of this nature, viz. an analysis of temporal and spatial diffusion patterns. Although the main emphasis in the work is placed on the diffusion of Hybrid Maize, this innovation is rarely, if ever, presented to the potential adopters separately. Hybrid Maize is generally presented as part of a package including fertilizers, pesticides as well as improved managerial practices.

A close examination of the adoption data, reveals that this is also the way in which Hybrid Maize has been adopted, i.e. adoption takes place in distinct combinations — 'bundles' — made up from the whole package or in different combinations of parts of the package. Thus, instead of focusing on the adoption of individual innovations, which does not give very many clues to the overall adoption processes, two and four adoption-categories have been defined for Igana and Kodoch West respectively. When studying these, a difference in the adoption patterns between the two sub-locations emerged.

In Igana, Hybrid Maize came to be an innovation that was added to an already established practice of adoptions related to the production of cash-crops. As not all initial adopters continue with the adoption of Hybrid Maize, it is assumed that those doing so belong to the more successful initial adopters. In Kodoch West, the complete adoption process centres around the Hybrid Maize package, as no substantial initial adoption of the related innovations studied exists there. This, among other things, seems to lead to a larger diversity in the types of combinations which are adopted. For both sub-locations it can also be noted that the rapidly increasing prices of fertilizers, after 1973, has affected the overall adoption process and, thus, the combinations adopted.

Finally, in Chapter VI attention is turned to the spatial manifestations of the adoption. In this analysis a very clear 'Market and Infrastructural Perspective' is applied, if, however, only at a low level of aggregation. Two particular aspects are being looked at. First, the applicability of the applied perspective on this scale is being looked at. Second, and related to the first point, the emerging patterns are considered with respect to the extent to which they conform to the postulates of the spatial diffusion theory. Implicit in the latter point lies the question, whether the frequently applied wave-analogies are applicable at this level of aggregation or if this is a scale-dependent phenomenon.

Basically, the analysis of the diffusion patterns mapped for the defined adoption-categories (Maps 6.1-6.13), concludes that both perspectives are applicable at this level of aggregation, viz. the adoption patterns show traits which link the process to the organization of the distributional network, as well as to the established infrastructure in the sub-locations. In addition, once adoption had been established, the familiar traits of spatial diffusion patterns seemed to be operative, i.e. the creation of primary diffusion centres, neighbourhood effects and secondary diffusion centres etc.

At the same time, however, fairly large deviations were found from the norms, particularly in Kodoch West. Here it turned out that the different adoption-categories came to occupy more or less separate parts of the sub-location — parts that could roughly be defined as quadrants of a co-ordinate system with the origin in the 'middle' of the sub-location. Although a link to the distributional network could generally be established as a prerequisite for the start of the process, and the spatial clustering of the adoption-categories can be seen as the outcome of strong neighbourhood effects, the deviations from the norms are so large that they will have to be explained by additional forces affecting the emergent adoption patterns — forces over and above the ones already mentioned. These are also the topics which are discussed in the two final chapters of the analysis.

In Chapter VII an attempt is made to find significant relationships between a large set of 'independent variables' and adoption of the different adoption-categories by means of a 'correlation analysis'. In terms of results, however, this part of the analysis did not yield anything substantial which could give further insight into the processes studied. The strong correlations found should mostly be categorized as 'autocorrelations', i.e. subsets correlated with their corresponding summary variables and variables expressing ratios correlated with their corresponding absolute values etc. Generally, however, the correlation coefficients were fairly low. The 'correlation analysis' has, thus, not been very enlightning.

In one sense though, some of the results have been useful in that they have pointed out ways in which the continued analysis could be pursued. Primarily this refers to the correlations found between distance variables and adoption variables. It appears that, although neither of the correlation coefficients are very large, they show marked trends — the time of adoption is distinctly negatively correlated with the distance variables. In Igana, different adoption-categories were related to different distance variables, which could be explained by the phases through which adoption in Igana has passed. The main value of the indication of a distance related adoption process was that it pointed out the spatial dimension as one of the 'criterion variables' that should be used in the sub-divisions of the adoption-categories in the analysis in Chapter VIII.

In Chapter VIII a very detailed analysis is made of the different adoption-categories. The principal aim of this analysis is to try to pinpoint some of the factors that trigger off adoption and in particular the differentials in these factors leading to adoption of more or less complex combinations from the complete innovation package.

A significant part of the analysis in this chapter deals with the consequences of the diffusion of the particular innovations being looked at. The latter is a natural extension of the analysis, as it turns out that marked differences in the values of the 'independent variables' exist between the adopters of the different adoption-categories. In an analysis of non-adopters vs adopters these differences are further accentuated. Although the observations above partly anticipate the presentation of the results, it can also be mentioned at this point that an explicit consideration of non-adopters is rarely found in diffusion studies.

At the beginning of the chapter some methodological comments are made describing the course of the analysis to be pursued. From this the attention is turned to the analysis proper, again following a funnelling approach, in the sense that the focus is first on the broad dichotomy between adopters and non-adopters, generally as well as in a spatial perspective. Figure 8.2 clearly shows a stratification between the two groups — adopters invariably display higher values on the variables shown, even though overlaps can be seen in the confidence intervals. These differences between adopters and non-adopters are also clear when the two groups are regarded from a spatial point of view (Figures

8.3-8.5). To an extent, however, the latter figures, when linked to the noted 'outward' movement of the adoption processes, also indicate that the differences are not a static feature but also one that may be accentuated by the adoption.

Finally, attention is focused on details of the adoption of the defined adoption-categories. The first observation concerning these is that they differ depending on the complexity of the adopted package. Generally, the more complex the adopted package, the higher the adopters tend to rate in the economic-, socio-economic- and informational-hierarchies defined by the 'independent variables'. Similar differences are generally found within the adoption-categories as well — i.e. between the relatively early vs the later adopters. In addition the analysis shows that early adoption and adoption of the more complex packages are related to what is here called the 'functional aspects' (links reaching beyond the immediate surroundings of the adopters). In sum, the analysis suggests that adoption is strongly related to the existing social- and economic-stratification in the sub-locations and that this stratification is further emphasised by the adoption process, the implications of this will be the principle topic in the next section.

9.3 Conclusions & Outlook

Two main conclusions can be drawn from the analyses presented. First, at face value, the adoption processes investigated at a low level of aggregation show traits that conform to the more general statements of spatial diffusion theory. This leads to the conclusion that diffusion patterns observed at higher levles of aggregation and then also the frequently used wave-analogies concerning these, are actually the sum of a large number of similar patterns at micro-levels. In a sense, the aggregated patterns observed seem to be scale-dependent in that the patterns seem not to be generated by a gradually moving diffusion wave, but are the sum of a large number of such diffusion patterns. At the same time they are not scale-dependent, as the macro-patterns are reflected in similar micro-patterns. From these observations it is not possible to state that the explanations for these patterns, particularly in the early theoretical formulations, are fully and directly applicable here. As indicated in Chapter II these explanations have generally been put in terms of the flow of information and that this flow is affected by distance-decay functions.

Information is naturally of critical importance in any diffusion process. The point here, however, concerns the relative importance of the informational factor. There is also the question concerning the extent to which the neighbourhood patterns inferred from the mapped diffusion patterns are attributable to information factors. Quite a large 'randomness' is also seen in the mapped diffusion patterns and it could be asked whether the inferred neighbourhood effects are truly such. As already quoted, Blaikie (1975:138) notes that: "if one look for contagious effects, ...neighbourhood effect in innovation diffusion, one will find it, ...".

The points raised in the preceding paragraph are related to the second main finding from the study, i.e. the adoption of the innovations studied is strongly related to the position of the potential adopters in the existing economic-, socio-economic- and informational-hierarchies. At this stage it is necessary to point out once again, that the conclusions drawn in the study are mainly from a relatively limited set of material — basically from sample surveys in two sub-locations involving 357 farm-units in all. In the drawing of more general conclusions, this reservation must be kept in mind.

A second reservation, which has been indicated but not dealt with explicitly, concerns the 'environment' into which the innovations are introduced. This refers to environmental aspects of an ecological nature, as well as in terms of a general level of development and integration into the existing market economy (for the latter cf. i.a. Kenyatta 1938 and Kitching 1980). Although the factors mentioned could cater for some of the differences found between, as well as within, the survey areas, it is not assumed that they would radically alter the conclusions drawn. If anything, they could only somewhat modify these. In a possible future study with a similar approach, the 'environmental aspects' ought to be included more explicitly.

The second main conclusion also indicates that adoption is related to the existing stratification in the sub-locations studied and that this existing stratification could be further strengthened by adoption. Stratification is defined here in terms of land-ownership, economic-position, the reception of incomes from sources other than farming, and the integration into networks operating at higher levels of aggregation than those constituting the sub-locations as such. A third reservation is necessary at this stage — the study focuses on only parts of the total farm economy. Thus, the observed processes of a stratification, naturally, cannot be ascribed to the adoption of the innovations studied only. It is, however, assumed that the adoption is a strong reflection of a general process of stratification and, moreover, is instrumental in enforcing this process.

That innovations of the type studied, have a stratifying effect on the societies of the Third World, into which they have been introduced, has been noted in several places in the more recent literature on the diffusion of innovations. The 'Green Revolution' technology, which basically is what is being studied here, and its effects, have largely been studied in an Asian context and similar, or worse, effects have been found (cf. Pearse 1980 — see also Lappé & Collins 1977). Empirical findings from other parts of the world, as well as more theoretical approaches to the problems, are found in for example Bengtsson (1983), Brown (1981) and Rogers (1983).

In the Kenyan perspective the conclusions drawn by different authors on the topic are slightly conflicting. Gerhart (1975) observes a relationship between farm-size, frequency of extension contacts and early adoption. He does not, however, see this as "preclusive of subsequent adoption by smaller farmers" (ibid.:47-8). Bager (1980), studying the Co-operative movement in Kenya, concludes that he finds no evidence of an increasing polarization among small-holders in Kenya — at least one caused by the co-operative movement. The status differences he finds within the co-operatives (between committee members and the rest of the peasants) he claims are "a difference of degree, not a qualitative difference." (ibid.:93).

Contrary to the views expressed by Bager, Carlsen (1980) concludes that the development in the rural areas of Kenya is characterized by a capital accumulation by rich-households "while poor-households are turned into a landless proletariat, ..." (ibid.:221). Kitching concludes that the "agrarian revolution" which followed the land enclosures and other measures taken as a consequence of the Swynnerton Plan in the mid 1950s, has not contributed to a lessened stratification in the rural areas. Rather the effect has been an increased stratification. He also concludes that the differentiation caused by the "agrarian revolution" meant a continuation of a process that was established already before the 1950s — actually a process which had been in operation throughout the colonial era and one which in

fact had been the consequence of a number of colonial policies. One important point he notices, is the fact that access to off-farm incomes is a very important factor in explaining the continued stratification. The latter point is
also made by Collier (1980), but then related to innovative
behaviour of smallholders. Both Kitching's and Collier's
conclusions concerning the importance of off-farm incomes
are in line with the conclusions drawn concerning the so
called 'functional aspects' in Chapter VIII.

Land-ownership is also an important factor influencing
the possibilities of participating or not in the "agrarian
revolution". Kitching (op.cit.) claims that those with less
than three acres are only rarely likely to participate.
Also in the present study, land-ownership has been noted
as an important factor in influencing adoption of the innovations studied. In some instances it seems as if the rural
societies in Africa are perceived as fairly egalitarian,
not least with respect to the distribution of land. This
has been refuted by Rudengren (1981) and in Dickenson et
al. (1983:106) a skewed land distribution in Kenya is obvious. From ILO (1981) it is possible to estimate that
about 75 per cent of the land holdings in Kenya are smaller
than 2 hectares and occupy only about 16 per cent of the
total arable area. About 54 per cent of the land holdings
are smaller than 1 hectare and occupy less than 8 per cent
of the total arable land. In contrast large farms constitute less than 3 per cent of the land holdings but occupy
about 30 per cent of the total arable land.

In view of the observations made above, it is necessary
to place the results from the present study into a perspective of the overall Kenyan development. To an extent it is
possible to agree with Bager (op.cit.) that the differences
found between adopters and non-adopters, as well as the
within and between adoption-category differences, are more
a matter of degree than definite qualitative differences.
In several instances the differences found are not very
great and the trends that could be inferred from the results do not always unequivocally point in a definite direction for each of the studied 'independent variables'.
In a wider perspective, judging from the combined results
given by the fairly large set of 'independent variables'
looked at for each defined sub-group (Appendices 1-30), the
conclusion must be one of an existing and probably growing
stratification in the rural areas of Kenya.

The adopter-categories studied seem to form fairly distinct strata, where the non-adopters are found at the bot-

tom and the adopters of the complete package are found at the top of generalized status/development hierarchies. Moreover, those found at the higher levels of these hierarchies, clearly receive preferential treatment from the different bodies created to support agricultural development — extension service, credit organizations etc. — which further enhances their possibilities of a future positive development in comparison with those at the lower levels. Thus, the results seem to indicate that the development of the Kenyan rural areas, follows a path similar to the one observed in many other places in the Third World, not least when this development is linked to the diffusion of innovations which are supposed to better the situation of the poor. What Pearse (1980:5) refers to as the "Talents-effects" are operative here as well.

> "For unto everyone that hath shall be
> given and he shall have abundance: but
> from him that hath not shall be taken
> away even that which he hath."
> (Matthew, Ch. 5, v 29)

A large number of issues are raised by this observation. The first issue is whether this is an acceptable development or not. Hydén (1983) may seem to claim that it is and, furthermore, that it may be a prerequisite for a positive development in Africa as well as, perhaps, the only way of bringing Africa out of its present crisis. His line of argument rests on the assumption that Africa is still largely in a pre-capitalist phase of development, where the peasants are poorly, if at all, integrated into a formal market-oriented economy. Furthermore, he argues that the state does not have the managerial capacity to promote development through a "Blueprint Approach", i.e. a macro-economic planning (ibid.:63-67).

In line with the title of his work he also claims that there are "No Shortcuts to Progress" and that the African societies will have to go through a capitalist state of development in order to drag the "uncaptured peasantry" out of their pre-capitalist mode of production into a market-oriented mode in which a formal national economy could be established. In the process, an internal bourgeoisie must be allowed to develop and the class conflicts that exist must be further strenghtened. In order to mitigate some of the negative effects of such a development he suggests that an emphasis should be put on supporting Non-Government organizations and other local initiatives. Thus, in sum, the proposals put forward by Hydén are such that an increasing stratification is not necessarily evil. Instead it could be seen as a means of achieving an integration of the peasantry into a market economy, as well as fostering a class-polarization and class-consciousness that in the long run should lead to a positive development.

The latter discussion also leads back to the quotation with which the present work started. The two critical concepts in Mabogunje's quotation (1980:114) are effective and innovations. In a sense Mabogunje's claim is truistic — of course development has as a prerequisite, the diffusion of innovations, be it in the form of implements, seed or organizational structures. The two key concepts are not value-free, however. Innovations of different kinds are more or less suited to different groups in a society — cf. the concepts "Landlord-biased", "Neutral" and "Peasant-biased" innovations introduced by Griffin (1972). The efficiency criterion must also be placed in perspective of the development that is envisaged. As is obvious from this one, as well as a large number of other studies, the diffusion of innovations can lead to a differential impact for different groups of potential adopters. In taking a "Welfare approach" (Brown 1981:Ch.8) as opposed to a purely capitalistic development (which essentially also is what Mabogunje does in his work) the efficiency criterion must be formulated in terms of a wide coverage of adoption and, thus, that a majority of the potential adopters gain access to the benefits which should accrue from adoption.

To achieve a situation that could cater for a 'Welfare approach' in the dissemination of innovations, particularly the kinds of innovations studied here, would in the present situation call for a number of measures at different levels. The principal criterion in all of these, is to increase the access to the innovations combined with increased access to principal factors of production for a larger number of the potential adopters. With this must also be considered that the innovations function and are generally adopted as 'Bundles of Innovations'. If proper information is disseminated on the necessary managerial aspects, the full potential of the Hybrid Maize component of the 'Bundle' can be utilized. Thus, the interdependencies of the innovations must be maintained as an integral part of the suggested recommendations.

On the one hand, this would entail an easier access to supply points for the innovations involved. Although, in the cases looked at here, access to Hybrid Maize seed is generally good, it should be noted that the mobility space of the majority of farmers is often very restricted and, thus, even the present day network may be to thinly spread to enable a wide adoption.

On the other hand, it will be necessary to increase access to credit, in kind or cash, in order to promote adoption. Today, adoption as shown here as well as in Carlsen (1980), Collier (1980) and Kitching (1980), is very much dependent on off-farm sources of income. From a 'welfare' point of view it is not acceptable that the diffusion of innovations in the rural areas should depend on such incomes — incomes that in turn are dependent on the demographic structure of individual rural households and the regional availability of off-farm incomes. A viable rural development must naturally be dependent on farmers being able to reap their livelihood from their farms.

Also among the measures to be taken at a fairly low and direct level, would be to improve the extension service. Criticism against the functioning of the extension service has been levelled by several authors writing on widely different areas (cf. i.a. Rogers 1983). In the Kenyan context a lot of this criticism is summarized by Heyer (1976). This study, as well as many others, has brought up the fact that extension agents give a preferential treatment to already well-off farmers. One possible way out of this, would be to engage more in group extension activities as suggested by Ascroft et al. (1971) and also by Rogers (1983).

The most important measure, however, would be to distribute the factors of production more evenly among the potential adopters and then pricipally land. Pearse (1980) notes that the only places where the 'Green Revolution Techiques' could be said to have been successful are where a determined effort has been made to redistribute this resource and then add the supporting activities necessary for an effective diffusion. The countries he refers to are Japan, Taiwan and China and it is thus not possible to infer any direct political implications from these. The important lesson to learn, however, is that land-redistribution must be backed by and followed up by a very clear political determinination to achieve a genuine redistribution. This determination must not restrict itself to only a reshuffling of land-ownership, but must also create viable production opportunities for those being allocated land. The latter entails an active policy to integrate the farmers in the newly redistributed areas into the wider economy beyond mere subsistence. More concretely it includes the practical measures already discussed, viz. the creation of supply nodes, credit facilities, marketing facilities, infrastructural development etc. The number of failed and dilluted land-reforms, where this political will has not been present, are almost too numerous to mention. In the Kenyan case a determined land-redistribution policy should be a prerequisite for any rural development — disregarding the innovation diffusion aspect — in the light of the figures presented above from ILO (1981).

A 'Welfare approach' to rural development is to the present author the more acceptable of the options given here. The situation and the prospects for a majority of countries in the Third World, perhaps particularly so in Africa, is today not very encouraging. The possibility of achieving such a development could, with Hydén (1983), be rightfully questioned. In the short term, at least, no signs exist that indicate such a clear political determination as would be necessary to achieve a viable rural development. From there to conclude that a purely capitalist development is the only feasible road out of the stagnation/regression, seen today in several African countries, and elsewhere, is a step that the present author is not prepared to take.

Bibliography

Acland, J.D. (1971): East African Crops, An introduction to the production of field and plantation crops in Kenya, Tanzania and Uganda. Longman, FAO. Singapore.

Allen, A.Y. (1969): Maize Diamonds. Appendix to Ogada, F. (1969).

---(1970): Early planting of maize is essential for high yields. Kenya Farmer, March 1970. Reprint from Kenya Seed Company Ltd.

---(1972): Nitrogen is essential for high maize yields. Tran Nzoia Post Show Supplement. Reprint by Kenya Seed Co. Ltd.

---(1974): Will fertilizers be profitable on maize in the future?. Tranz Nzoia Post Show Supplement. Reprint by Kenya Seed Co. Ltd.

Ascroft, J.R., Chege, F.E., Kariuki, J.F., Roling, N.G. (1971): Accelerating the flow of new ideas to rural people. A proposal for a pilot extension training project in Nyeri. Institute of Development Studies, Discussion Paper No. 133. Nairobi.

Bager, T. (1980): Marketing Co-operatives and Peasants in Kenya. Scandinavian Institute of African Studies. Uppsala.

Bengtsson, B.M.I. (1983): Rural Development Research and Agricultural Innovations, A comparative study of agricultural changes in a historical perspective, and agricultural research policy for rural development. Swedish University of Agricultural Sciences, Dep. of Plant Husbandry. Uppsala.

Blaikie, P.M. (1973): The Spatial Structure of Information Networks and Innovative Behaviour in the Ziz Valley, Southern Morocco. Geografiska Annaler, Vol. 55B, No. 2. Stockholm.

---(1975): Family Planning in India, Diffusion and Policy. Edward Arnold. London.

---(1978): The Theory of the Spatial Diffusion of Innovations: a spacious cul-de-sac. In Progress of Geography 1978/2. Edward Arnold. London.

Blaut, J.M. (1977): Two Views of Diffusion. Annals of the Association of American Geographers, Vol. 67, No. 3.

Brookfield, H. (1975): Interdependent Development. Methuen & Co. Ltd. London.

Brown, L.A. (1968a): Diffusion Processes and Location, A conceptual framework and bibliography. Regional Science Research Institute. Philadelphia.

---(1968b): Diffusion Dynamics, A review and revision of the quantitative

232

theory of the spatial diffusion of innovations. Lund Studies in Geography, Ser. B. Human Geography, No. 29. Gleerup. Lund

---(1975): The Market and Infrastructure Context of Adoption: A spatial perspective on the diffusion of innovation. Economic Geography, Vol. 51, No. 3. Clark University. Worcester.

---(1981): Innovation Diffusion, A new perspective. Methuen. New York.

Brown, L.A. & Cox, K.R. (1971): Empirical Regularities in the Diffusion of Innovations. Annals of the Association of American Geographers, Vol. 61, No. 3.

Brown, L.A. and Moore, E.G. (1969): Diffusion Research in Geography: a perspective. In Progress in Geography, Vol. 1. Edward Arnold. Bristol.

Brown, L.A. and Lentnek, B. (1973): Innovation Diffusion in a Developing Economy: A Meso-Scale View, Studies in the Diffusion of Innovations, Discussion Paper Series, No. 14. Dep. of Geography, Ohio State University.

Byrnes, F.C. (1968): Some Missing Variables in Diffusion Research and Innovation Strategy. The Agricultural Development Council Inc. New York.

Campell, P.A. (1975): Appropriate Technology Innovation for Rural Industrialization in LDC:s. Institute of Development Studies, University of Nairobi, Working Papers No. 252. Nairobi.

Carlsen, J. (1980): Economic and Social Transformation in Rural Kenya. Scandinavian Institute of African Studies. Uppsala.

Carlstein, T. (1970a): Tidsorganisation och Social Struktur hos Tanala. Inst. för Socialantropologi/Etnografi, Göteborgs Universitet. Göteborg.

---(1970b): Införandet av Skolgång i ett Agrart Bysamhälle. Inst. för Kulturgeografi och Ekonomisk Geografi, Lunds Universitet. Lund.

---(1973): Population Activities and Settlement as a System, The case of shifting cultivation. Dep. of Geography, Univ. of Lund. Lund.

---(1974): Time Allocation, Innovation and Agrarian Change, Outline of a research project. Dep. of Geography, Univ. of Lund. Lund.

---(1977): Innovation, Time Allocation and Time-Space Packing. Dep. of Geography, Univ. of Lund. Rapporter och Notiser No. 35. Lund.

Collier, P. (1980): Poverty and Growth in Kenya. World Bank Staff Working Paper No. 389.

Cone, L.W. & Lipscomb, J.F. (1972): The Histroy of Kenya Agriculture. University Press of Africa. Nairobi.

Coughenour, C.M. (1964): The Rate of Technological Diffusion among Locality Groups. American Journas of Sociology, Vol. LXIX, No. 4.

Dickenson, J.P. et al. (1983): A Geography of The Third World. Methuen & Co. London.

Dodd, S.C. (1955): Diffusion is Predictable: Testing Probability Models for Laws of Interaction. American Sociological Review, No. 4.

Dumont, R. (1969): Tanzanian Agriculture after the Arusha Declaration.

The United Republic of Tanzania. Dar es Salaam.

Edmonson, M.S. (1961): Neolithic Diffusion Rates. Current Anthropology, Vol. 2, No. 2.

Fawcett, J.T.; Somboonsuk, A.; Khaisang, S. (1967): Thailand: An Analysis of Time and Distance Factors at an IUD Clinic in Bangkok. Studies in Family Planning, No. 19. Population Council. New York.

Fuller, G. (1974): On the Spatial Diffusion of Fertility Decline: The Distance to Clinic Variable in a Chilean Community. Economic Geography, Vol. 50, No. 4. Clark University. Worcester

Garst, R.D. (1972): The Spatial Diffusion of Agricultural Innovations in Kisii District, Kenya. PhD Thesis, Michigan State University, Department of Geography.

---(1974a): Spatial Diffusion in Rural Kenya: The impact of Infrastructure and Centralized Decision Making. Studies in the Diffusion of Innovations, Discussion Paper Series No. 17. Dep. of Geography, The Ohio State University.

---(1974b): Innovation Diffusion among the Gusii of Kenya. Economic Geography, Vol. 50, No. 4. Clark University. Worcester.

Gerhart, J.D. (1974): The Diffusion of Hybrid Maize in Western Kenya. PhD Thesis, Princeton University.

---(1975): The Diffusion of Hybrid Maize in Western Kenya. Abridged by CIMMYT - Centro Internacional de Mejorament de Maiz y Trigo. Mexico City.

Girling, P. (1968): The Diffusion of Banks in the United States, 1781 to 1861. Masters Thesis, Penn State University.

Gould, P. (1960): Transportation in Ghana. Northwestern Studies in Geography, No. 5. Evanston.

---(1969): Spatial Diffusion. Commission on College Geographic Resource Paper No. 4. Association of American Geographers. Washington DC.

---(1979): "Geography 1957-1977: The Augean Period". Annals of the Association of American Geographers, Vol. 69, No. 1.

Grabner, F. (1911): Methode der Ethnologie. Heidelberg (Germany), Carl Winter (cited in Heine-Geldern 1968).

Griffin, K. (1972): The green revolution: an economic analysis. United Nations Research Institute for Social Development - UNRISD. Geneva.

Grigg, D. (1982): The Dynamics of Agricultural Change. Hutchinson University Library. London.

Grilchies, Z. (1957): Hybrid Corn: An Explanation in the Economics of Technological Change. Econometrica, Vol 25, No. 4.

Gyllström, B. (1977a): Ekonomiska Utvecklingsstrategier - en diskussion av perspektiv och teoribildningar. Dep. of Social and Economic Geography, Rapporter och Notiser No. 31, Univ. of Lund. Lund.

---(1977b): The Organization of Production as a Space-Modelling Mechanism in Underdeveloped Countries, The case of Tea Production in Kenya. Gleerup. Lund.

Hanham, R.Q. (1973): Diffusion of Innovations from a Supply Perspective:

An application to the artificial insemination of cattle in Southern Sweden. PhD Thesis, The Ohio State University.

Hansen, F. (1979): Kulturgeografiens object: Samfundsmæssige processer opfattet som rum. Häften för Kritiska Studier, Nr. 2-3. Lund.

Harvey, D. (1973): Social Justice and the City. Edward Arnold. London.

Hazelden, E.J.R. (1976): Maize production in Lake Shore Nyanza. Mimeographed report from KSC, Kitale.

Heine-Geldern, R. (1968): Cultural Diffusion. In Sills, D.L. (ed); International Encyclopedia of the Social Sciences, Vol. 4 (pp. 167-73). Macmillan & The Free Press. New York.

Hesselmark, O. (1976): Maize yields in Kenya 1975. Maize and Produce Board. Nairobi.

Hettne, B. (1982): Development Theory and the Third World. SAREC - Swedich Agency for Research Coopreation with Developing Countries, R2:1982. Stockholm.

Heyer, J. (ed.) (1976): Agricultural Development in Kenya. East African Publishing House. Nairobi.

Heyer, J.; Ireri, D.; Morris, J. (1971): Rural Development in Kenya. East African Publishing House. Nairobi.

Huang, J-C. and Gould, P. (1974): Diffusion in an Urban Hierarchy: The case of Rotary Clubs. Economic Geography, Vol. 50, No. 4. Clark University. Worcester.

Hudson, J.C. (1972): Geographical Diffusion Theory. Northwestern Studies in Geography, No. 19. Evanston.

Huke, R.E. & Duncan, J. (1969): Spatial Aspects of HYV Diffusion. Studies in the Diffusion of Innovations. Discussion Paper Series, No. 6. Dep. of Geography, The Ohio State University.

Hydén, G. (1983): No Shortcuts to Progress, African development management in perspective. Heineman. London.

Hägerstrand, T. (1952): The Propagation of Innovation Waves. Lund Studies in Geography, Ser. B. Human Geography, No. 4. Gleerup. Lund.

---(1953): Innovationsförloppet ur Korologisk Synpunkt. Meddelanden från Lunds Universitets Geografiska Institution. Avhandlingar XXV. Gleerup. Lund.

---(1965a): A Monte-Carlo Approach to Diffusion. European Journal of Sociology, Vol. 6.

---(1965b): Quantiative Techniques for Analysis of the Spread of Information on Technology. In Anderson, C.A. and Bowman, M.J. (eds.) (1965): Education and Economic Development. Aldine Publishing Co. Chicago.

---(1966): Aspects of Spatial Structure of Social Communication and the Diffusion of Innovations. Regional Science Association Papers, Vol. XVI.

---(1968): The Diffusion of Innovations. In Sills, D.L. (ed.) International Encyclopedia of the Social Sciences, Vol. 4 (pp. 174-78). Macmillan & The Free Press, New York.

---(1974): On the Socio-Technical Ecology and the study of Innovations. Dep. of Geography, Univ. of Lund, Rapporter och Notiser No. 10, Lund.

IDR (1973): Dualism and Rural Development in East Africa. Institute of Development Research. Copenhagen.

ILO (1972): Employment Incomes and Equality - a strategy for increasing productive employment in Kenya. International Labour Office. Geneva.

ILO (1981): Rural Development, Employment and Incomes in Kenya. International Labour Office - Jobs and Skills Programme for Africa (JASPA). Prepared by Ian Livingstone. Addis Ababa.

Johnson, E.A. (1970): The Organization of Space in Developing Countries. Harvard University Press. Cambridge.

Jones, G.E. (1963): The Diffusion of Agricultural Innovations. Journal of Agricultural Economics, Vol. XVI, No. 3.

Jonsson, J. (1975): Diffusion of Agricultural Innovations in Chilalo Awraja, Ethiopia. Institute of Development Research, Haile Sellassie I University. Addis Ababa.

Josefsson, G. & Lindström, B. (1979): Om rumsbegreppet inom samhällsgeografin. Häften för Kritiska Studier, Nr. 2-3. Lund.

Katz, E. (1968): Interpersonal Influence. In Sills, D.L. (ed.) International Encyclopedia of the Social Sciences, Vol. 4 (pp. 178-85). Macmillan & The Free Press. New York.

Katz, E.; Levin, M.L. and Hamilton, H. (1963): "Traditions of Research on the Diffusion of Innovations. American Sociological Review.

Kitching, G. (1980): Class and Economic Change in Kenya, The making of an African Petite-Bourgeoisie. Yale University Press. New Haven and London.

Kenyatta, J. (1938): Facing Mount Kenya, The tribal life of the Gikuyu. Secker & Warburg, London.

KSC - Kenya Seed Company Ltd., Kitale, Kenya.

---(undated): Recommendations for Planting Hybrid Maize. Information sheet in english and kiswahili in each packet of seed.

---(1967): Report on the Distribution of Hybrid Seed Maize, Fertilizers and Chemical in the Small-Scale Farming Areas. 1966/67 Season. Kenya Seed Co. Ltd. Kitale.

---(1972): Hybrid Seed maize Stockists 1971/72. Kenya Seed Co. Ltd. Kitale.

---(1975): Kenya Seed Company Limited - Hybrid Seed 1975/75 Sales Figures. Kenya Seed Co. Ltd. Kitale.

---(1976): Hybrid Seed Maize Stockists 1975/76. (Mimeographed) Kenya Seed Co. Ltd. Kitale.

Kuhn, T. (1962): The Structure of Scientific Revolutions. Univ. of Chicago Press. Ghicago.

Lappé, F.M. & Collins, J. (1977): Food First, Beyond the Myth of Scarcity. Houghton Mifflin Co. Boston.

Lele, U. (1975): The Design of Rural Development, Lessons from Africa.

Published for the World Bank by the John Hopkins University Press.
Baltimore and London.

Lewis, W.A. (1978): The Evaluation of the International Economic Order.
Princeton University Press.

Linton, R. (1936): The study of man. Appelton Century Crafts. New York.
(cited in Rogers & Shoemaker 1971)

Lundqvist, J. (1975): Local and Central Impulses for Change and
Development, A case study of Morogoro District, Tanzania. Meddelanden
från Göteborgs Universitets Geografiska Institutioner, Ser. B,
Nr. 44. Universitetsforlaget, Bergen-Oslo. Tromsø

Mabogunje, A.L. (1980): The Development Process, A spatial perspective.
Hutchinson University Library. London.

Maclennan, D. (1973): A re-examination and Reconsideration of the
Neighbourhood Effect in the Diffusion of Innovations at the Micro-
Scale. (Mimeographed) Dep. of Geography, University of Glasgow.

Manners, R.A. (1962): Land Use, Labour and the Growth of the Market
Economy in Kipsigis Country. Ch. 19 in Bohanan, P. and Dalton, G.
(eds.) (1962) Markets in Africa. Northwestern University Press.

Mayfield, R.C. & Yapa, L.S. (1974): Information Fields in Rural
Mysore. Economic Geography, Vol. 50, No. 4. Clark University.
Worcester.

Mbithi, R.M. (1972): Innovation in Rural Development. Institute for
Development Studies, Univ. of Nairobi. Discussion Paper No. 158.
Nairobi.

Mellor, J.W. (1966): The Economics of Agricultural development.
Cornell University Press. Ithaca.

Miller, C. (1973): The Lunatic Express, An entertainment in imperia-
lism. Ballentines Books INC. New York.

Misra, R.P. (1968): Diffusion of Agricultural Innovations. Univ. of
Mysore. Mysore.

Morrill, R.L. and Manninen, D. (1975): Critical Parameters of Spatial
Diffusion Processes. Economic Geography, Vol. 51, No. 3. Clark
University. Worcester.

Mosher, A.T. (1969): Creating a Progressive Rural Structure to Serve
a Modern Agriculture. Agricultural Development Council. New York.

Mott, F.L. and Mott, S.H. (1980): Kenya's Record Population Growth:
A Dilemma of Development. population Bulletin, Vol. 35, No. 3.
Population Reference Bureau Inc. Washington DC.

Naidu, N. (1975): Spatial Aspects of Social change, A Social Geography
of the Kikuyu. Summary written by Appalraju, J. and Rundquist F-M.
Lund Studies in Geography, Ser. B. human Geography, No. 41.
Gleerup. Lund.

Norcliffe, G.B. (1977): Inferential Statistics for Geographers.
Hutchinson University Library. London.

Nordström, O. (1957): Plogen som Innovation. Svensk Geografisk Årsbok,
Årgång 33. Gleerup. Lund.

Odingo, R.S. (1971): The Kenya Highlands, Land Use and Agricultural
    Development. East African Publishing House. Nairobi.
Ogada, F. (1969): The Role of Maize Research in Stimulating Agricul-
    tural Progress in Kenya. Paper presented and The East African
    Agricultural Economics Society Conference 1969.
Pearse, A. (1980): Seeds of Plenty, Seeds of Want, Social and Economic
    Implications of the green Revolution. Oxford University Press.
    Clarendon Press. Oxford.
Pedersen, P-O. (1971): Innovation Diffusion in Urban Systems. In
    Hägerstrand, T. and Kuklinski, A.R. (eds.) (1971): Information
    Systems for Regional Development - A seminar. Lund Studies in
    Geography, Ser. B. Human Geography, No. 37. Gleerup. Lund.
Pyle, G. (1969): The Diffusion of Cholera in the United States in
    the Nineteenth Century. Geographical Analysis, Vol. 1.
Ramachandran, R. (1969): Spatial Diffusion of Innovations in Rural
    India: A case study of the spread of irrigation. PhD Thesis,
    Clark University. Worcester.
RoK - Republic of Kenya.
---(1970a): National Atlas of Kenya, Third edition 1970. Republic of
    Kenya. Nairobi.
---(1970b): Kenya population Census 1969, Volume I. republic of Kenya.
    Nairobi.
---(1972): Ministry of Agriculture, Annual Report of the Research Di-
    vision 1970. Republic of Kenya. Nairobi.
---(1974): Development Plan 1974-78. Republic of Kenya. Nairobi.
---(1975): Statistical Abstracts 1975. Cenral Bureau of Statistics.
    Ministry of Finance and Planning. Republic of Kenya. Nairobi.
---(1976): Economic Survey 1976: Central Bureau of Statistics. Mini-
    stry of Finance and Planning. Republic of Kenya. Nairobi.
---(1977): IRS - Integrated Rural Survey 1974-75. Central Bureau of
    Statistics. Ministry of Finance and Planning. Republic of Kenya.
    Nairobi.
---(1980): Statistical Abstracts 1980. Central Bureau of Statistics.
    Ministry of Economic Planning and Development. Republic of Kenya.
    Nairobi.
---(1981a): Statistical Abstracts 1981. Central Bureau of Statistics.
    Ministry of Economic Planning and Development. Republic of Kenya.
    Nairobi.
---(1981b): Sessional Paper No. 4 of 1981 on National Food Policy.
    Republic of Kenya. Nairobi.
Riddell, J.B. (1970): The Spatial Dynamics of Modernization in Sierra
    Leone. Northwestern University Press. Evanston.
Rogers, E.M. (1962): Diffusion of Innovations. The Free Press. New York.
---(1983): Diffusion of Innovations, Third Edition. The Free Press.
    New York.
Rogers, E.M. & Shoemaker, F.F. (1971): Communication of Innovations.

The Free Press. New York.

Roling, N.; Chege, F. and Ascroft, J. (1973): Innovation and Equity in Rural Development Research and Field Experiments in Kenya. Institute of Development Studies, University of Nairobi. Working Paper, No. 84. Nairobi.

Rudengren, J. (1981): Peasants by Preference? Socio-Economic and Environmental Aspects of Rural Development in Tanzania. EFI - The Economic Research Institute, Stockholm School of Economics. Stockholm.

Rundquist, F-M. (1977): "Settlement Schemes" i Kenya. Geografiska Notiser, 1977:3. Lund.

---(1982): Befolkningstillväxt och befolkningsomfördelning i Tanzania 1967-78. Geografiska Notiser 1982:2. Lund.

Ryan, B. and Gross, N.C. (1943): The Diffusion of Hybrid Seed Corn in Two Iowa Communities. Rural Sociology, 8:15-24. (Cited in Hägerstrand 1952, Rogers 1962, Rogers & Shoemaker 1971 and Rogers 1983)

Schrimpf, N. (1966): Maize, Cultivation and Fertilization. Ruhr-Stickstoff AG. bochum.

Semple, R.K. and Brown, L.A. (1974): Cones of Resolution in Spatial Diffusion Studies: A perspective. Studies in the Diffusion of Innovations. Discussion Paper Series, No. 2. Dep. of Geography, The Ohio State University.

Semple, R.K. & Brown, L.A. & Brown, M.A. (1975): Propagator Supported Diffusion Processe: Agency Strategies and the Innovation Establishment Interface. Studies in the Diffusion of Innovations. Discussion Paper Series, No. 18. Dep. of Geography, The Ohio State University.

Smith, D.M. (1979): Where The Grass is Greener, Living in an Unequal World. Penguin Books Ltd. Harmondsworth.

Soya, E.W. (1968): The Geography of Modernization in Kenya. A spatial analysis of Social, Economic and Political Change. Syracuse University Press. Syracuse.

Swedish Univ. of Agricultural Sciences (1981): Kenya: A study of the Agricultural Sector. Rural Dev. Studies, No. 11. Swedish Univ. of Agricultural Sciences. Uppsala.

Tarde, G. (1903): The Laws of Imitation (tr. by Parson, E.C.). Holt. New York. (Cited in Rogers & Shoemaker 1971)

Thrift, N. (1977): An Introduction to Time-Geography. Geo Abstracts Ltd. University of East Anglia. Norwich.

Törnqvist, G. (1967): TV-ägandets utveckling i Sverige 1956-65. Industriens Utredningsinstitut. Almqvist & Wiksell. Stockholm.

Verburgt, W.H. (1969): The Kenya Seed Company Ltd. and the Diffusion of Hybrid Seed Maize in Kenya. Paper presented at The East African Agricultural Economic Society Conference.

Webster, C.C. & Wilson, P.W. (1966): Agriculture in the Tropics. Longman. London.

White, P. and Woods, R. (eds.) (1980): The geographical impact of Migration. Longman. London.

Widberg, J. (1979): <u>Traditionell och radikal geografi</u> - en översikt.
Häften för Kritiska Studier, Nr. 2-3. Lund.

Woods, R. <u>Theoretical Population geography</u>. Longman. London.

Yapa, L.S. (1977): <u>The Green Revolution: A Diffusion Model</u>. Annals
of the Association of American Geographers, No. 67.

Yapa, L.S. and Mayfield, R.C. (1978): <u>Non-adoption of Innovations:</u>
<u>Evidence from Discrimant Analysis</u>. Economic Geography, Vol. 54,
No. 2. Clark University. Worcester.

Zelinsky, W. (1967): <u>Classical Town Names in the United States</u>.
Geographical Review, Vol. LVII.

Aquist, A-C. (1981): <u>Kuhns Paradigmteori: Ett försök till tillämpning</u>
<u>på kulturgeografi</u>. Institutionen för Kulturgeografi och Ekonomisk
Geografi vid Lunds Universitet. Rapporter och Notiser, Nr. 61.
Lund.

IGANA

APPENDIX 1:A Total Population broken down on DIST/SO - MEAN VALUES.

TOTAL POP.	S	n	VAL/ LS	VAL/ BH	VAL/ CA	EXP/ LA	EXP/ HO	INC/ ATO	VAL/ CAT	LO/ LR	LO/ ADL	LO/ LOT	LAB/ HP	LAB/ HT	EXT/ FQ	LAB/ EQ	FQV/ MA	ARE/ HM	ARE/ M	ARE/ CC	ARE/ RC	PC/ HMTA	PC/ MTA	PC/ CCTA	PC/ HMA
T.POP.		172	191	118	92	395	475	2061	458	1.6	0.5	2.1	1.1	0.2	11.7	4.3	2.9	0.2	0.5	0.3	0.0	8.1	29.7	13.6	32.0
T.POP.//	1	44	181	124	65	554	371	2082	413	1.9	0.7	2.6	0.3	0.3	12.2	3.7	3.4	0.1	0.4	0.3	0.0	6.4	22.2	12.2	29.1
DIST/SO	2	87	183	121	107	399	456	2088	474	1.5	0.5	2.0	0.2	0.2	10.9	4.3	2.6	0.2	0.6	0.3	0.0	9.0	31.2	13.6	33.7
	3	41	217	105	88	217	629	1980	473	1.6	0.2	1.8	0.1	0.1	12.9	5.2	3.1	0.1	0.5	0.2	0.0	8.2	34.7	14.9	31.7
T.POP.//	1	74	209	131	73	516	385	2027	468	1.9	0.6	2.7	0.3	0.3	10.9	4.3	3.1	0.2	0.5	0.3	0.0	8.4	25.1	12.9	37.1
DIST/SO	2	98	177	108	106	304	545	2087	450	1.4	0.3	1.7	0.2	0.2	12.3	4.4	2.8	0.1	0.5	0.2	0.0	7.9	33.3	14.1	28.2

APPENDIX 1:B Total Population broken down on DIST/SO - MEDIAN VALUES

TOTAL POP.	S	n	VAL/ LS	VAL/ BH	VAL/ CA	EXP/ LA	EXP/ HO	INC/ ATO	VAL/ CAT	LO/ LR	LO/ ADL	LO/ LOT	LAB/ HP	LAB/ HT	EXT/ FQ	LAB/ EQ	FQV/ MA	ARE/ HM	ARE/ M	ARE/ CC	ARE/ RC	PC/ HMTA	PC/ MTA	PC/ CCTA	PC/ HMA
T.POP.		172	150	89	43	2	301	1021	345	1.5	0.01	1.7	0.2	0.2	2.4	3.9	2.1	0.03	0.4	0.2	0.0	0.1	26.7	10.5	4.1
T.POP.//	1	44	98	89	33	2	375	977	287	1.5	0.02	1.8	0.2	0.2	2.5	3.8	2.2	0.02	0.4	0.2	0.0	0.1	18.1	7.6	5.0
DIST/SO	2	87	150	89	48	2	300	1011	361	1.4	0.02	1.8	0.1	0.2	2.4	3.8	2.0	0.03	0.6	0.2	0.0	0.1	30.8	10.5	8.8
	3	41	179	88	42	1	398	1100	369	1.6	0.03	1.7	0.1	0.1	2.3	5.2	2.1	0.02	0.4	0.2	0.0	0.2	33.2	13.8	23.2
T.POP.//	1	74	149	90	48	3	365	1162	362	1.6	0.02	1.9	0.2	0.2	3.5	3.9	2.2	0.03	0.4	0.2	0.0	0.1	23.2	10.0	5.4
DIST/SO	2	98	150	89	37	1	300	957	321	1.3	0.01	1.6	0.1	0.1	2.1	3.9	2.0	0.02	0.4	0.2	0.0	0.1	31.3	11.8	6.7

APPENDIX 1:C Total Population broken down on DIST/MA - MEAN VALUES.

TOTAL POP.	S	n	VAL/ LS	VAL/ BH	VAL/ CA	EXP/ LA	EXP/ HO	INC/ ATO	VAL/ CAT	LO/ LR	LO/ ADL	LO/ LOT	LAB/ HP	LAB/ HT	EXT/ FQ	LAB/ EQ	FQV/ MA	ARE/ HM	ARE/ M	ARE/ CC	ARE/ RC	PC/ HMTA	PC/ MTA	PC/ CCTA	PC/ HMA
T.POP.//	1	70	222	117	135	2	299	1084	527	1.6	0.5	2.1	0.3	0.3	10.2	4.4	3.4	0.03	0.5	0.3	0.0	9.5	28.1	14.1	38.0
DIST/MA	2	40	191	123	62	2	300	934	433	1.5	0.1	1.6	0.2	0.2	16.5	4.7	2.2	0.05	0.5	0.3	0.0	9.2	34.5	18.1	32.5
	3	62	155	116	62	2	401	914	396	1.7	0.7	2.4	0.2	0.2	10.2	4.0	2.9	0.1	0.5	0.2	0.0	5.9	28.6	10.1	25.0
T.POP.//	1	79	213	112	125	2	365	1083	503	1.6	0.4	2.0	0.2	0.2	9.3	4.5	3.2	0.1	0.5	0.3	0.0	8.9	28.4	14.4	35.0
DIST/MA	2	93	171	123	64	2	400	976	420	1.6	0.5	2.1	0.2	0.2	13.7	4.2	2.7	0.2	0.5	0.2	0.0	7.5	30.9	12.9	29.6

APPENDIX 1:D Total Population broken down on DIST/MA - MEDIAN VALUES

TOTAL POP.	S	n	VAL/ LS	VAL/ BH	VAL/ CA	EXP/ LA	EXP/ HO	INC/ ATO	VAL/ CAT	LO/ LR	LO/ ADL	LO/ LOT	LAB/ HP	LAB/ HT	EXT/ FQ	LAB/ EQ	FQV/ MA	ARE/ HM	ARE/ M	ARE/ CC	ARE/ RC	PC/ HMTA	PC/ MTA	PC/ CCTA	PC/ HMA
T.POP.//	1	70	190	90	49	2	299	1084	391	1.6	0.02	1.9	0.1	0.2	2.5	3.9	2.2	0.03	0.4	0.2	0.0	0.1	23.6	12.6	9.5
DIST/MA	2	40	148	89	37	2	300	934	321	1.4	0.02	1.6	0.1	0.2	2.5	4.7	1.9	0.05	0.4	0.2	0.0	0.4	33.7	11.1	24.1
	3	62	91	89	33	2	401	914	252	1.4	0.02	1.7	0.2	0.2	2.2	3.8	2.2	0.1	0.4	0.2	0.0	0.1	28.6	7.0	8.7
T.POP.//	1	79	180	89	45	2	299	1083	376	1.6	0.01	1.9	0.1	0.2	2.4	4.0	2.1	0.03	0.4	0.2	0.0	0.1	25.1	12.5	8.3
DIST/MA	2	93	101	89	37	2	400	976	289	1.4	0.02	1.7	0.1	0.1	2.5	3.9	2.0	0.02	0.4	0.2	0.0	0.1	30.8	8.3	10.8

APPENDIX 2:A   Total values for the studied Adoption-Categories - MEAN VALUES

ADOPT. CAT.	n	LS	VAL/BH	VAL/CA	VAL/LA	EXP/HO	INC/ATO	VAL/CAT	LO/LR	LO/ADL	LO/LOT	LAB/HP	LAB/HT	EXT/FQ	LAB/EQ	FQV/MA	ARE/HM	ARE/M	ARE/CC	ARE/RC	PC/HMTA	PC/MTA	PC/CCTA	PC/HMA
ADY/SFP	52	301	156	169	885	512	3993	686	1.8	0.8	2.6	0.5	0.5	20.0	4.5	3.2	0.5	0.5	0.4	0.0	22.9	24.7	16.8	94.5
ADY/FP	45	181	110	72	196	523	1605	444	1.7	0.5	2.2	0.1	1.0	13.6	4.9	3.0	0.0	0.0	0.3	0.0	0.0	31.8	16.8	0.0

APPENDIX 2:B   Total values for the studied Adoption-Categories - MEDIAN VALUES

ADOPT. CAT.	n	LS	VAL/BH	VAL/CA	VAL/LA	EXP/HO	INC/ATO	VAL/CAT	LO/LR	LO/ADL	LO/LOT	LAB/HP	LAB/HT	EXT/FQ	LAB/EQ	FQV/MA	ARE/HM	ARE/M	ARE/CC	ARE/RC	PC/HMTA	PC/MTA	PC/CCTA	PC/HMA
ADY/SFP	52	270	95	95	100	498	1489	584	1.7	0.02	1.9	0.3	0.5	12.1	4.7	2.1	0.40	0.4	0.4	0.0	21.2	23.2	13.0	99.1
ADY/FP	45	150	89	47	2	300	1210	361	1.6	0.02	1.9	0.1	0.1	4.0	4.5	2.1	0.00	0.6	0.2	0.2	0.0	31.3	12.5	0.0

APPENDIX 3   Comparison between Adopters and Non-Adopters broken down on DIST/SO and DIST/MA - MEAN VALUES

	S	n	LS	VAL/BH	VAL/CA	VAL/LA	EXP/HO	INC/ATO	VAL/CAT	LO/LR	LO/ADL	LO/LOT	LAB/HP	LAB/HT	EXT/FQ	LAB/EQ	FQV/MA	ARE/HM	ARE/M	ARE/CC	ARE/RC	PC/HMTA	PC/MTA	PC/CCTA	PC/HMA
NON-AD. T.		65	112	96	40	171	438	1404	291	1.4	0.3	1.7	0.1	0.1	4.3	3.9	2.5	0.0	0.0	0.5	0.1	0.0	32.6	9.1	0.0
ADOP. T.		107	238	131	123	531	498	2460	562	1.7	0.6	2.3	0.3	0.3	16.2	4.6	3.2	0.3	0.3	0.6	0.3	13.1	28.0	16.3	51.5
NON-AD.// DIST/SO	1	17	78	99	42	222	321	1433	254	1.6	0.7	2.3	0.2	0.2	3.8	3.6	3.6	0.0	0.0	0.4	0.1	0.0	26.3	2.7	0.0
	2	32	97	97	34	117	527	1136	275	1.3	0.2	1.5	0.1	0.1	2.6	3.8	1.8	0.0	0.0	0.4	0.1	0.0	30.6	11.8	0.0
	3	16	178	90	49	225	385	1910	361	1.4	0.0	1.4	0.1	0.1	8.1	4.9	2.6	0.0	0.0	0.6	0.1	0.0	43.4	10.3	0.0
ADOP.// DIST/SO	1	27	245	139	79	763	402	2492	515	2.0	0.7	2.7	0.4	0.4	17.4	4.1	3.3	0.2	0.2	0.4	0.3	10.5	19.7	18.2	47.4
	2	55	233	135	150	563	414	2643	591	1.7	0.6	2.3	0.3	0.3	15.7	4.5	3.0	0.3	0.3	0.6	0.3	14.2	31.6	14.6	53.3
	3	25	241	115	113	212	785	2024	546	1.6	0.3	1.9	0.1	0.1	16.0	5.3	3.4	0.2	0.2	0.5	0.3	13.4	29.1	17.9	52.0
NON-AD.// DIST/MA	1	18	147	75	34	83	238	667	278	1.9	0.0	1.9	0.1	0.1	4.7	3.8	2.4	0.0	0.0	0.5	0.1	0.0	28.7	8.4	0.0
	2	17	133	122	54	318	552	2267	364	1.1	0.1	1.2	0.2	0.2	7.6	4.4	2.3	0.0	0.0	0.4	0.1	0.0	37.8	13.4	0.0
	3	30	80	93	36	141	494	1358	256	1.4	0.5	1.9	0.1	0.1	2.1	3.7	2.7	0.0	0.0	0.5	0.1	0.0	32.0	7.0	0.0
ADOP.// DIST/MA	1	52	248	131	169	666	430	2973	615	1.5	0.6	2.1	0.3	0.3	12.2	4.6	3.7	0.3	0.3	0.5	0.3	12.8	28.0	16.0	51.2
	2	23	234	123	69	273	755	2013	486	1.8	0.1	1.9	0.1	0.1	23.0	4.9	2.1	0.3	0.3	0.6	0.4	16.0	31.8	21.5	56.5
	3	32	225	138	87	498	424	1948	530	2.0	0.8	2.8	0.3	0.3	17.8	4.3	3.1	0.3	0.3	0.6	0.3	11.3	25.3	13.0	48.4

IGANA

APPENDIX 4   The studied Adoption-Categories broken down according to Time (ADY/...) - MEAN VALUES

	|T	n	VAL/ LS	VAL/ BH	VAL/ CA	EXP/ LA	EXP/ HO	INC/ ATO	VAL/ CAT	LO/ LR	LO/ ADL	LO/ LOT	LAB/ HP	LAB/ HT	LAB/ FQ	EXT/ FQ	LAB/ EQ	FQV/ MA	ARE/ HM	ARE/ M	ARE/ CC	ARE/ RC	PC/ HMTA	PC/ MTA	PC/ CCTA	PC/ HMMA
ADY/SFP	1	10	339	216	110	1806	609	5065	677	2.2	1.1	3.3	1.0	2.7	23.1	3.8	2.9	0.4	0.5	0.4	0.0	14.6	17.2	15.9	87.9
	2	20	334	153	274	897	602	4261	840	1.6	0.8	2.4	0.5	2.0	25.3	4.7	3.1	0.5	0.5	0.4	0.0	23.0	25.6	21.8	93.3
	3	22	254	132	95	456	386	1843	557	1.7	0.6	2.3	0.2	3.2	13.9	4.6	3.5	0.5	0.6	0.3	0.0	26.4	27.2	12.7	98.5
ADY/FP	1	11	202	117	107	191	278	1608	495	1.9	1.1	3.0	0.1	0.6	22.3	5.3	3.8	0.0	0.4	0.5	0.0	0.0	17.5	20.2	0.0
	2	16	181	128	69	156	917	1975	469	1.8	0.3	2.1	0.1	0.8	11.4	5.2	2.8	0.0	0.8	0.3	0.0	0.0	41.3	16.6	0.0
	3	18	168	90	53	234	323	1274	392	1.6	0.2	1.8	0.1	1.5	10.1	4.4	2.7	0.0	0.5	0.2	0.0	0.0	32.0	14.8	0.0

APPENDIX 5   The studied Adoption-Categories broken down according to Space (DIST/..) - MEAN VALUES

	|S	n	VAL/ LS	VAL/ BH	VAL/ CA	EXP/ LA	EXP/ HO	INC/ ATO	VAL/ CAT	LO/ LR	LO/ ADL	LO/ LOT	LAB/ HP	LAB/ HT	LAB/ FQ	EXT/ FQ	LAB/ EQ	FQV/ MA	ARE/ HM	ARE/ M	ARE/ CC	ARE/ RC	PC/ HMTA	PC/ MTA	PC/ CCTA	PC/ HMMA
ADY/SFP //	1	13	302	197	104	1188	474	3610	681	2.0	0.9	2.9	0.6	2.9	21.0	3.3	3.2	0.4	0.5	0.4	0.0	19.6	21.7	17.4	90.7
DIST/SO	2	27	329	161	237	1042	531	4020	792	1.9	0.8	2.7	0.5	3.4	18.6	4.7	3.1	0.6	0.6	0.4	0.0	23.8	24.7	14.5	97.5
	3	12	236	100	77	204	512	1746	466	1.5	0.6	2.1	0.2	0.8	22.0	5.4	3.4	0.4	0.5	0.4	0.0	24.3	27.9	21.4	91.8
ADY/FP //	1	22	160	111	71	164	295	1262	410	1.4	0.4	1.8	0.1	0.3	12.1	4.8	3.5	0.0	0.5	0.3	0.0	0.0	32.5	19.3	0.0
DIST/MA	2	9	177	108	78	134	1231	2170	466	2.1	0.0	2.1	0.0	2.1	18.2	5.6	1.8	0.0	0.7	0.3	0.0	0.0	35.8	17.9	0.0
	3	14	215	110	70	283	425	1780	486	2.0	0.9	2.9	0.1	1.5	12.9	4.7	3.0	0.0	0.7	0.3	0.0	0.0	28.1	12.1	0.0

APPENDIX 6   The studied Adoption-Categories broken down according to Space/Time (DIST/.../ADY/...) - MEAN VALUES

	|ST	n	VAL/ LS	VAL/ BH	VAL/ CA	EXP/ LA	EXP/ HO	INC/ ATO	VAL/ CAT	LO/ LR	LO/ ADL	LO/ LOT	LAB/ HP	LAB/ HT	LAB/ FQ	EXT/ FQ	LAB/ EQ	FQV/ MA	ARE/ HM	ARE/ M	ARE/ CC	ARE/ RC	PC/ HMTA	PC/ MTA	PC/ CCTA	PC/ HMMA
DIST/SO //	1	11	369	224	116	1355	470	3735	762	1.9	1.0	2.9	0.7	2.8	20.6	3.9	2.9	0.4	0.5	0.4	0.0	19.6	21.4	17.7	91.9
ADY/SFP	2	13	293	147	103	642	423	2214	628	2.1	0.4	2.5	0.3	3.4	10.1	4.2	3.3	0.6	0.6	0.3	0.0	23.2	23.9	12.5	97.4
	2	7	286	156	584	1836	1142	9031	1090	1.3	1.7	3.0	0.9	3.0	35.6	4.7	3.3	0.4	0.5	0.5	0.0	15.6	21.6	22.3	85.7
DIST/MA //	1	17	252	103	89	265	359	1670	506	1.6	0.4	2.0	0.2	1.8	20.7	5.2	3.4	0.5	0.5	0.3	0.0	28.4	29.4	17.1	98.0
ADY/FP	2	15	162	118	86	120	317	1437	442	1.6	0.5	2.1	0.3	0.3	15.2	5.3	3.9	0.0	0.6	0.4	0.0	0.0	30.7	19.1	0.0
	2	10	135	95	40	195	265	913	315	1.4	0.1	1.5	0.1	0.4	4.4	3.7	2.4	0.0	0.5	0.2	0.0	0.0	34.9	17.2	0.0
	2	6	183	76	54	350	358	1431	330	2.6	1.1	3.7	0.2	0.5	21.5	5.0	3.0	0.0	0.8	0.6	0.0	0.0	31.5	22.1	0.0
	2	14	233	127	87	212	999	2553	590	1.8	0.4	2.2	0.1	2.6	14.9	5.3	2.5	0.0	0.7	0.2	0.0	0.0	30.9	11.7	0.0

IGANA

APPENDIX 9 "Functional asp." broken down acc. to Space and Time - MEAN VALUES for INC/ATO

	N|AT/	AT/	COOP/	TR/	CRED
	STY|FTC	AGS	M	INC	
DIST/SO//	110| 2259	3522	976	2579	1851
	1	4732	3841	3932	4024	4025
ADY/SFP	120| 2326	2099	853	1570	2340
	1	2084	2473	2328	2766	2158
	210| 7060	5865	-	4321	1980
	1	11658	16945	9031	10914	14319
	220| 1344	1391	-	1514	1153
	1	2137	2070	1670	1847	1952
DIST/MA//	110| 1496	1232	-	1431	2880
	1	1052	2001	1436	1441	1334
ADY/FP	120| 913	755	-	985	-
	1| -	2335	913	841	913
	210| 1519	1120	-	1758	1020
	1	1256	2987	1431	1104	1513
	220| 2121	2380	-	1046	-
	1	5370	2000	2353	2710	23553

APPENDIX 8 "Functional Asp." broken down acc. to Space and Time - MEAN VALUES for VAL/CAT

	N|AT/	AT/	COOP/	TR/	CRED
	STY|FTC	AGS	M	INC	
DIST/SO//	110| 642	612	81	901	357
	1	837	833	808	724	821
ADY/SFP	120| 613	593	971	615	729
	1	637	695	595	632	577
	210| 957	880	-	571	330
	1	1260	1604	1087	1293	1654
	220	500	357	503	443	528
	1	514	712		571	490
DIST/MA//	110| 431	444		381	452
	1	509	436	442	482	441
ADY/FP	120| 314	280		343	-
	1| -	613	314	284	314
	210	287	313		327	164
	1	412	409	329	331	361
	220| 482	618		368	-
	1	1481	211	589	649	589

APPENDIX 11 "Functional Asp." broken down acc. to Space and Time - MEAN VALUES for EXT/FQ

	N|AT/	AT/	COOP/	TR/	CRED
	STY|FTC	AGS	M	INC	
DIST/SO//	110| 12.7	12.2	12.0	9.0	12.0
	1| 25.9	24.8	21.2	23.5	21.9
ADY/SFP	120| 8.1	7.9	1.0	8.8	12.3
	1| 12.3	15.0	10.8	11.1	9.1
	210| 28.0	42.2	-	24.0	37.0
	1| 45.7	19.0	35.6	40.2	34.5
	220| 22.6	27.6		22.4	35.5
	1| 18.0	10.9	20.7	18.8	12.6
DIST/MA//	110| 16.4	8.2		9.2	99.0
	1| 7.5	34.5	15.2	19.2	9.2
ADY/FP	120| 4.4	2.2		2.2	-
	1| -	24.0	4.4	6.6	4.4
	210| 16.3	6.2		17.7	3.0
	1| 32.0	18.0	21.5	25.3	25.2
	220| 15.2	15.2		13.0	-
	1| 12.0	12.0	14.9	15.5	14.9

APPENDIX 7 "Functional Asp." broken down acc. to Space and Time - Absolute Nos.

	N|AT/	AT/	COOP/	TR/	CRED
	STY|FTC	AGS	M	INC	
DIST/SO //	110| 6	5	1	3	2
	1	9	10	14	1	13
ADY/SFP	120| 7	9	1	6	4
	1	6	4	12	7	9
	210| 4	5	-	2	3
	1	3	2	7	5	4
	220| 10	10	-	9	6
	1	7	7	17	8	11
DIST/MA //	110| 13	11		6	1
	1	2	4	15	9	14
ADY/FP	120| 10	9		5	-
	1| -	1	1	5	10
	210	4	5		3	5
	1	2	1	6	3	1
	220| 13	13		3	-
	1	1	7	1	11	14

APPENDIX 10 "Functional Asp." broken down acc. to Space and Time - MEAN VALUES for LO/LOT

	N|AT/	AT/	COOP/	TR/	CRED
	STY|FTC	AGS	M	INC	
DIST/SO//	110| 1.6	2.2	1.0	3.1	1.5
	1| 3.8	3.3	3.11	2.9	3.2
ADY/SFP	120| 2.5	2.2	1.3	2.2	2.7
	1| 2.5	3.2	2.6	2.8	2.5
	210| 2.1	2.4	-	1.4	2.1
	1| 4.1	4.5	3.0	3.6	3.6
	220| 1.6	2.0		2.2	2.0
	1| 2.7	2.2	2.1	1.9	2.1
DIST/MA//	110| 2.0	1.9		2.2	1.6
	1| 2.9	2.6	2.1	2.0	2.1
ADY/FP	120| 1.5	1.4		1.7	-
	1| -	2.2	1.5	1.3	1.5
	210| 4.7	3.9		5.6	3.0
	1| 1.7	2.5	3.7	1.7	3.8
	220| 2.1	2.2		2.2	-
	1| 3.5	2.3	2.2	2.2	2.2

APPENDIX 12 Comparison between Adopters and Non-Adopters broken down on DIST/SO and DIST/MA - MEDIAN VALUES

	s	n	VAL/LS	VAL/BH	VAL/CA	EXP/LA	EXP/HO	INC/ATO	VAL/CAT	LO/LR	LO/ADL	LO/LOT	LAB/HP	LAB/HT	EXT/FQ	LAB/EQ	FOV/MA	ARE/HM	ARE/M	ARE/CC	ARE/RC	PC/HMTA	PC/MTA	PC/CCTA	PC/HMMA
NON-AD. T.		65	76	52	23	8	300	533	213	1.3	0.01	1.5	0.0	0.7	0.0	3.6	2.0	0.00	0.4	0.0	0.0	0.0	30.8	0.1	0.0
ADOP. T.		107	190	90	67	3	302	1257	442	1.6	0.02	1.9	0.2	0.3	11.7	4.5	2.1	0.15	0.4	0.3	0.0	5.4	25.0	13.0	70.8
NON-AD.//	1	17	42	80	18	30	313	600	123	1.4	0.02	1.6	0.1	0.2	3.0	3.0	2.3	0.00	0.4	0.0	0.0	0.0	13.8	0.4	0.0
DIST/SO	2	32	75	53	20	8	300	500	214	1.3	0.03	1.3	0.0	0.4	0.1	3.0	1.9	0.00	0.4	0.1	0.0	0.0	30.7	0.3	0.0
	3	16	155	65	28	120	298	538	281	1.7	0.00	1.7	0.1	0.3	0.0	5.1	2.2	0.00	0.7	0.1	0.0	0.0	36.6	5.2	0.0
ADOP.//	1	27	200	90	61	3	381	1257	390	1.5	0.04	2.0	0.3	0.3	11.9	3.9	2.1	0.10	0.4	0.4	0.0	5.7	18.2	14.3	28.6
DIST/SO	2	55	190	90	70	4	300	1251	463	1.6	0.02	1.9	0.3	0.2	11.7	4.4	2.1	0.17	0.6	0.2	0.0	5.4	30.8	11.8	83.9
	3	25	210	91	67	2	450	1310	442	1.5	0.07	1.7	0.2	0.2	4.0	5.2	2.1	0.10	0.4	0.2	0.0	2.7	26.7	16.7	53.8
NON-AD.//	1	18	138	66	25	44	205	508	281	1.7	0.01	1.7	0.0	0.0	1.5	3.3	1.9	0.00	0.4	0.1	0.0	0.0	25.2	2.3	0.0
DIST/MA	2	17	48	67	27	120	297	750	181	0.9	0.06	1.0	0.1	0.0	0.3	4.2	2.2	0.00	0.4	0.0	0.0	0.0	36.4	1.7	0.0
	3	30	43	88	19	10	400	508	135	1.3	0.06	1.6	0.0	0.0	0.3	2.0	2.0	0.00	0.4	0.0	0.0	0.0	31.0	0.1	0.0
ADOP.//	1	52	221	90	72	2	310	1477	457	1.6	0.02	1.9	0.2	0.2	3.5	4.2	2.4	0.17	0.4	0.2	0.0	5.5	23.5	13.9	66.7
DIST/MA	2	23	178	90	54	4	302	1220	386	1.7	0.04	1.7	0.1	0.3	12.1	5.1	1.7	0.16	0.5	0.4	0.0	8.7	31.3	16.7	61.5
	3	32	153	90	68	4	404	1238	390	1.6	0.03	2.0	0.2	0.3	12.1	3.9	2.0	0.05	0.5	0.2	0.0	0.3	22.9	8.7	25.0

APPENDIX 13 The studied Adoption-Categories broken down according to Time (ADY/....) - MEDIAN VALUES

	T	n	VAL/LS	VAL/BH	VAL/CA	EXP/LA	EXP/HO	INC/ATO	VAL/CAT	VAL/LR	LO/ADL	LO/LOT	LAB/HP	LAB/HT	EXT/FQ	LAB/EQ	FOV/MA	ARE/HM	ARE/M	ARE/CC	ARE/RC	PC/HMTA	PC/MTA	PC/CCTA	PC/HMMA
ADY/SFP	1	10	235	103	99	1850	500	4381	621	1.7	0.60	1.9	1.0	2.8	14.6	3.8	1.3	0.23	0.3	0.4	0.0	10.2	13.5	10.8	97.3
	2	20	315	96	113	23	302	1268	625	1.7	0.08	2.0	0.3	0.3	11.8	4.8	2.3	0.41	0.4	0.4	0.0	21.2	23.7	14.4	98.1
	3	22	223	92	77	100	475	1311	498	1.6	0.04	2.0	0.1	2.8	12.0	3.8	2.2	0.41	0.4	0.2	0.0	23.3	23.3	12.0	99.2
ADY/FP	1	11	189	90	134	33	283	1483	452	1.5	0.04	2.0	0.1	0.1	12.0	5.6	2.4	0.00	0.4	0.4	0.0	0.0	20.0	16.7	0.0
	2	16	103	89	43	17	311	1212	320	1.7	0.06	1.9	0.0	0.1	4.0	5.0	1.8	0.00	0.7	0.3	0.0	0.0	33.5	13.8	0.0
	3	18	113	85	38	3	305	722	288	1.6	0.04	1.8	0.1	0.3	3.2	3.5		0.00	0.5	0.2	0.0	0.0	33.3	8.7	0.0

APPENDIX 14 The studied Adoption-Categories broken down according to Space (DIST/....) - MEDIAN VALUES

	S	m	VAL/LS	VAL/BH	VAL/CA	EXP/LA	EXP/HO	INC/ATO	VAL/CAT	VAL/LR	LO/ADL	LO/LOT	LAB/HP	LAB/HT	EXT/FQ	LAB/EQ	FOV/MA	ARE/HM	ARE/M	ARE/CC	ARE/RC	PC/HMTA	PC/MTA	PC/CCTA	PC/HMMA
ADY/SFP	1	13	270	98	118	200	480	2184	722	1.5	0.13	2.0	0.4	2.8	12.1	3.7	2.0	0.38	0.4	0.4	0.0	14.5	19.9	10.1	98.1
	2	27	310	98	112	110	400	1624	633	1.7	0.03	2.1	0.3	3.1	12.0	5.0	2.2	0.43	0.4	0.3	0.0	23.4	23.6	12.4	98.7
	3	12	153	90	68	13	453	1333	442	1.6	0.10	2.0	0.1	0.2	12.1	2.0		0.38	0.4	0.4	0.0	22.6	23.9	15.4	93.5
ADY/FP	1	22	163	89	48	3	294	1008	378	1.3	0.02	1.8	0.1	0.1	3.8	4.2	2.3	0.00	0.4	0.2	0.0	0.0	27.1	16.6	0.0
	2	9	120	90	61	100	288	1220	345	1.9	0.00	1.9	0.0	0.8	3.3	5.6	1.6	0.00	0.8	0.3	0.0	0.0	34.3	10.1	0.0
	3	14	113	87	29	3	325	1024	267	1.8	0.04	2.3	0.1	0.2	11.7	4.4	2.1	0.00	0.8	0.2	0.0	0.0	28.6	7.0	0.0

APPENDIX 15   The studied Adoption-Categories broken down according to Space/Time (DIST/..//ADY/...) - MEDIAN VALUES

IGANA

	ST	n	VAL/LS	VAL/BH	VAL/CA	EXP/LA	EXP/HO	INC/ATO	VAL/ATO	VAL/CAT	LO/LR	LO/ADL	LO/LOT	LAB/HP	LAB/HT	EXT/FQ	LAB/EQ	FQV/MA	ARE/HM	ARE/M	ARE/CC	ARE/RC	PC/HMTA	PC/MTA	PC/CCTA	PC/HMMA
DIST/SO//	1	1	15	360	225	124	1200	460	2725	718	1.6	0.40	1.9	0.6	3.0	12.1	4.3	2.0	0.39	0.41	0.4	0.4	0.0	20.0	21.1	12.6	98.4
ADY/SFP	2		13	308	95	91	103	475	1385	619	2.0	0.11	2.3	0.2	3.0	11.8	3.9	2.4	0.41	0.41	0.4	0.2	0.0	19.5	23.1	10.1	98.6
	2	1	7	260	98	112	1080	500	3923	572	1.4	0.60	1.9	0.8	1.1	12.0	5.0	1.8	0.30	0.30	0.4	0.4	0.0	17.6	20.0	12.8	91.7
	2	17	7	224	90	70	7	413	1310	461	1.4	0.05	1.7	0.1	0.4	12.4	5.3	2.1	0.41	0.41	0.4	0.2	0.0	26.7	26.7	14.8	99.0
DIST/MA//	1	1	15	160	90	59	64	300	1476	390	1.5	0.02	2.0	0.0	0.1	11.6	5.2	3.0	0.00		0.4	0.2	0.0	0.0	26.7	16.7	0.0
ADY/FP	2	10	105	63	31	13	288	495	188		1.3	0.03	1.7	0.1	0.1	2.2	3.7	1.8	0.00		0.5	0.2	0.0	0.0	30.8	10.3	0.0
	2	1	6	130	65	26	75	300	1254	205	1.9	0.45	1.8	0.1	0.3	12.0	5.0	2.0	0.00		0.8	0.5	0.0	0.0	29.5	16.7	0.0
	2	14	5	125	90	62	5	325	918	326	1.7	0.02	1.8	0.0	0.5	11.7	3.9	1.9	0.00		0.8	0.2	0.0	0.0	33.3	7.4	0.0

KODOOH WEST

APPENDIX 16:A   Total Population broken down on DIST/SO - MEAN VALUES

TOTAL POP.	S	n	LS	BH	CA	LA	HO	ATO	CAT	LO/LR	LO/ADL	LO/LOT	LAB/HP	LAB/HT	EXT/FQ	LAB/EQ	FQV/MA	ARE/HM	ARE/M	ARE/CC	PC/HMTA	PC/MTA	PC/CCTA	PC/RCTA	PC/HMMA
T.POP.		186	368	78	50	99	572	1433	607	2.6	0.1	2.7	0.0	3.2	2.9	3.8	5.8	0.3	0.7	0.2	9.3	27.1	0.7	8.3	29.0
T.POP.//	1	56	280	49	36	65	467	1144	453	1.9	0.4	2.3	0.0	2.8	3.7	3.1	5.4	0.4	0.7	0.0	14.0	30.8	1.3	8.7	36.7
DIST/SO	2	71	390	68	50	107	775	1719	608	2.7	0.1	2.8	0.0	3.2	2.8	4.0	5.5	0.2	0.7	0.2	7.3	25.1	0.8	6.9	27.4
	3	59	425	119	62	122	427	1363	752	3.3	0.0	3.3	0.1	3.5	2.1	4.2	6.6	0.2	0.9	0.3	7.1	26.0	0.1	9.8	23.7
T.POP.//	1	88	300	59	40	60	503	1307	493	2.2	0.3	2.5	0.0	3.0	3.4	3.4	5.4	0.3	0.7	0.2	11.8	27.4	0.9	8.7	35.9
DIST/SO	2	98	429	96	58	134	634	1546	709	3.0	0.1	3.0	0.0	3.3	2.4	4.1	6.2	0.2	0.8	0.2	7.0	26.8	0.5	8.0	22.9

APPENDIX 16:B   Total Population broken down on DIST/SO - MEDIAN VALUES

TOTAL POP.	S	n	LS	BH	CA	LA	HO	ATO	CAT	LO/LR	LO/ADL	LO/LOT	LAB/HP	LAB/HT	EXT/FQ	LAB/EQ	FQV/MA	ARE/HM	ARE/M	ARE/CC	PC/HMTA	PC/MTA	PC/CCTA	PC/RCTA	PC/HMMA
T.POP.		186	340	50	38	44	400	1086	534	2.0	0.01	2.2	0.0	2.9	0.4	3.8	7.6	0.03	0.5	0.0	0.0	25.0	0.0	8.3	0.2
T.POP.//	1	56	281	50	28	21	499	933	454	1.7	0.04	1.8	0.0	0.5	0.5	2.8	7.6	0.04	0.5	0.1	0.1	25.0	0.0	7.1	0.2
DIST/SO	2	71	351	55	36	48	398	1240	558	2.0	0.00	2.0	0.0	3.1	0.3	4.1	6.0	0.02	0.5	0.0	0.1	23.1	0.0	6.9	0.7
	3	59	391	51	52	48	396	1090	611	2.2	0.00	2.2	0.0	3.4	0.3	4.2	7.9	0.02	0.6	0.2	0.1	25.0	0.1	11.1	0.2
T.POP.//	1	88	281	50	28	39	482	1008	432	1.8	0.02	2.0	0.0	2.1	0.4	3.3	7.6	0.04	0.4	0.0	0.2	22.2	0.0	8.3	0.2
DIST/SO	2	98	429	50	50	48	360	1201	643	2.2	0.01	2.2	0.0	3.2	0.4	4.2	7.8	0.02	0.6	0.1	0.1	25.0	0.0	9.1	0.2

KODOCH WEST

APPENDIX 17:A Total values for the studied Adoption-Categories - MEAN VALUES

ADOPT. CAT.	n	VAL/ LS	VAL/ BH	VAL/ CA	VAL/ LA	EXP/ HO	INC/ ATO	VAL/ CAT	LO/ LR	LO/ ADL	LO/ LOT	LAB/ HP	LAB/ HT	EXT/ FQ	LAB/ EQ	FQV/ MA	ARE/ HM	ARE/ M	ARE/ CC	ARE/ RC	PC/ HMTA	PC/ MTA	PC/ CCTA	PC/ RCTA	PC/ HMMA
ADY/SFP	15	484	81	69	115	397	2089	777	2.4	0.3	2.7	0.1	4.7	4.3	4.8	7.3	0.5	0.5	0.0	0.3	18.8	19.7	0.6	8.5	97.8
ADY/S	23	321	51	46	158	971	1706	510	2.8	0.3	3.1	0.1	3.4	4.0	3.3	3.4	0.7	0.8	0.0	0.2	24.6	28.7	0.0	5.6	89.0
ADY/SF	9	435	50	48	128	489	1444	634	2.0	0.4	2.4	0.0	6.6	5.3	2.9	5.2	1.3	1.5	0.0	0.2	50.1	58.3	1.8	6.7	85.7
ADY/SP	17	462	196	85	283	567	1619	876	3-4	0.2	3.6	0.2	2.7	6.5	4.8	6.2	0.7	1.3	0.0	0.5	24.9	37.4	0.0	11.6	65.7

APPENDIX 17:B Total values for the studied Adoption-Categories - MEDIAN VALUES

ADOPT. CAT.	n	VAL/ LS	VAL/ BH	VAL/ CA	VAL/ LA	EXP/ HO	INC/ ATO	VAL/ CAT	LO/ LR	LO/ ADL	LO/ LOT	LAB/ HP	LAB/ HT	EXT/ FQ	LAB/ EQ	FQV/ MA	ARE/ HM	ARE/ M	ARE/ CC	ARE/ RC	PC/ HMTA	PC/ MTA	PC/ CCTA	PC/ RCTA	PC/ HMMA
ADY/SFP	15	463	51	70	98	316	1746	662	1.9	0.08	2.0	0.0	4.3	0.3	4.7	8.1	0.38	0.4	0.0	0.1	16.7	16.7	0.3	10.0	98.8
ADY/S	23	212	50	43	31	502	1007	405	2.0	0.03	2.2	0.1	3.0	1.8	3.3	2.3	0.63	0.6	0.0	0.1	23.5	28.6	0.0	0.0	98.8
ADY/SF	9	362	50	43	100	425	1445	563	1.9	0.16	2.5	0.0	8.6	2.3	2.8	6.8	1.20	1.2	0.0	0.0	53.3	53.3	1.0	0.4	91.7
ADY/SP	17	373	52	99	42	503	1349	673	2.6	0.09	2.6	0.2	2.1	3.3	4.7	6.3	0.58	0.7	0.0	0.2	22.2	33.3	0.0	12.7	65.8

APPENDIX 18 Comparison between Adopters and Non-Adopters broken down on DIST/SO - MEAN VALUES

	S	n	VAL/ LS	VAL/ BH	VAL/ CA	VAL/ LA	EXP/ HO	INC/ ATO	VAL/ CAT	LO/ LR	LO/ ADL	LO/ LOT	LAB/ HP	LAB/ HT	EXT/ FQ	LAB/ EQ	FQV/ MA	ARE/ HM	ARE/ M	ARE/ CC	ARE/ RC	PC/ HMTA	PC/ MTA	PC/ CCTA	PC/ RCTA	PC/ HMMA
NON-AD. T.		122	344	69	69	58	525	1247	565	2.6	0.1	2.7	0.0	2.8	1.8	3.7	6.1	0.0	0.6	0.0	0.2	0.0	24.0	0.9	8.5	0.0
ADOP. T.		64	413	96	62	177	661	1736	690	2.8	0.3	3.1	0.1	4.0	4.9	4.0	5.3	0.8	1.0	0.0	0.3	26.9	33.1	0.4	8.0	84.4
NON-AD. //	1	32	223	47	26	39	474	986	380	2.0	0.2	2.2	0.0	1.7	2.9	3.0	5.6	0.0	0.5	0.0	0.2	0.0	24.3	1.4	9.9	0.0
DIST/SO	2	49	367	61	45	77	665	1464	569	2.6	0.1	2.7	0.0	2.9	1.8	3.8	6.0	0.0	0.6	0.0	0.2	0.0	24.2	1.1	7.0	0.0
	3	41	412	95	54	49	397	1272	705	3.1	0.1	3.1	0.0	3.4	0.8	4.0	6.5	0.0	0.8	0.0	0.2	0.0	23.4	0.2	9.2	0.0
ADOP. //	1	24	356	52	49	97	457	1354	553	1.8	0.6	2.4	0.0	4.4	4.9	3.3	5.2	0.8	1.0	0.0	0.2	32.7	39.5	1.0	7.1	85.6
DIST/SO	2	22	441	83	62	173	1019	2288	698	3.0	0.1	3.1	0.1	3.7	5.0	4.3	4.5	0.7	0.8	0.0	0.2	23.7	27.2	0.0	6.4	88.5
	3	18	453	173	79	287	497	1571	862	3.7	0.0	3.7	0.2	3.7	4.9	4.5	6.6	0.7	1.1	0.0	0.5	23.1	31.6	0.0	11.2	77.8

KOODOCH WEST

APPENDIX 19 The studied Adoption-Categories broken down according to Time (ADY/...) - MEAN VALUES

	T	n	VAL/LS	VAL/BH	VAL/CA	EXP/LA	EXP/HO	INC/ATO	VAL/CAT	LO/LR	LO/ADL	LO/LOT	LAB/HP	LAB/HT	EXT/FQ	LAB/EQ	FQV/MA	ARE/HM	ARE/M	ARE/CC	ARE/RC	PC/HMTA	PC/MTA	PC/CCTA	PC/RCTA	PC/HMMA
ADY/SFP	1	6	438	58	61	183	392	2849	699	1.8	0.0	1.8	0.2	3.5	4.0	4.5	8.0	0.3	0.4	0.0	0.2	17.8	20.2	0.0	10.9	94.4
	2	9	515	97	74	70	400	1583	855	2.8	0.4	3.2	0.0	5.6	4.6	5.0	6.9	0.6	0.6	0.0	0.3	19.4	19.4	0.9	6.9	100.0
ADY/S	1	9	626	54	51	198	644	1626	826	3.3	0.0	3.3	0.1	3.6	3.3	3.7	2.2	1.0	1.0	0.0	0.3	22.9	27.2	0.0	8.0	81.9
	2	14	125	48	42	132	1180	1758	309	2.4	0.0	2.4	0.1	3.3	4.4	4.2	3.0	0.6	0.7	0.0	0.3	22.9	29.6	0.0	8.0	100.0
ADY/SF	1	4	320	50	40	108	450	1738	512	2.1	0.6	2.7	0.0	6.0	6.3	3.2	5.3	1.4	1.5	0.1	0.2	48.5	54.9	4.0	4.2	85.4
	2	5	528	50	55	144	520	1208	734	1.9	0.4	2.3	0.0	7.0	4.6	2.7	5.2	1.3	1.5	0.0	0.2	51.4	61.1	0.0	8.7	85.9
ADY/SP	1	9	623	291	101	234	539	1835	1204	4.7	0.3	5.0	0.0	2.8	7.7	5.8	7.0	1.7	1.7	0.0	0.7	23.1	36.9	0.0	12.9	64.4
	2	8	278	90	68	337	599	1377	514	2.0	0.0	2.0	0.3	2.5	5.3	3.6	5.3	0.4	0.7	0.0	0.2	27.0	38.6	0.0	10.2	67.1

APPENDIX 20 The studied Adoption-Categories broken down according to Space (DIST/SO) - MEAN VALUES.

	S	n	VAL/LS	VAL/BH	VAL/CA	EXP/LA	EXP/HO	INC/ATO	VAL/CAT	LO/LR	LO/ADL	LO/LOT	LAB/HP	LAB/HT	EXT/FQ	LAB/EQ	FQV/MA	ARE/HM	ARE/M	ARE/CC	ARE/RC	PC/HMTA	PC/MTA	PC/CCTA	PC/RCTA	PC/HMMA
ADY/SFP //	1	6	318	58	77	168	450	1769	570	1.7	0.6	2.3	0.2	4.2	6.3	4.3	5.7	0.5	0.6	0.1	0.2	20.8	23.2	1.4	8.1	94.4
DIST/SO	2	4	606	50	48	75	438	2831	845	1.6	0.0	1.6	0.0	5.8	0.0	4.6	8.3	0.3	0.3	0.1	0.1	18.3	18.5	0.0	7.5	100.0
	3	5	586	134	75	84	300	1881	983	3.9	0.0	3.9	0.0	4.6	5.4	5.5	8.6	0.7	0.7	0.0	0.5	16.7	16.7	0.0	9.7	100.0
ADY/S //	1	7	289	49	35	25	447	1049	453	1.4	1.0	2.4	0.0	3.0	2.7	2.9	4.4	0.6	0.7	0.0	0.2	25.1	34.8	0.0	7.5	81.0
DIST/SO	2	13	392	52	53	260	1373	2297	606	3.7	0.0	3.7	0.0	3.9	5.5	3.7	2.8	0.8	0.9	0.0	0.2	24.1	25.9	0.0	4.2	91.7
	3	3	87	50	39	25	450	682	243	2.3	0.0	2.3	0.0	2.0	0.3	2.7	4.0	0.6	0.6	0.0	0.2	25.2	26.3	0.0	6.7	96.3
ADY/SF //	1	9	435	50	48	128	489	1444	635	2.0	0.4	2.4	0.0	6.6	5.3	2.9	5.2	1.3	1.5	0.0	0.2	50.1	58.3	1.8	6.7	85.7
DIST/SO	-	-	-	-	-	-	-	-	-	-	-	-	-	-	-	-	-	-	-	-	-	-	-	-	-	-
ADY/SP //	1	2	341	48	21	0	365	769	481	2.5	0.0	2.5	0.0	0.0	6.0	3.3	6.0	0.5	1.1	0.0	0.1	16.4	20.2	0.0	4.2	75.0
DIST/SO	2	5	437	190	95	26	5651	1831	827	2.5	0.6	3.1	0.0	1.4	7.6	5.9	5.8	1.1	0.7	0.0	0.3	26.9	37.7	0.0	11.2	71.1
	3	10	498	229	93	468	609	1684	987	4.1	0.0	4.1	0.3	3.8	6.1	4.5	6.4	1-5	0.8	0.0	0.6	25.7	40.7	0.0	13.3	61.2

APPENDIX 21:A The studied Adoption-Categories broken down according to Space/Time (DIST/SO//ADY/...) - MEAN VALUES

	ST	n	VAL/LS	VAL/BH	VAL/CA	EXP/LA	EXP/HO	INC/ATO	VAL/CAT	LO/LR	LO/ADL	LO/LOT	LAB/HP	LAB/HT	EXT/FQ	LAB/EQ	FQV/MA	ARE/HM	ARE/M	ARE/CC	ARE/RC	PC/HMTA	PC/MTA	PC/CCTA	PC/RCTA	PC/HMMA
DIST/SO//	111	6	438	58	61	183	392	2849	699	1.8	0.0	1.8	0.2	3.5	4.0	4.5	8.0	0.3	0.4	0.0	0.2	17.8	20.2	0.0	10.9	94.4
ADY/SFP	21	3	392	50	85	36	600	1283	528	1.0	1.3	2.3	0.0	6.0	4.7	4.3	3.3	0.5	0.5	0.11	0.1	22.8	22.8	2.8	4.4	100.0
	121	-	-	-	-	-	-	-	-	-	-	-	-	-	-	-	-	-	-	-	-	-	-	-	-	-
	2	6	626	120	69	87	300	1735	989	3.7	0.0	3.7	0.0	5.3	4.5	5.3	8.7	0.7	0.7	0.0	0.4	17.8	17.8	0.0	8.1	100.0
DIST/SO//	111	2	782	50	42	10	600	834	949	1.9	3.4	5.3	0.0	4.5	2.0	3.6	1.5	1.5	1.5	0.0	0.3	27.4	27.4	0.0	6.1	100.0
ADY/S	12	12	124	49	43	25	554	1071	308	2.4	0.0	2.4	0.0	3.3	4.1	3.2	4.3	0.5	0.9	0.0	0.3	20.7	28.3	0.0	7.6	79.9
	21	7	581	56	51	251	657	1852	791	3.7	0.0	3.7	0.1	3.3	3.7	3.7	2.4	0.9	0.9	0.1	0.1	27.2	27.2	0.0	0.6	100.0
	2	2	130	48	37	773	4937	5882	315	2.4	0.0	2.4	0.5	3.0	6.0	2.0	4.0	0.8	0.8	0.0	0.3	35.6	37.2	0.0	10.0	94.4

248

APPENDIX 21:B The studied Adoption-Categories broken down according to Space/Time (DIST/SO//ADY/....) - MEAN VALUES

	ST	n	VAL/ LS	VAL/ BH	VAL/ CA	VAL/ LA	EXP/ HO	INC/ ATO	VAL/ CAT	LO/ LR	LO/ ADL	LO/ LOT	LAB/ HP	LAB/ HT	EXT/ FQ	LAB/ EQ	FOV/ NA	ARE/ HM	ARE/ M	ARE/ CC	ARE/ RC	PC/ HMTA	PC/ MTA	PC/ CCTA	PC/ RCTA	PC/ HMMA
DIST/SO//	111	4	320	50	40	108	450	1738	512	2.1	0.6	2.7	0.0	6.0	6.3	3.2	5.3	1.4	1.5	0.1	0.2	48.5	54.9	4.0	4.2	85.4
ADY/SF	21	5	528	50	55	144	520	1208	734	1.9	0.4	2.3	0.0	7.0	4.6	2.7	5.2	1.3	1.5	0.0	0.2	51.4	61.1	0.0	8.7	85.9
	2	-	-							-					-							-				-
DIST/SO//	111	3	456	173	83	17	617	1501	843	3.2	0.9	4.1	0.0	1.0	12.0	5.6	6.3	0.8	1.3	0.0	0.4	21.8	31.6	0.0	10.3	71.2
ADY/SP	2	2	217	50	34	0	553	773	353	2.4	0.0	2.4	0.0	0.0	6.0	3.5	5.5	0.5	0.6	0.0	0.1	19.8	23.6	0.0	4.5	75.0
	21	6	707	349	110	343	500	2002	1385	5.5	0.0	5.5	0.2	3.7	5.5	5.9	7.3	1.1	2.0	0.0	0.8	23.8	38.7	0.0	14.2	61.1
	2	6	301	103	78	449	615	1579	569	1.9	0.0	1.9	0.3	3.3	5.0	3.6	5.2	0.4	0.8	0.0	0.2	29.4	43.7	0.0	12.0	64.5

APPENDIX 22 "Functional Asp." broken down acc. to Space and Time - Absolute Nos.

	N STY	AT/ FTC	IAT/ AGS	COOP/ M	TR/ INC	CRED
DIST/SO//	110	1	2	5	1	5
ADY/SFP	120	5	6	1	5	1
	1	1	1	2	2	-
	210	2	2	1	1	3
	1	-	-	-	-	-
	220	-	-	6	3	6
	1	6	6	-	3	-
DIST/SO//	110	2	2	2	1	2
ADY/S	120	10	8	12	2	12
	1	2	4	-	10	-
	210	7	5	7	3	7
	1	-	2	-	4	-
	220	2	1	2	2	2
	1	1	1	-	2	-

APPENDIX 22 "Functional Asp." broken down acc. to Space and Time - Absolute Nos. (cont.)

	N STY	AT/ FTC	IAT/ AGS	COOP/ M	TR/ INC	CRED
DIST/SO//	110	2	1	3	2	3
ADY/SF	120	2	4	1	1	4
	1	1	1	4	4	1
	210	1	1	-	-	-
	1	-	-	-	-	-
	220	-	-	1	1	1
	1	-	-	-	-	-
DIST/SO//	110	3	2	3	2	3
ADY/SP	120	2	2	1	1	1
	1	1	1	1	1	1
	210	6	1	6	2	6
	1	5	5	-	-	-
	220	6	3	6	1	6
	1	3	3	-	5	-

APPENDIX 23 "Functional Asp." broken down acc. to Space and Time - MEAN VALUES for VAL/CAT

	N STY	AT/ FTC	IAT/ AGS	COOP/ M	TR/ INC	CRED
DIST/SO//	110	606	-	627	192	627
ADY/SFP	120	713	695	1039	796	1039
	1	792	792	553	633	-
	210	394	394	473	314	526
	1	-	-	-	-	-
	220	-	-	985	1195	985
	1	985	985	-	774	-
DIST/SO//	110	948	948	948	1098	948
ADY/S	120	336	277	306	798	307
	1	160	366	-	143	-
	210	790	790	790	339	790
	1	-	1044	-	228	-
	220	314	578	314	1211	314
	1	-	50	-	314	-

KOOOOH WEST

APPENDIX 23 (cont.) "Functional Asp." broken down acc. to Space and Time - MEAN VALUES for VAL/CAT

	N STY	AT/ FTC	AT/ AGS	COOP/ M	TR/ INC	CRED
DIST/SO//	110	425	626	444	595	444
	1	595	471	708	425	708
ADY/SF	120	803	1552	673	974	528
	1	453	529	974	673	1552
	210	-	-	-	-	-
	1					
	220	-	-	-	-	-
	1	-	-	-	-	-
DIST/SO//	110	839	958	839	-	839
	1	-	603	-	839	-
ADY/S	120	351	351	351	839	457
	1	-	-	-	457	244
	210	1381	711	1381	1973	1381
	1	-	1515	-	1085	-
	220	565	765	565	1333	565
	1	-	365	-	411	-

APPENDIX 24 "Functional Asp." broken down acc. to Space and Time - MEAN VALUES for INC/ATO

	N STY	AT/ FTC	AT/ AGS	COOP/ M	TR/ INC	CRED
DIST/SO//	110	1430	-	2894	1746	2894
	1	3133	2849	2628	3070	2628
ADY/SFP	120	1176	1176	1263	1250	-
	1	1337	1337	1323	1350	1283
	210	-	-	-	-	-
	1					
	220	-	-	1733	1804	1733
	1	1733	1733	-	1661	-
DIST/SO//	110	834	834	834	660	834
	1	-	-	-	1007	-
ADY/S	120	1059	1027	1071	1270	1071
	1	1129	1158	-	1031	-
	210	1852	1466	1852	574	1852
	1	-	2819	-	2811	-
	220	5882	963	5882	-	5882
	1	-	10800	-	5882	-
DIST/SO//	110	1150	1827	1836	2527	1836
	1	2327	1708	1445	1150	1145
ADY/SF	120	1097	1012	1266	978	1257
	1	1654	1257	978	1266	1012
	210	-	-	-	-	-
	1					
	220	-	-	-	-	-
	1					
DIST/SO//	110	1501	-	1695	1501	1501
	1	-	1114	1501	1501	-
ADY/SP	120	773	773	773	668	877
	1	2002	2402	2002	1729	668
	210	-	1921	-	2138	2001
	220	1579	1740	1579	1034	1579
	1	-	1418	-	1689	-

APPENDIX 25 "Functional Asp." broken down acc. to Space and Time - MEAN VALUES for LO/LOT

	N STY	AT/ FTC	AT/ AGS	COOP/ M	TR/ INC	CRED
DIST/SO//	110	3.6		1.6	1.2	1.6
	1	1.5	1.8	2.8	2.0	2.8
ADY/SFP	120	1.2	1.2	1.6	2.4	-
	1	2.8	2.8	3.6	1.9	2.2
	210	-	-	-	-	-
	1					
	220	-	-	-	2.5	3.7
	1	3.7	3.7	3.7	4.9	-
DIST/SO//	110	5.3	5.3	5.3	4.1	5.3
	1	-	-	-	6.4	-
ADY/S	120	2.1	2.0	2.5	4.3	2.5
	1	4.3	3.4	-	2.1	-
	210	3.7	2.5	3.7	2.6	3.7
	1	-	6.8	-	4.6	-
	220	2.4	3.0	2.4	-	2.4
	1	-	1.8	-	2.4	-
DIST/SO//	110	2.7	1.1	2.7	2.7	2.7
	1	2.7	3.2	2.5	6.4	2.5
ADY/SF	120	2.3	3.2	2.1	2.9	2.0
	1	2.2	2.0	2.9	2.1	3.2
	210	-	-	-	-	-
	1					
	220	-	-	-	-	-
	1					
DIST/SO//	110	4.1	4.8	4.1	4.1	4.1
	1	-	2.8	-	4.1	-
ADY/SP	120	2.4	2.4	2.4	2.2	2.6
	1	-	-	-	2.6	2.2
	210	5.5	1.5	5.5	6.4	5.4
	1	-	6.2	-	5.0	-
	220	1.9	3.0	1.9	2.6	1.9
	1	-	0.7	-	1.7	-

APPENDIX 26 "Functional Asp." broken down acc. to Space and Time - MEAN VALUES
for EXT/FQ

	N	AT/ STY FTC	AT/ AGS	COOP/ M	TR/ INC	CRED
DIST/SO//	110	0.0	-	0.0	0.0	0.0
	1	4.8	4.0	24.0	4.8	24.0
ADY/SFP	120	0.0	0.0	6.0	1.0	-
	1	7.0	7.0	2.0	12.0	4.7
	210	-	-	-	-	-
	1	-	-	-	-	-
	220	-	-	4.5	0.0	4.5
	1	4.5	4.5	-	9.0	-
DIST/SO//	110	2.0	2.0	2.0	2.0	2.0
	1	-	-	-	2.0	-
ADY/S	120	4.1	5.9	4.1	12.0	4.1
	1	4.0	0.5	-	2.5	-
	210	3.7	2.4	3.7	1.0	3.7
	1	-	7.0	-	5.8	-
	220	6.0	0.0	6.0	-	6.0
	1	-	12.0	-	-	-

APPENDIX 26 "Functional Asp." broken down acc. to Space and Time - MEAN VALUES
(cont.) for EXT/FQ

	N	AT/ STY FTC	AT/ AGS	COOP/ M	TR/ INC	CRED
DIST/SO//	110	0.5	24.0	8.0	12.0	8.0
	1	12.0	0.3	1.0	0.5	1.0
ADY/SF	120	3.3	2.0	5.3	2.0	5.3
	1	10.0	5.3	2.0	5.3	2.0
	210	-	-	-	-	-
	1	-	-	-	-	-
	220	-	-	-	-	-
	1	-	-	-	-	-
DIST/SO//	110	12.0	6.0	12.0	-	12.0
	1	-	24.0	-	12.0	-
ADY/SP	120	6.0	6.0	6.0	0.0	12.0
	1	-	-	-	12.0	0.0
	210	5.5	0.0	5.5	3.5	5.5
	1	-	6.6	-	6.5	-
	220	5.0	5.0	5.0	3.0	5.0
	1	-	5.0	-	5.4	-

APPENDIX 27 Comparison between Adopters and Non-Adopters broken down on DIST/SO - MEDIAN VALUES

	S	n	VAL/ LS	VAL/ BH	VAL/ CA	VAL/ LA	EXP/ HO	INC/ ATO	VAL/ CAT	LO/ LR	LO/ ADL	LO/ LOT	LAB/ HP	LAB/ HT	EXT/ FQ	LAB/ EQ	FOV/ MA	ARE/ HM	ARE/ M	ARE/ CC	ARE/ RC	PC/ HMTA	PC/ MTA	PC/ CCTA	PC/ RCTA	PC/ HMMA
NON-AD. T.	1	122	307	50	30	41	398	933	517	2.0	0.01	2.0	0.0	2.5	0.2	3.6	7.7	0.0	0.4	0.0	0.1	0.0	22.2	0.0	8.3	0.0
ADOP. T.	1	64	352	50	46	51	497	1350	604	2.1	0.02	2.2	0.1	3.3	1.9	3.9	5.8	0.59	0.7	0.0	0.2	22.2	30.0	0.1	8.3	99.8
NON-AD.//	1	32	102	49	18	2	500	799	291	1.7	0.02	1.8	0.0	0.3	0.3	2.8	7.6	0.00	0.4	0.0	0.2	0.0	22.5	0.0	7.4	0.0
DIST/SO	2	49	342	50	30	48	343	1230	549	2.0	0.00	2.0	0.0	3.1	0.3	4.1	7.7	0.00	0.4	0.0	0.1	0.0	21.4	0.0	6.3	0.0
	3	41	391	50	45	41	360	986	575	2.2	0.00	2.2	0.0	3.6	0.1	4.0	7.9	0.00	0.5	0.0	0.1	0.0	23.5	0.1	10.5	0.0
ADOP.//	1	24	337	50	43	52	410	1177	501	1.7	0.06	2.2	0.0	3.5	1.8	3.0	7.6	0.60	0.6	0.0	0.1	25.7	33.0	0.4	6.9	99.8
DIST/SO	2	22	352	50	46	43	503	1512	604	2.2	0.07	2.2	0.1	3.2	1.8	4.1	3.8	0.65	0.7	0.0	0.2	23.1	28.6	0.0	8.3	99.3
	3	18	383	52	80	80	495	1352	668	2.6	0.00	2.6	0.1	3.3	2.8	4.2	8.0	0.43	0.7	0.0	0.3	18.3	30.3	0.0	12.7	75.4

APPENDIX 28:A The studied Adoption-Categories broken down according to Time (ADY/...) - MEDIAN VALUES

	T	n	VAL/ LS	VAL/ BH	VAL/ CA	VAL/ LA	EXP/ HO	INC/ ATO	VAL/ CAT	LO/ LR	LO/ ADL	LO/ LOT	LAB/ HP	LAB/ HT	EXT/ FQ	LAB/ EQ	FOV/ MA	ARE/ HM	ARE/ M	ARE/ CC	ARE/ RC	PC/ HMTA	PC/ MTA	PC/ CCTA	PC/ RCTA	PC/ HMMA
ADY/SFP	1	6	109	53	23	117	325	2594	323	1.3	0.00	1.3	0.1	3.5	2.4	3.3	8.0	0.25	0.3	0.0	0.2	14.1	14.1	0.0	10.2	96.7
	2	9	474	76	67	325	1350	695		2.0	0.14	2.6	0.0	5.8	0.4	4.7	8.3	0.43	0.4	0.0	0.1	21.1	21.1	0.5	2.8	100.0
ADY/S	1	9	705	53	40	331	494	1007	832	2.3	0.17	4.0	0.1	3.3	2.3	4.0	2.0	0.90	0.9	0.0	0.0	30.0	30.0	0.0	0.6	100.0
	2	14	1	49	44	8	510	965	162	1.9	0.02	1.8	0.0	2.7	0.5	3.1	3.5	0.35	0.5	0.0	0.2	18.2	20.0	0.0	9.3	97.5

KODOOH WEST

APPENDIX 28:B   The studied Adoption-Categories broken down according to TIME (ADY/...) - MEDIAN VALUES

	T	n	VAL/ LS	VAL/ BH	VAL/ CA	VAL/ LA	EXP/ HO	EXP/ ATO	INC/ CAT	VAL/ LR	LO/ ADL	LO/ LOT	LAB/ HP	LAB/ HT	EXT/ FQ	LAB/ EQ	FOV/ MA	ARE/ HM	ARE/ M	ARE/ CC	RC	PC/ HMTA	PC/ MTA	PC/ CCTA	PC/ RCTA	PC/ HMA
ADY/SF	1	4	353	50	38	116	400	1636	595	2.0	0.30	2.7	0.0	7.5	0.5	2.5	5.5	1.50	1.5	0.1	0.1	40.6	37.9	2.7	2.8	95.8
	2	5	362	50	44	100	425	1012	543	1.7	0.20	2.2	0.0	8.3	3.0	2.8	5.7	0.90	1.0	0.0	0.0	53.3	53.3	0.0	6.7	80.0
ADY/SP	1	9	609	400	100	47	513	2108	1128	2.8	0.18	2.8	0.1	2.3	4.0	6.0	8.2	0.70	1.1	0.0	0.4	22.2	33.3	0.0	13.3	65.8
	2	8	221	50	46	35	510	896	458	2.1	0.00	2.1	0.2	1.7	3.0	3.8	4.0	0.38	0.5	0.0	0.0	20.2	32.3	0.0	9.8	52.3

APPENDIX 29   The studied Adoption-Categories broken down according to Space (DIST/SO) - MEDIAN VALUES

	S	n	VAL/ LS	VAL/ BH	VAL/ CA	VAL/ LA	EXP/ HO	INC/ ATO	VAL/ CAT	LO/ LR	LO/ ADL	LO/ LOT	LAB/ HP	LAB/ HT	EXT/ FQ	LAB/ EQ	FQV/ MA	ARE/ HM	ARE/ M	ARE/ CC	RC	PC/ HMTA	PC/ MTA	PC/ CCTA	PC/ RCTA	PC/ HMA
ADY/SFP// DIST/SO	1	6	281	53	72	81	500	1364	540	0.9	0.25	1.9	0.1	3.5	1.0	4.8	6.3	0.45	0.5	0.0	0.2	21.3	21.3	0.8	7.3	96.7
	2	4	129	50	23	83	325	2124	377	1.3	0.00	1.3	0.0	7.0	0.0	3.5	8.2	0.25	0.3	0.0	0.1	13.5	13.5	0.0	9.2	100.0
	3	5	472	103	76	87	300	1781	695	2.8	0.00	2.8	0.0	4.3	1.0	5.0	8.7	0.40	0.4	0.0	0.3	15.0	15.0	0.0	12.5	100.0
ADY/S // DIST/SO	1	7	57	50	40	8	400	948	178	1.3	0.15	1.7	0.0	1.1	1.7	2.3	2.3	0.40	0.6	0.0	0.1	22.0	32.8	0.0	11.1	93.3
	2	13	351	49	44	50	510	1227	535	2.2	0.00	2.3	0.1	3.8	3.0	4.0	2.2	0.76	0.8	0.0	0.0	25.0	25.0	0.0	0.4	98.5
	3	3	2	50	37	30	500	673	89	2.2	0.00	2.2	0.0	2.3	0.3	2.8	4.0	0.60	0.6	0.0	0.2	26.7	30.0	0.0	5.0	97.2
ADY/SF// DIST/SO	1	9	362	50	50	43	425	1445	563	1.9	0.16	2.5	0.0	8.6	2.3	2.8	6.8	1.20	1.2	0.0	0.0	53.3	53.3	1.0	0.4	91.7
	2	–	–	–	–	–	–	–	–	–	–	–	–	–	–	–	–	–	–	–	–	–	–	–	–	–
	3	–	–	–	–	–	–	–	–	–	–	–	–	–	–	–	–	–	–	–	–	–	–	–	–	–
ADY/SP// DIST/SO	1	2	341	48	21	21	365	769	479	2.5	0.00	2.5	0.0	0.0	6.0	3.3	6.0	0.40	0.5	0.0	0.1	16.3	20.2	0.0	4.2	75.0
	2	5	457	105	94	38	600	2244	711	2.2	0.35	2.2	0.0	1.8	2.0	6.0	3.0	0.68	0.8	0.0	0.2	25.0	33.3	0.1	11.1	66.7
	3	10	383	55	103	53	510	1379	692	2.6	0.00	2.6	0.2	2.5	3.5	4.2	6.5	0.43	0.4	0.0	0.4	18.8	40.6	0.0	14.3	50.4

APPENDIX 30   The studied Adoption-Categories broken down according to Space/Time (DIST/SO//ADY/...) - MEDIAN VALUES

	ST	n	VAL/ LS	VAL/ BH	VAL/ CA	VAL/ LA	EXP/ HO	VAL/ ATO	INC/ CAT	VAL/ LR	LO/ ADL	LO/ LOT	LAB/ HP	LAB/ HT	EXT/ FQ	LAB/ EQ	FQV/ MA	ARE/ HM	ARE/ M	ARE/ CC	RC	PC/ HMTA	PC/ MTA	PC/ CCTA	PC/ RCTA	PC/ HMA
DIST/SO// ADY/SFP	1	6	109	53	23	117	325	2594	323	1.3	0.00	1.3	0.1	3.5	2.4	3.3	8.0	0.25	0.3	0.0	0.2	14.1	14.1	0.0	10.2	96.7
	2	3	295	50	78	40	600	1323	473	0.8	1.00	1.9		6.8	2.0	4.7	2.8	0.40	0.4	0.1	0.1	22.2	22.2	2.1	2.8	100.0
	2	6	480	92	40	90	300	1517	698	2.7	0.00	2.7		4.5	0.8	4.6	8.8	0.45	0.5	0.0	0.2	15.4	15.4	0.0	1.4	100.0
DIST/SO// ADY/S	1	2	782	50	42	10	600	834	948	1.9	3.40	5.3	0.0	4.5	2.0	3.6	1.5	1.50	1.5	0.0	0.3	27.4	27.4	0.0	6.1	100.0
	2	12	1	49	44	3	500	950	162	1.8	0.02	1.7	0.0	1.0	0.5	3.3	3.5	0.30	0.5	0.0	0.2	18.2	18.2	0.0	9.3	97.6
	2	7	695	53	38	55	488	1906	832	2.3	0.00	2.3	0.1	3.3	3.0	4.0	2.1	0.80	0.8	0.0	0.0	30.0	30.0	0.0	0.3	100.0
	2	2	130	48	37	773	4937	5882	314	2.4	0.00	2.4	0.5	3.0	6.0	2.0	4.0	0.80	0.9	0.0	0.3	35.6	37.2	0.0	10.0	94.4
DIST/SO// ADY/SF	1	4	353	50	38	116	400	1636	595	2.0	0.30	2.7	0.0	7.5	0.5	2.5	5.5	1.50	1.5	0.1	0.1	40.6	37.9	2.7	2.8	95.8
	2	5	362	50	44	100	425	1012	543	1.7	0.20	2.2	0.0	8.3	3.0	2.8	5.7	0.90	1.0	0.0	0.1	53.3	53.3	2.7	6.7	80.0
DIST/SO// ADY/SP	1	3	346	50	79	13	600	1114	603	2.8	0.70	2.8	0.0	0.0	12.0	6.0	6.0	0.70	1.1	0.0	0.1	22.6	30.6	0.0	9.8	80.0
	2	2	217	50	34	0	553	773	351	2.4	0.00	2.4	0.0	0.0	2.4	3.5	5.5	0.45	0.6	0.0	0.1	19.8	23.6	0.0	4.5	63.6
	2	6	628	405	102	50	500	2146	1136	2.7	0.00	2.7	0.1	2.5	3.5	5.8	8.3	0.70	0.9	0.0	0.4	18.9	34.0	0.0	13.6	75.0
	2	6	229	50	99	45	545	1064	478	1.2	0.00	1.2	0.3	2.3	3.0	4.1		0.38	0.2	0.0	0.2	20.2	42.3	0.0	12.3	66.2

APPENDIX 31

CONFIDENTIAL: (Information given by individuals will be treated strictly confidential)

Date of interview:........
Enumerator:........
Time commenced:........
Time completed:........

Name of Farmer:........
District:........
Location:........
Farm identity code:........

The interview should preferably be conducted with the owner of the farm. If the owner or other responsible person on the farm gives permission, interviewers may also be conducted with other persons on the farm e.g. male relative working on the farm or wife of the owner.

The interview conducted with ....owner
....other person /specify below/

Interview conducted with:........
Relationship to owner:........
Reason for interviewing other person than owner:........

1. Which is the size of this farm? ....acres (....hectares)

2a. Is this all the land you have, or do you also claim rights to land somewhere else:
....Yes, this is all the land /carry on to question 3/
....No, I have other land as well /ask question 2b/

b. Into how many separate pieces is your land divided and what is the distance to these places?
....Places The distance is: 1..... 2..... 3.....
What is the size of these pieces: 1..... 2..... 3.....
/If possible, try to get an exact location of these pieces/
1..... 2..... 3.....

3. How many people are presently living on the farm?
/Spent last night on the farm/
....owner
....wives ....boys ....girls
....children ....males ....females
....grandparents ....males ....females
....relatives ....males ....females
....other ....males ....females
/comments about the composition of the people living on the farm/

4. What are the ages of the children you mentioned above? Could you also say if they are attending school and what type of school they are attending?
/MARK: - for not attending school; otherwise indicate level by using e.g. S1 for Standard 1 etc. and F1 for Form 1 etc. Try also to indicate if it is a Government of Harambee School by using G or H. Standard 3 in a Harambee School would then be marked S3H./

Boys:	Age	School	Girls	Age	School
A	....	....	F	....	....
B	....	....	G	....	....
C	....	....	H	....	....
D	....	....	I	....	....
E	....	....	J	....	....

5a. What are the occupations of the people living on the farm? How many are engaged in the work on the farm full-time, part-time and what is the occupation of those not engaged in farm work?
....No, full-time Who?........
....No, part-time Who?........

Occupation of those not engaged in farm work:........

b. Those who only work part-time on the farm, do they have other occupations outside the farm?
....No
....Yes What?........

6a. What kind of livestock do you have on the farm?
....None /carry on to question 7/
....Cows (....improved ....unimproved)
....Bulls (....improved ....unimproved)
....Goats
....Sheep
....Poultry
....Pigs

b. Who is taking care of them? ....

7. What crops are grown on the farm and on what (approximative) acreage?
/Specify under these headings: a. planted during the long rains; b. planted during the short rains; c. interplanted with; mark - if not interplanted; d. number of pure stands; e. acreage of pure stands; f. year of adoption (to be used on the crops marked + only)/

	a	b	c	d	e	f
1. Maize improved+	....	....	....	....	....	.....
2. Maize unimproved+	....	....	....	....	....	xxxxx
3. Millet	....	....	....	....	....	xxxxx
4. Sorghum	....	....	....	....	....	xxxxx
5. Beans	....	....	....	....	....	xxxxx
6. Sweet potatoes	....	....	....	....	....	xxxxx
7. English Potatoes+	....	....	....	....	....	xxxxx
8. Cassava	....	....	....	....	....	xxxxx
9. Yams	....	....	....	....	....	xxxxx
10. Bananas	....	....	....	....	....	xxxxx
11. Cabbage	....	....	....	....	....	xxxxx
12. Sunflower+	....	....	....	....	....	xxxxx
13. Sugar+	....	....	....	....	....	xxxxx
14. Cotton+	....	....	....	....	....	xxxxx
15. Sisal+	....	....	....	....	....	xxxxx
16. Pasture	....	....	....	....	....	xxxxx
17. Tobacco+	....	....	....	....	....	xxxxx
18.						
19.						

8. Have you or anybody else on the farm attended any courses at a Farmers Training Centre (FTC)?
....No
....Yes, I have ....Yes
Which FTC? ....

/The questions in this questionnaire should be given to those farmers, who answered YES on any of the alternatives given in question 11e./

District: ....
Location: ....
Farm identity code: ....

A1. Which of the crops (see question 7) are grown with purchased seed (planting material)?
....

A2a. Are you buying and using fertilizers on all your crops?
....Yes
....No /ask question A2b./

b. On which of the crops are you using fertilizers? ....

A3. You said that you bought seeds, fertilizers, pesticides, herbicides, insecticides (mention the appropriate ones). Could you get all these from the same source (place)?
....Yes Where is that? .... in ....
....No   What different sources do have for them?
Seeds   at........... in ....
Fertilizers at........... in ....
Pesticides   at........... in ....
Insecticides at........... in ....
             at........... in ....

A4a. Are you a member of a co-operative?
....No
....Yes Which?

b. Are some of the goods you buy for use on the farm delivered through the co-operative?
....No   /carry on to question A5a./
....Yes all of them /as question A4d./
....Yes some of them /ask question A4c. and then A4d./

c. Which of the goods are delivered through the co-operative? ....

d. On which of the places you mentioned earlier (question A3) are you getting the goods from the co-operative?
.... at........... in ....
.... at........... in ....
.... at........... in ....

A5a. In order to buy these goods do you apply for credit from someone or from any organization?
....No   /carry on to question A6. - then carry on to A8./
....Yes /ask question A5b. - then carry on to question A7./

b. From whom/where have you applied for credit?
From .... at........... in ....

---

9. Have you or anybody else on the farm visited any of the following meetings during the last year?
....Chief's Baraza   Who visited?...........
                           Where was it?...........
....Crop Demonstration   Who visited?...........
                           Where was it?...........
....Agricultural Show   Who visited?...........
                           Where was it?...........
....No, no one on the farm has visited any of these meetings.

10a. Which market place do you usually visit? /Where they usually go to buy or sell goods./
.... in ....

b. How often do you visit this market place?
....times/week ....times/month ....times/year

c. How do you usually travel to the market place?
....by foot ....by bus ....by bicycle ....other What?...........

11a. Do you ever at this or any other market place buy improved-seeds and/or fertilizers, herbicides, pesticides, insecticides which you will use on your farm?
....No /as question 11b./
....Yes Seeds
....Yes Fertilizers
....Yes Herbicide/Pesticide/Insecticide
....Yes all types of these goods

b. Have you ever bought any of these goods and then stopped buying them?
....No
....Yes /ask question 11c./

c. Why did you stop buying them?

/12/ /Mark here what you can observe about the houses lived in by the household members, and about the items to be found on the farm. Ask only if you are not sure about the presence of a specific item./

House: ....Mud and wood ....Stone and brick ....other
Roof: ....Thatch ....Iron ....Tin ....other
Floors: ....Earth ....Wood ....Cement ....other
Windows: ....Glass ....Wood ....other
Items: ....Pangas ....Jembes ....Saw ....Wheelbarrow ....Bike ....Cart
          ....Plow ....Harrow ....Tractor ....Car ....Parafin Stove/Lamp
          ....Clock ....Radio ....other
Fencing: ....Wire ....Hedge ....other

/If the answer to question 11e. is YES on any of the alternatives go on and ask the questions marked with a capital A. If the answer is NO on question 11e. go on and ask the questions marked with a capital B. Furthermore, try to remember the alternatives mentioned in this question. What is marked as the goods in the following questions is referring to the alternatives mentioned here. This must then be put into the questions at appropriate places./

A6a. How do you finance the purchase of these goods?
....By selling the surplus from my last harvest of food-crops /e.g. maize, beans etc./
....Through my incomes from my cash-crops ....../....../....../......
/e.g. cotton, coffee etc./ /write which cash-crop/
....By selling livestock

b. What and where do you sell your food-crop surplus/cash-crops/livestock?
...... at .... in ....
...... at .... in ....
...... at .... in ....

A7. Is the selling of farm products your major source of income or do you also have other sources of income?
....Yes it is the only source of income
....No I have other sources as well
What other sources? ....

A8. On what do you spend most of the incomes you receive from employment, cash-crops, livestock and food-crops? Could you also say how much (approximately) you spend per year on these different things?
....School-fees   about ......shs.
....Seeds   about ......shs.
....Fertilizers   about ......shs.
....Pesticides   about ......shs.
....Insecticides   about ......shs.
....Labour pay   about ......shs.
....   about ......shs.

A9. Approximately how much of your incomes are used on the things you mentioned above? Is it all of your incomes or some other part of your incomes? /note volume by using 1/1: 3/4: 1/2: 1/4/
....of the income is used for these things ....

A10. How do you transport the goods you are buying from the market place ('duka') to the farm?
....They are carried
....They are taken on bicycle/cart /underline which/
....They are taken on bus/'matatu' /underline which/
....other Which? ....

A11. How did you find out about these types of goods?
....From extension agents
....From neighbours/relatives /underline which/
....I have seen them in the market place/'duka' /underline which/
....other Which? ....

A12a. How often does the extension agent visit you?
....Never
....Every week ....Every month ....Time/year

b. When did the extension agent last visit you?
....weeks ago ....months ago ....years ago

c. Can you remember when the extension agent first started to visit you?
....months ago ....years ago

A13. Can you also remember when you first started to use these goods?
Seeds   ....months ago ....seasons ago ....years ago
Fertilizers ....months ago ....seasons ago ....years ago
Pesticides   ....months ago ....seasons ago ....years ago
Insecticides ....months ago ....seasons ago ....years ago

A14a. When you first heard about these things, that you could buy and use on your farm, did you then immediately begin to use them?
....months/seasons/years ago /underline which/
....Yes When was that? 1..........
....No /as question A14b./ 2..........

b. When did you begin to use these goods?
What was the first thing you began to use? 1..........
Then what did you begin to use? 1......... 2......... 3..........

A15a. Which of the sources from which you received information, was the most influential for your decision to begin use these goods?
....Extension agents
....Relatives/Neighbours /underline which/
....other Which? ....

b. The source you mentioned above, is that the one you think of as the most reliable and which you usually consult in matters concerning changes on the farm and buying new things to the farm?
....Yes ....No Who do you usually consult in these matters? ....

A16. These good, that you are buying, when do you go an purchase them?
....Well in advance before sowing (use)
....Just prior to sowing (use)
....other Which? ....
/If possible, try to get the month when each type is bought/

A17. In what quantities do you usually buy these goods?
....bags of seed (....kilos)
....bags of fertilizers (....kilos)
....

A18a. Do you usually try to buy all the goods you will need during one growing season at the same time?
....Yes /carry on to question A19./
....No /ask question A18b./

b. How many trips do you usually make and when do you make these trips?
....Number of trips
....Whenever I need a specific type of commodity
....When I can find the time during the growing season
....The trips are made before the growing season
....other Which? ....

c. Why do you make several trips to buy the goods you need?
....it is the only way of transporting it
....The distance to the market makes it impossible to take it all at the same time
....other Which? ....

A19a. When you sell the surplus from your production, do you then sell it all at the same time?

....I never have any surplus /carry on to question A20./
....No, it is not sold at the same time /ask question A19b. and A19c./
....Yes, it is all sold at the same time
        When is that? ....immediately after harvest
                        ....other ....

b. When do you sell this surplus?
....When I need cash
....When the price is good
....other ....

c. Why do you split up your surplus and sell it in smaller portions?
....It is the only way of transporting it
....The distance to the market makes it impossible to take it all at the same time
....other ....

A20a. When did you plant your last maize crop?
....Weeks before the rains
....Weeks after the rains
....other ....
Is that the time you usually plant your maize?
....Yes ....No /Comments:.................

b. Did you plant your maize in rows and what spacing did you use?
....Yes ....No Spacing:.................
Is this the way you usually do?
....Yes ....No /Comments:.................

c. Did you apply fertilizers to your maize?
....Yes ....No When?.................
Do you usually apply fertilizers to your maize?
....Yes ....No /Comments:.................

d. Did you weed your maize after it had been planted and how many times did you weed it?
....Yes ....No Number of times:.................
Do you usually weed your maize after it has been planted?
....Yes ....No /Comments:................./.

e. Did you apply insecticides to the growing maize?
....Yes ....No
Do you usually apply insecticides to your maize?
....Yes ....No /Comments:.................

f. After you had harvested the maize, did you apply any insecticides to protect it during storage?
....Yes ....No
Do you usually do this?
....Yes ....No /Comments:................./

g. Do you buy fresh seed every year?
....Yes ....No

A21. When you buy fertilizers/pesticides/insecticides/.........do you then spread them equally among your crops or are some given more than others?
....I spread them equally among my crops
....Some are given more than others
        Which crops are that? 1.......... 2.......... 3..........

A22a. Do you hire any extra labour for your farm work?
....No /carry on to question A23./
....Yes /ask question A22b./

b. How many do you hire and when do you hire these?

Number permanently hired:......   When?.................
Number seasonally hired:......

A23. So we have reached the final question. Is there any specific factors you can think of, which is preventing you from developing your farm as much as you would like, and what is this?
....Lack of credit/ready cash /underline which/
....The distance to the place where the goods are being sold is to long
....I can't get the goods in the 'duka' when I need them
....other ....

What do you think one should do about this, and which is the most urgent point for you?
....
....
Most urgent point:.................

/The questions in this questionnaire should be given to those farmers who answered NO on question 11e./

District:.................
Location:.................
Farm identity code:.................

B1a. Where do you get your seeds and planting material from?
....It is taken from my last harvest /carry on to question B2a./
....From neighbours/relatives /underline which/- ask question B1b./
....other Which? /ask question B2b./

b. Could you tell the location from which you get your seeds/planting material?
at .... in ....
What is the distance to that place? ....

B3a. How often does the extension agent visit you?
....Never ....Every week ....Every month ....Times/year

b. When did the extension agent last visit you?
....Weeks ago ....Months ago ....Years ago

c. Can you remember when the extension agent first started to visit you?
....Years ago ....Months ago ....Weeks ago

B4. Are you a member of a co-operative?
....No ....Yes Which? .... at .... in ....

B5a. Have you applied for and received credit for the improvement of your farm?
....No /carry on to question B6./
....Yes /ask question B5b./

b. From where/whom did you apply for credit, and did you also receive any credit?
From: .... at .... in ....
....Yes I did receive a credit
....No I did not receive a credit

B6a. Which of your farm products do you sell and where do you sell them?
....I never have any /carry on to question B7./
.... is sold at .... in ....
.... is sold at .... in ....
/carry on to question B6b./

b. Do you sell all your surplus at the same time?
....No /ask question B6c./
....Yes When is that? ....Immediately after harvest
....other What?

c1. When do you sell this surplus?
....When I need cash
....When the price is good
....other Which?

c2. Why do you split up your surplus and sell it in smaller portions?
....It is the only way of transporting it
....The distance to the market makes it impossible to take it all at the same time
....other Which?

B7. How do you transport the things you sell and buy on the market place to the and from the farm?
....They are carried ....They are taken on bus/'matatu' /underline which/
....They are taken on bicycle/cart /underline which/
....other Which?

B8. Is the selling of farm products your major source of income or do you have other sources of income?
....Yes it is the Major source of income
....No I have other sources as well
What other sources are those? ....

B9a. On what do you spend most of the incomes you receive from employment, cash-crops, livestock and food-crops? Could you also say how much (approximately) you spend per year on these different things?
....School-fees about ....shs.
....Labour pay about ....shs.
.... about ....shs.
.... about ....shs.

b. Approximately how much of your incomes are used on the things you mentioned above? Is it all of your incomes, half your incomes or some other part of your incomes?
....of the income is used for these things /Note volume by using 1/1: 3/4: 1/2: 1/4/

B10a. When did you plant your last maize crop?
....Weeks before the rains
....Weeks after the rains
....other Which?
Is that the time when you usually plant your maize?
....Yes ....No /Comments: ..../

b. Did you plant your maize in rows and what spacing did you then use?
....Yes ....No Spacing: ....
Is this the way you usually do?
....Yes ....No /Comments: ....

c. Did you weed your maize after it had been planted and how many times did you weed it?
....Yes ....No Number of times: ....
Do you usually weed your maize after it has been planted?
....Yes ....No /Comments: ..../

B11a. Do you hire any extra labour for your farm work?
....No /carry on to question B12./
....Yes /ask question B11b./

b. How many do you hire and when do you hire these?
Number permanently hired: .... When?
Number seasonally hired: ....

B12a. Do you think you will begin to use improved seeds, fertilizers, pesticides/insecticides in the future?
....No /ask question B12b./
....Yes /carry on to question B13./

b. Why don't you think you will begin to use them in the future?

B13. So we have reached the final question. Is there any specific factors you can think of, which is preventing you from developing your farm as much as you would like, and what is this?
....Lack of credit/ready cash /underline which/
....The distance to the place where the goods are being sold is to to long
....I can't get the goods in the 'duka' when I need them
....other ....
What do you think one should do about this, and which is the most urgent point for you?
....
Most urgent point: ....

APPENDIX 32

LIST OF VARIABLES USED

Var. Name | var. No.   Description of variable content

ADOPTION VARIABLES FOR THE STUDIED INNOVATIONS

ADY/ST | V061   Adoption Year - Total Hybrid Maize Seed (S) adoption
ADY/FT | V063   Adoption Year - Total Fertilizer (F) adoption
ADY/PT | V065   Adoption Year - Total Pest-/Insecticide (P) adoption
ADY/SFP | V157   Adoption Year - S, F, P adoption (Seed adoption criterion)
ADY/FP | V158   Adoption Year - F, P adoption only (Fertilizer adoption criterion)
ADY/S | V161   Adoption Year - S only (Seed adoption criterion)
ADY/SF | V162   Adoption Year - S, F (Seed adoption criterion)
ADY/SP | V163   Adoption year - S, P (Seed adoption criterion)

Note. V061, V063, V065 and V157 are used in both sub-locations
      V158 is used in Igana only.
      V161, V162 and V163 are used in Kodoch West only.

DISTANCE VARIABLES

DIST/SO | V070   Distance to Source of Innovation (kms)
DIST/MA | V104   Distance to most frequented Market (kms)

"INDEPENDENT VARIABLES"

ADY/CC | V169   Adoption Year - Cash-Crop
ARE/CC | V167   Area (ha) under main Cash-Crop in Long Rains 1975/76
ARE/HM | V165   Area (ha) under Hybrid Maize in Long Rains 1975/76
ARE/M | V166   Total Area (ha) under Maize in Long Rains 1975/76
ARE/RC | V170   Are (ha) under 'Risk-Crop' (cassava) in Long Rains 1975/76
AT/AGS | V046   Attended Agricultural Show in the last year - Yes/No
AT/FTC | V040   Attended Course at Farmers Training Centre - Yes/No
COOP/M | V073   Membership in Co-operative - Yes/No
CRED | V077   Have received Credits - Yes/No
EXP/HO | V092   Expenditure Household/Other
EXP/LA | V091   Expenditure Labour (time of survey)
EXT/FQ | V107   Extension Visits Frequency/Year
FQV/MA | V105   Frequency of Visits to most frequented Market
INC/ATO | V093   Annual Income/Turnover
LAB/EQ | V156   Labour Eqvivalents (calculated with weights for each individual)
LAB/HP | V113   Hired Labour Permanently (no.)
LAP/HT | V114   Hired Labour Temporary (no.)
LO/ADL | V008   Land Ownership - Additional Land (ha)
LO/LOT | V143   Total Land Ownership (V143=V006+V008)
LO/LR | V006   Land Ownership (farm size) from Land Registry (ha)
PC/CCTA | V173   Percentage share Cash-Crop out of Total Area
PC/HMMA | V175   Percentage share Hybrid Maize our of total Maize Area
PC/HMTA | V171   Percentage share Hybrid Maize out of Total Area
PC/MTA | V172   Percentage share Maize out of Total Area
PC/RCTA | V174   Percentage share 'Risk-Crop' out of total Area
TR/INC | V076   Transfers of Income - Yes/No
VAL/BH | V052   Value of 'Best' House
VAL/CA | V054   Value of tools and Capital Assets
VAL/CAT | V145   Value of Total Capital Assets (V145=V051+V053+V054)
VAL/LS | V051   Value of Livestock
(VAL/TH | V053   Value of all Houses)

MEDDELANDEN FRÅN LUNDS UNIVERSITETS GEOGRAFISKA INSTITUTION

Serie Avhandlingar

LXXIV. *Raul Nino Guerrero:* Rural to Urban Drift of the Unemployed in Colombia. (1975).

LXXV. *Ulf Erlandsson:* Företagsutveckling och utrymmesbehov. (1975).

LXXVI. *Sture Öberg:* Methods of Describing Physical Access to Supply Points. (1976).

LXXVII. *Bo Lenntorp:* Paths in Space-time Environments. A time-geographic Study of Movement Possibilities of Individuals. (1976).

LXXVIII. *Richard Åhman:* Palsar i Nordnorge. En studie av palsars morfologi, utbredning och klimatiska förutsättningar i Finnmarks och Troms fylke. (1977).

LXXIX. *Björn Gyllström:* The Organization of Production as a Space-Modelling Mechanism in Underdeveloped Countries. (1977).

LXXX. *Anders Järnegren - Fosco Ventura:* Tre samhällens förändringshistoria. Exploateringen av den fysiska miljön i historisk belysning. (1977).

LXXXI. *Tommy Book:* Stadsplan och järnväg i Storbritannien och Tyskland. (1978).

LXXXII. *Jan O Mattsson - Leif Börjesson:* Lokalklimatiska temperaturstudier inom ett skånskt fruktodlingsdistrikt med särskilt beaktande av frostlänt-heten. (1978).

LXXXIII. *Bjørn Terje Asheim:* Regionale ulikheter i levekår. (1979).

LXXXIV. *Solveig Mårtensson:* On the Formation of Biographies in Space-Time Environments. (1979).

LXXXV. *Erik Wallin:* Vardagslivets generativa grammatik - Vid gränsen mellan natur och kultur. (1980).

LXXXVI. *Reinhold Castensson:* Välja för framtid - om markanvändningsval och förtroendemannainflytande i kommunal planering. (1980).

LXXXVII. *Kerstin Montal:* Industri och vatten. Den vattenförorenande industrins lokaliseringsproblem i Malmöhus län. (1980).

LXXXVIII. *Tommy Carlstein:* Time Resources, Society and Ecology. (1980).

LXXXIX. *Jonas Akerman:* Studies on periglacial geomorphology in West Spitsbergen. (1980).

XC. *Leif Engh:* Karstområdet vid Lummelunds bruk, Gotland, med speciell hänsyn till Lummelundagrottan. (1980).

XCI. *Karna Lidmar-Bergström:* Pre-quaternary Geomorphological Evolution in Southern Fennoscandia. (1982).

XCII. *Lars-Olof Olander:* Staten, kommunerna och servicen. (1984).

XCIII. *Bo Malmström och Owe Palmér:* Glacial och periglacial geomorfologi på Varangerhalvön, Nordnorge. (1984).

XCIV. *Franz-Michael Rundquist:* Hybrid Maize Diffusion in Kenya. (1984).